Kpele Lala

Mediums Sing *Kpele* Songs

Kpele Lala ;

Ga Religious Songs and Symbols

Marion Kilson

IP 4 B

Harvard University Press
Cambridge, Massachusetts
1971

For Martin, Jenny, Peter, and Hannah

Preface

This study of Ga religious songs is based upon ethnographic material collected in Ghana during ten months in 1964-65 and three months in 1968. These research trips were supported by grants from the Charles E. Merrill Trust Fund, Radcliffe College, and the Institute of African Studies, University of Ghana, in 1964-65, and from the Joint Committee on African Studies of the American Council of Learned Societies and the Social Science Research Council in 1968. In Ghana the directors of the Institute of African Studies, Professor Thomas Hodgkin in 1964 and Professor J. H. K. Nketia in 1968, generously provided research facilities at the Institute. The leisure and facilities for writing this study were provided by the Radcliffe Institute and partially supported by a Younger Scholar Fellowship from the National Endowment for the Humanities.

Among the individuals who assisted in the preparation of this book, I wish to acknowledge my special indebtedness to Thomas O. Beidelman, Yoomo Dantserebi, and Martin Kilson. Professor Beidelman, who enabled me to complete my graduate studies, graciously has assumed the subsequent role of critical advisor. I am extremely grateful to him both for commenting on drafts of this book and for contributing a critical foreword to it. Yoomo Dantserebi, the *Olila* medium, not only instructed me in *kpele* ritual and thought but gave me insight into the emotional meaning of the *kpele* religion to its adherents. In her company I spent my most intellectually absorbing and delightful hours in Ghana, whether talking in her compound, trudging through the bush, observing her perform ritual, or listening to her sing. Martin Kilson, who turned my ethnographic interests to Africa and enabled me to do research in West Africa in 1960, 1962, and 1964-65, has shared the conjugal joys and trials associated with writing this book. Without the unique contribution of each of these individuals, this study could not have been completed.

I also wish to express my gratitude to several friends who made this study possible. Inestimable contributions were made by three Ga associates: E. A. Ammah, who introduced me to Ga culture; Henry Adjei, who mediated the linguistic barriers between me and my Ga informants, and Gladys Adjei, who assisted in the transcription and translation of interviews. Edna Sargent and Cynthia Reddy Benjamins, as loving mother-surrogates to my children, have given me the incalculable gift of leisure time in which to pursue my ethnographic interests.

M.K.

Radcliffe Institute
Cambridge, Massachusetts
January 1970

Contents

Illustrations

Tables

Foreword by T. O. Beidelman

It is a double pleasure to write a foreword to Dr. Kilson's fine study of Ga songs and ritual. First, it is gratifying to have some formal association with a valuable work in the ethnography of West African folklore and cosmology. Secondly, it is equally gratifying to survey the work of a former student and find that she has become an accomplished colleague contributing by both research and scholarly devotion to the advancement of a field to which one is committed, the study of Africa and its peoples.

The proper purpose of a foreword is to provide a commentary which supplements an author's study. Modesty and a sense of scholarly propriety often inhibit an author from clearly indicating the values of his own work. Furthermore, whatever the enthusiasm and skill lavished on an ethnographic report, no such study ever provides all of the data one might wish, and this too may contribute to a scholar's reticence about his achievements. I feel that Dr. Kilson has modestly underemphasized the value of her findings, and in the next few pages I try to indicate the values her work has for the study of folklore, symbolism, and society and how this may contribute to social theory. Perhaps I can best do this with reference to some of the previous work of this type done in Africa, especially West Africa, for, having examined the literature, I believe the present study is the finest available sociological analysis of texts for West Africa.

Whatever their differences, most scholars agree that there has been insufficient recording and publication of African oral literature, whether this be ritual songs and chants, folk-tales, myths, legends, riddles, proverbs, etc. In his useful though now outdated survey, Bascom takes stock of the material available for sub-Saharan Africa.[1] In an earlier essay, Berry surveys the material for West Africa.[2] Both scholars express a measured gratitude that even such uneven data are available, but each goes on to suggest the weaknesses in these works. Most scholars lament the lack of volume in these data, the lack of a wide range of types of texts from any particular society, and the lack of extensive original texts to go with these translations. But some of the most perceptive criticism reflects more difficult and subtler theoretical problems in which the data cannot be separated from the aims to which these are put by the analyst. Three interconnected but somewhat different issues are stressed: (1) There is a problem in accurately transcribing a language. For the most part this issue is emphasized by linguists primarily interested in the structure of various languages; their needs would seem best served by intensive tape recording and interviews by linguists themselves, collecting a wide range of types of speech. This poses requirements beyond the capabilities (and even the needs) of most social anthropologists. But even the social anthropologist requires original texts, even if somewhat crude, in order to check the use and context of key terms; moreover, since opinions vary regarding just what indigenous terms and notions are relevant to research in alien ideology and thought, all texts must be available. (2) Some social anthropologists, including myself, have emphasized the ways by which such material may be used both as keys to understanding the cosmology or world view of a particular society and as means of discerning certain problematical social situations. (3) Still others insist that this material is best considered in and of itself. Personally, I consider the last of these a poorly conceived approach, but one worth discussing further if only

1. W. Bascom, "Folklore Research in Africa," *Journal of American Folklore* 77, no. 303:12-31 (1964).
2. J. Berry, *Spoken Art in West Africa,* School of Oriental and African Studies, University of London (London, 1961).

because it has been strongly advocated by Dr. Finnegan, one of the more intelligent and sophisticated contemporary researchers in the study of West African oral literature.[3] This also seems the implicit view of the editors of the influential series, the Oxford Library of African Literature.

Dr. Finnegan's arguments so neatly illustrate some of the difficulties involved in the study of traditional oral literature that they provide a convenient point of departure for an assessment of the kinds of information and understanding which such data may provide. Dr. Finnegan, as a student of Professor Evans-Pritchard, makes a laudable plea for the resuscitation of folklore studies in Africa, but in the course of her advocacy she somewhat unfairly blames the decline of interest in such studies in Britain upon the students of social structure:

> Under the influence of the 'structure and function' approach, the impression has been implicitly given that such narratives must *either* have a clear and discoverable function (usually maintaining the *status quo*) — in which case they are to be analyzed 'sociologically' (i.e. according to one particular theoretical approach) *or* that they are 'merely' art—in which case they are irrelevant to the serious sociologist or social anthropologist. Hence, any detailed investigation of oral literature in its own terms has been ignored. Little interest has been taken, for instance, in the social contexts and aims of particular genres or individual artists in particular societies, in the nature and roles of narrator or audience, in the local classification of literature, and so on.[4]

It is arguable that this may describe the attitudes of some British social anthropologists in the 1940s and 1950s, but it is surely an inaccurate stereotype incompatible with postwar structuralism, with its roots in French sociology and in such

3. See R. Finnegan, *Limba Stories and Storytelling*, Oxford Library of African Literature (Oxford: Clarendon Press, 1967).
4. R. Finnegan, "Attitudes to the Study of Oral Literature in British Social Anthropology," *Man*, n.s. 4, no. 1: 59-69 (1969), p. 65.

original minds as Hocart, Freud, Dumézil, and the folklorist Propp. It also suggests a gross misunderstanding of sociology. In any case, this seems a false quandary; today, indeed, art and symbolism, what Leach calls the identity of aesthetics with social ethics, are viewed as the core of any moral (social) system.[5] Dr. Finnegan's conception of the scope of social anthropology seems far from Mauss's notion of a "total social phenomenon." If folklore has any lasting merit as a field of study by anthropologists, it is in its relation to other spheres of society and social action. Indeed, this too is the relevance of literature.

One of the main virtues of Dr. Kilson's work is her ability to tie in *Kpele* songs and associated ritual with the central ideology and, therefore, normative features of Ga society. Such an approach, of course, is axiomatic with a proper study of any ritual, which in some sense always relates to the basic concepts that provide the means for ordering a society.

In contrast, Dr. Finnegan seems to imply that only myth, ritual, and legend would interest the ordinary social anthropologist. While Dr. Kilson's present work deals essentially with ritual situations, perhaps a few remarks on the topic of folktales, as they relate to oral literature, would not be entirely out of place. Somehow the entertaining and "artificial" qualities of folktales or poetry might be wrongly dismissed as mere epiphenomena. Even Bascom, whose own view is very different from Dr. Finnegan's, discusses the social functions of folklore, such as its didactic, mnemonic, and cathartic functions, but he writes little of its potential as a vehicle for depth analysis of tensions and basic patterns and forms within culture.[6] However, in fairness to Bascom, one must concede that such interpretations are implicit in his concept of the didactic and cathartic functions of oral literature. The epiphenomenal quality of some folklore data may well be their greatest social significance. One can express dangerous and

5. E. R. Leach, *Political Systems of Highland Burma* (Cambridge, Mass.: Harvard University Press, 1954), p. 12.
6. See W. Bascom, "Folklore and Literature," in *The African World*, ed. R. A. Lystad, pp. 469-490 (New York: Praeger, 1965).

perplexing quandaries with impunity in the guise of harmless and humorous tales, often described by the tellers themselves as fit more for children than adults. Similarly, Freud made much of seemingly irrelevant verbal slips as clues to fundamental perplexities and tensions in the mind. Edgar Wind, a master of symbolic analysis of visual forms, puts the matter well in describing the great nineteenth-century art critic, Morelli:

> To identify the hand of the master, and distinguish it from the hand of a copyist, we must rely on small idiosyncrasies which seem inessential, subordinate features which look so irrelevant that they would not engage the attention of any imitator, restorer or forger; the shape of a finger-nail or the lobe of an ear. As these are inexpressive parts of a figure, the artist himself, no less than his imitator, is likely to relax in their execution; they are the places where he lets himself go, and for that reason they reveal him unmistakably. This is the core of Morelli's argument: an artist's personal instinct for form will appear at its purest in the least significant parts of his work because they are the least laboured.[7]

Similarly, folklore, in its unguarded quality of play, may provide comparable clues about the most fundamental, but less consciously realized, qualities of values and thoughts. Dr. Kilson suggests similar problems in her discussion of variation in Ga songs, although she does not here expand this point further.

One problem is that "folklore" itself is an unsuitable term. As Dr. Finnegan rightly points out, the term has sometimes been used in an ethnocentric and demeaning manner to cover all oral literature which, not being committed to script, we consider less important than our own. At one level of analysis, all literature is of a piece for a society; at another it is of such different types that one may well question how we can properly apply the same analytical tools to all of it. For ex-

---

7. *Art and Anarchy* (New York: Vintage Books, 1969), p. 40.

ample, it is clear that the social contexts in which key myths are recited and the significance which these have are very different, say, from the context for a set of proverbs told to underscore a particular social opinion. It is one thing to suggest, as Lévi-Strauss sometimes does, that a myth works out at an imaginary level profound, potential paradoxes presented within a society;[8] it is quite another to be aware that many proverbs exist in contradictory sets which may lose their sense of contradiction once a particular situation is morally agreed upon in its definition. Thus, in any extensive written collection of proverbs, the contradictions would be obvious to a reader, but one would suppose that the actors involved could evaluate a particular situation in order to determine whether "Haste makes waste" were more appropriate than "A stitch in time saves nine." And these clear-cut judgments, too, would be different from the insinuating, ambiguous interpersonal hostility Evans-Pritchard claims for certain Zande witticisms.[9]

Style and context of particular literary forms are only the beginning to the study of oral literature, or any literature. Thus, one may reasonably assert that the problems posed by the study of a particular Elizabethan playright are different from those posed by another, and yet one may go on to study the broader form and significance of Elizabethan drama. More important still, one may apply even broader criteria and study Elizabethan literature as a whole, from drama to poetry, from historical narratives to essays. In doing so, one simply applies an understanding of the cosmology and sociological qualities of that time, even though these are refracted in terms of individual authors and literary modes. Doubtless, Dr. Berry is as justified in writing of the basic form of the West African riddle as others are in writing of Western European lyric poetry or drama.[10] But we must not be less critical

8. See his analysis of the myth of Asdiwal, "The Story of Asdiwal," in *The Structural Study of Myth,* ed. E. R. Leach, pp. 11-48 (London: Tavistock, 1967).

9. *"Sanza,* a Characteristic Feature of Zande Language and Culture," in *Essays in Social Anthropology,* pp. 204-238 (London: Faber, 1962).

10. *Spoken Art in West Africa,* p. 11.

of the first than the second as a possible overgeneralization. It seems to me that the finest of any literary criticism, such as that of G. Wilson Knight, Edmund Wilson, T. S. Eliot, Kenneth Burke, or Leslie Fiedler, to cite a rather arbitrarily chosen set of critics, resembles the best of symbolic and cosmological analyses in social anthropology, such as those by Leach, Horton, Middleton, Douglas, Turner, and others. These are successful to the extent that each is able to enter into the cosmological perspective of the society being analyzed. It is perplexing to determine how to take Dr. Finnegan's own concluding quote from Leavis that we must study literature "as literature"; it is surely only within a wider cultural context, including social relations and cosmology, that this can have any significance at all.[11] Without such considerations, social anthropologists studying folklore may resemble those aestheticians damned by Wind who seek the eradication of matter by form, much as Lévi-Strauss sometimes seems bent on some neo-Kroeberian misdirection in constructing pattern at the cost of cultural content.

Dr. Kilson's present study combines the best of various modes of analysis. (1) The songs are presented both in translations and in their original texts. (2) The technical structure of the songs and some of the bases for variation and style are discussed. But even her laudably detailed comments on textual variation still cannot penetrate the deeper levels in explaining the relation between individual motives and the choice of symbols which individuals try to use, nor can these wholly expose aesthetic criteria regarding qualities of sound and imagery, as conceived by the singers. This deeper level of analysis makes little sense to readers lacking some acquaintance with the actual language concerned. This is a universal limitation of comparative literature, even when it is presented in a social anthropological context. There seems no ready solution to the problem, though one could reasonably ask why such aesthetic criteria should be of particular interest to those

---

11. "Attitudes to the Study of Oral Literature."

not well acquainted with a language in the first place.[12]
(3) The social context in which a song is sung is recognized as essential to understanding its meaning. This involves not only a description of the social occasion itself but of the composition of the audience and its responses to the singers. Dr. Kilson's fine discussion of the songs sung at the installation of a chief nicely demonstrates the problems involved. (4) Ga cosmology is presented with clear relevance to the songs considered. Since any discussion of the content of literature must ultimately refer back to a cosmology, it seems odd to praise Dr. Kilson for having the common sense to provide the data essential to her problem; yet the background cosmology which she so rightly provides here is absent from most of the other studies of this nature, including nearly all of those cited by Bascom and Berry and is even very inadequate for Dr. Finnegan's material. (5) Finally, Dr. Kilson presents a broad picture of Ga social organization and its relation to cosmology. However, we still require further, supplementary publications on these topics before the broader picture of the relation of Ga thought and ritual to Ga social action and sentiments will be entirely clear. This Dr. Kilson is in the process of doing.

There are, however, two minor points regarding Dr. Kilson's interpretation of Ga cosmology with which I take issue, mainly because they suggest more complex issues regarding the origins and functions involved in constructing symbolic systems.

12. It is, of course, reasonable to demonstrate to students both the complexity and unique qualities of any particular literature. However, this does not mean that the deeper aesthetic levels of such literature can be grasped by nonspeakers. Indeed, any suggestions of this sort would seem to be a kind of ethnocentrism in that these minimize the inherent difficulties in such a task. But, most would admit that such oversimplification is less likely where the language is already written, especially if this is in an alien script. For example, many would concede that the complexities of Chinese and Arabic poetry and their intimate relation to calligraphy demand knowledge of both the spoken and written language; only a brash novice would suggest that even the best alien translations and discussions could wholly solve the problems of rendering a full meaning. The situation is surely similar regarding the complex relations of Ga song texts and Ga music and speech.

The first involves her explanation as to why Ga utilize so many anthropomorphic models in discussing nonhumans. She asserts that ". . . an anthropomorphic model of social relations within nonhuman classes of being not only makes relations within these classes intelligible to men, but creates the ideological basis for orderly interaction between members of these classes and human beings. Through the assimilation of the existence of nonhuman beings to human categories, interrelations between nonhuman beings and human beings become possible." (p. 66). I recognize that her essentially cognitive interpretation is both valid and useful, but I should prefer it supplemented with an affectual interpretation as well: man shackles animals by putting them into his image (as she suggests), but man also frees himself by describing himself in bestial, nonhuman terms. Since this problem is complex, some examples from Western popular imagery may help clarify my points. Thus, animals such as the deer Bambi or the dog Lassie are made sympathetic and both cognitively and affectually comprehensible through endowing them with anthropomorphized attributes, but they remain animals, nonetheless. In contrast, the animals in the Uncle Remus tales and Aesop, or cartoon characters such as those in the wistful-demonic worlds of Krazy Kat and Pogo, are hardly merely animals, nor are the frenetic characters in animated films; these are humanoid, all the more amusing but also disturbing because they represent complex conflations of attributes characterizing different organic and moral kingdoms. The ambiguous nature of men has often been expressed in this manner.[13] To view human attributes as exhibited therio-

---

13. These are humanoid in their absorption of some but not all human motives and values which they express in action, but these are also often dramatically expressed by deviation from natural posture, as seen in animals such as performing bears and dogs or cartoon animals assuming erect humanoid posture. For a long and involved discussion of this, see H. Hediger, *Man and Animal in the Zoo* (New York: Delacorte, 1969), pp. 121-123. The reverse of this holds for men. For example, the polluted king Nebuchadnezzar assumed quadrupedal posture (Daniel 4:25-30) and the "wild animal" lunatic assumed a bestial posture in the stage and film enactment of Peter Weiss's *Marat/Sade* (New York:

morphically may allow expression of feelings, motives, and acts sometimes disallowed full force in human shape.

The second point involves Dr. Kilson's use of an argument made famous by Durkheim. She writes that ". . . the most parsimonious explanation for the form of social relations within divine and animal classes is the Durkheimian hypothesis that Ga notions about the ordering of human society are the most readily available model for interrelations among nonhuman beings" (p. 66). While this characterizes the broadest assertion of Durkheim's classic analysis, his masterpiece contains a more subtle and ambiguous discussion of the interdependence between society and things in which he suggests that the categories of society and the natural categories of the physical world each exert influences upon the structure of thought. Despite a danger that such analysis may slip into a kind of Platonic, circular mysticism, the notion seems far nearer the state of affairs as to how cosmological systems developed:

> That the anthropomorphic instinct, with which the animists have endowed primitive men, cannot explain their mental condition is shown by the nature of the confusions of which they are guilty. In fact, these do not come from the fact that men have immoderately extended the human kingdom to the point of making all the others enter into it, but from the fact that they confound the most disparate kingdoms. They have not conceived the world in their own image any more than they have conceived themselves in the world's image: they have done both at the same time. Into the idea they have formed

---

Pocket Books, 1966; p. 53). Elsewhere, Hediger equates humanizing of animals with demonizing (*The Psychology and Behaviour of Animals in Zoos and Circuses* [New York: Dover, 1968], p. 84). Not only are such liminal animals and men ambiguous morally, but the forces of physical elements do not always affect them as they would ordinary creatures: men survive, even in physical conditions where they could not; cartoon creatures are hit by bricks or exploded and yet miraculously recover in seconds. This, of course, adds moral ambiguity to certain aspects of the violence presented, making it more acceptable.

of things, they have undoubtedly made human elements enter; but into the idea they have formed of themselves, they have made enter elements coming from things.[14]

But these are insignificant criticisms of an excellent and careful exposition of the thought of one African society. In her monograph, Dr. Kilson has advanced our understanding of the relations among cosmology, social structure, and the verbal aspects of ritual; in this study we have a distillation of what appear to be most of the basic features of Ga society and values. It demonstrates that even elementary appreciation of any African (non-Western) aesthetic modes of expression requires enormous care and thought. We remain in a very rudimentary stage in such interpretation. It is works such as Dr. Kilson's which will eventually show us the direction toward clearer understanding and appreciation, both for a new evaluation of human (social) possibilities and for our own individual pleasure and enrichment.

Dr. Kilson's work sustains a long and admirable tradition in social anthropology. In 1877, William Robertson Smith wrote:

Thus the quality of the poetic thought of each people is imprinted on its speech, while reciprocally the psychological and artistic peculiarities of the speech permanently control the national poetry, and form perhaps the strongest influence towards the preservation of a fixed character in the nation itself.[15]

Surely *Kpele* songs are such a formative national poetry for the Ga.

14. E. Durkheim, *The Elementary Forms of the Religious Life* (London: Allen and Unwin, 1934), p. 235.
15. "The Poetry of the Old Testament" (1877), in *Lectures and Essays of William Robertson Smith*, ed. J. S. Black and G. Chrystal, pp. 367-451 (London: A. & G. Black, 1912), p. 414.

Part I / *Kpele* Songs and Symbolism

The GA AREA

DEMU RIVER
AKWAPIM RANGE
SHAI HILLS
AYAWASO
ACCRA PLAINS
SAKUMƆ LAGOON
TEMA
NUNGUA
TESHI
KPESHI LAGOON
LABADI
KƆLE LAGOON
OSU
ACCRA
GULF of GUINEA

GHANA

UPPER VOLTA
IVORY COAST
TOGO
TAMALE
KUMASI
ACCRA
CAPE COAST
GULF of GUINEA

CENTRAL ACCRA and ENVIRONS

RING ROAD
AVENUE
INDEPENDENCE
KANESHI
ADABRAKA
KWAME NKRUMAH AVENUE
ABOSE OKAI
RAILWAY STATION
VICTORIABORG
BLACK STAR SQUARE
KƆLE LAGOON
RIPONSVILLE
HIGH STREET
HORSE ROAD
USSHER TOWN
USSHER FORT
JAMES TOWN
JAMES FORT
MAMPROBI
KƆLE GONNO
GULF of GUINEA

Central Accra

SCALE
0   ¼   ½   ¾   1 MILE

1 / Introduction

This book presents a collection of traditional religious songs which form part of the repertoire of the *kpele* cult of the Ga of southeastern Ghana. The texts are preceded by a discussion of the use of song *(lala)* in *kpele* ritual and an analysis of various aspects of the form and content of *kpele* songs in order to enrich and facilitate their appreciation and to demonstrate their value for understanding Ga conceptions. Underlying *kpele* ritual is a system of ideas about the ordering of the universe; *kpele* songs express aspects of this cosmology, especially the differentiation of moral categories and their modes of interrelationship. While certain aspects of *kpele* thought, such as anthropomorphic models of nonhuman reality, are conveyed exclusively through the verbal medium of songs, other notions relating to the differentiation and complementarity of moral categories are expressed not only in songs but even more effectively through the spatial and temporal properties of nonverbal ritual action. Consequently, I have utilized some nonverbal forms of ritual symbolism in describing and analyzing Ga cosmological conceptions.

The primary analytical value of *kpele* songs lies in their richness as sources of information about Ga conceptualizations of the universe. Although interest in the collection of the cosmological notions of preliterate peoples long antedates the founding of anthropology as a scholarly discipline, Durkheim and Mauss' classic and seminal essay, *Primitive*

Classification, published in 1903, represents the first systematic sociological analysis of such notions. In this essay Durkheim and Mauss postulate a causal relation between social classification and symbolic categorization. Although many contemporary scholars have rejected the notion of a causal connection between social and symbolic classifications, the correspondences between these orders continue to engage the attention of social anthropologists, particularly those interested in the analysis of ritual symbolism. This concern is especially evident in the analyses of ritual published in recent years by Beidelman, Middleton, Needham, Rigby, and Turner.[1] The sophisticated and often brilliant analyses of these contemporary students of ritual symbolism focus on the connotations of symbolic articles and/or ritual actions and the dynamic social and psychological implications of these connotations. Such analyses have led even to explicitly anti-Durkheimian hypotheses concerning the origins of symbolic classifications. For example, Turner concludes his paper, "Color Classification in Ndembu Ritual," by saying that

> . . . the three colors white-red-black for the simpler societies . . . are abridgments or condensations of whole realms of psychobiological experience . . . It is only by subsequent abstraction from these configurations that the other modes of social classification employed by mankind arose.[2]

Closely related to the problem of classification has been a continuing concern in social anthropology with the differentiation between "primitive" and "modern" modes of thought. This issue, which harks back to the formulations of prelogical mentality by Lévy-Bruhl, of mythical or pre-Copernican thought by Cassirer, and of primitive world view by Redfield, is relevant to the contemporary structural analyses of Lévi-Strauss. Mary Douglas eloquently characterizes the

---

1. See the Bibliography.
2. Victor W. Turner, *The Forest of Symbols*, p. 91.

personal nature of such a pre-Copernican world view:

> . . . a primitive world view looks out on a universe which is personal in several different senses. Physical forces are thought of as interwoven with the lives of persons. Things are not completely distinguished from persons and persons are not completely distinguished from their external environment. The universe responds to speech and mime. It discerns the social order and intervenes to uphold it.[3]

Such a characterization of world view is appropriate to Ga cosmology. In my subsequent analysis of Ga thought, however, I attempt to go beyond this assertion to explicate the logical modes of opposition and analogy whereby this personal world view is achieved.

Douglas and others assume that a corollary of such a personalized world view is a lack of interest in speculative thought in primitive societies. In several papers, Robin Horton effectively refutes this argument.[4] Horton suggests that primitive societies utilize personal explanatory models, because in such societies

> . . . people's activities in society present the most markedly ordered and regular area of their experience, whereas their biological and inanimate environment is by and large less tidily predictable. Hence it is chiefly to human activities and relationships that such communities turn for the sources of their most important explanatory models.[5]

In my analysis, I attempt to develop the basic explanatory model of the world which the Ga utilize and show its relationship to certain aspects of the Ga social order. In order to do this, I draw upon songs and other forms of ritual symbolism

3. Mary Douglas, *Purity and Danger*, p. 88.
4. "Ritual Man in Africa," *Africa* 34:85-104; "African Traditional Thought and Western Science," *Africa* 37:50-71, 155-187; "Neo-Tylorianism: Sound Sense or Sinister Prejudice?" Man, n.s. 3:625-634.
5. "Ritual Man in Africa," p. 99.

of the *kpele* cult and upon Ga exegeses of these data, because
I assume that ritual is, in Turner's words, "a storehouse of
traditional knowledge."[6]

Although Ga thought and ritual have not been analyzed in
this way before, information about many aspects of Ga society have been available in the West for more than a century.[7] Since the publication of Danniell's ethnographic essay
in 1856, a number of Ghanaian and Western scholars hàve
contributed to the study of Ga society. During the early
twentieth century, contributions to Ga ethnography were
made primarily by Ga writers and appeared in either the
Journal of the African Society or the *Gold Coast Review.* In
the former journal there appeared several ethnographically
useful papers on Ga political, kinship, and religious institutions by Quartey-Papafio and two essays on ethno-history
and marriage customs by Bruce-Myers; in the latter publication there are papers on beliefs and religious institutions by
Brown, Page, Welman, and Wright. The most influential
studies of Ga society, however, are M. J. Field's descriptive
monographs, *Religion and Medicine of the Ga People* and
Social Organisation of the Ga People, published in 1937 and
1940, respectively. Subsequently, several scholars have published limited but systematic studies relating to Ga society in
a variety of intellectual disciplines: Berry, Kropp, and Okun-
or in linguistics; Wilks and Ozanne in history; Allott and Pogucki in law; Adjei, Ammah, Nketia, and Quarcoo in ethnography; Acquah, Amarteifio *et al.*, Boateng, Munger, and Nypan in urban studies.

Within this fairly extensive body of literature on Ga society and culture, M. J. Field's descriptive monographs published in 1937 and 1940 constitute the most authoritative
ethnographic sources for social scientists. Thus, Manoukian's
description of Ga society in *Akan and Ga-Adangme Peoples
of the Gold Coast* relies almost exclusively on Field's data;

6. Victor W. Turner, *The Drums of Affliction*, p. 2.
7. See Bibliography for complete references.

Pogucki, Jack and Esther Goody, and Amarteifio *et al.* utilize Field's characterizations of Ga social institutions, particularly her analysis of kinship. While I fully appreciate Field's pioneering contribution to Ga ethnography, I must acknowledge that my interpretation of certain aspects of the Ga social system differs from hers. I, therefore, wish to note briefly two pertinent and significant differences in our understanding of Ga society and religion.

First, Field's interpretations of Ga social structure differ considerably from my own. While she characterizes Ga kinship as patrilineal, I consider that it is cognatic not only at the level of ideology but at the level of social transaction.[8] Thus, Ga phrase kinship relations in the physiological idiom of blood (*la*) which they say is transmitted by both parents to their offspring; Ga also say that a larger proportion of a person's blood is obtained from his father, which is consistent with the patrilateral emphasis of their kinship notions. Ga acquire property and accede to office through matrilateral and patrilateral affiliations. It may be that the fundamental difference between Field's and my interpretations of Ga kinship is due to the fact that our research has been conducted in different parts of the Ga area; she has worked primarily in Tema and Nungua, while I have worked in Accra. I am inclined to consider, however, that the difference relates to changes in conceptual orientations in social anthropology during the decades that intervene between our research.

Secondly, Field and I differ in our understanding of the Ga pantheon. While the notion of a supreme being is central to my analysis of *kpele* cosmology, Field not only makes only occasional references to such a being but does not present any analysis of such a conception.[9] Her description of Ga re-

8. "The Ga have a patrilineal system of succession" (M. J. Field, *Social Organisation of the Ga People*, p. 52n). "The members of the House are called *webii* (house-children) and are all descendants of the founder of the House counting only the children of male members" (ibid., p. 1).

9. M. J. Field, *Religion and Medicine of the Ga People*, pp. 18, 34, 61-62.

ligious institutions consists of a somewhat haphazard cata-
logue of deities and rites in different Ga towns. Although her
encyclopedic orientation towards Ga deities may account for
her failure to appreciate the significance of a supreme being,
Bruce-Myers discusses this notion in "Origins of the Gas"
which appeared a decade before the publication of her
book.[10] Although I do not wish to underestimate Field's contribution to Ga ethnography, I think that it is important to
indicate that I have found her data not infrequently at vari-
ance with my own.

Since this book concerns *kpele* songs, I wish to review
briefly previous publications which deal with these data. A
number of texts and/or translations have been recorded by
several scholars. In "Origins of the Gas," Bruce-Myers presents two texts with free translations. Field publishes a translation of one *kpele* song in *The Social Organisation of the Ga
People* and translations of twenty-five *kpele* songs, eleven of
which are accompanied by indigenous texts, in *Religion and
Medicine of the Ga People*. Nketia publishes the text and
translation of one song in "Prayers at Kple Worship" and two
untranslated texts in *African Music in Ghana*. Finally, E. A.
Ammah utilizes textual fragments in his essays, "Ghanaian
Philosophy" and *Materialism in Ga Society*.[11] Ammah's essays are the only previous publications which acknowledge
and draw upon the conceptual richness of *kpele* song texts.
Although Field records a number of texts, she does not attempt to analyze their content. Her attitude toward these
data is expressed clearly in the following statement:

> Like all Ga religious songs they are pleasant and full of
> life to hear, but extremely disappointing when the words

10. J. M. Bruce-Myers, "The Origin of the Gas," *Journal of the African Society* 27:70.

11. Field, *Social Organisation*, p. 12; Field, *Religion and Medicine*,
pp. 13, 16, 18, 22, 25, 31, 32, 34, 58, 71; J. H. K. Nketia, "Prayers at
Kple Worship," *The Ghana Bulletin of Theology* 2:21; J. H. K. Nketia,
African Music in Ghana, pp. 56-57, 127-129; E. A. Ammah, "Ghanaian
Philosophy," *The Ghanaian*, October 1961-June 1962, passim; E. A.
Ammah, *Materialism in Ga Society*, passim.

are written down, for they are mostly proverbs, memorable sayings of dead and gone people and references to obscure incidents in history.[12]

Her sources of regret are my sources of joy, for, as I hope to demonstrate, these frequently pithy, sometimes obscure texts are a treasure trove of Ga cosmological conceptions.

Ga Society

The contemporary Ga, who speak a Kwa language and numbered 236,210 in the 1960 census, are an ethnically and culturally diversified people.[13] Their cultural heterogeneity arises from a variety of factors which include penetrable natural boundaries, the entrepreneurial role of the Ga in prehistoric and historic times, the Akwamu domination of Ga society during the late seventeenth and early eighteenth centuries, and the location of the center of colonial and later national authority and international commercial activity at Accra. However much contemporary Ga culture may owe to contact with other African peoples, to say nothing of Europeans during the past three hundred years, Ga perceive their cultural heritage as unique and distinct from other Ghanaian cultures.

The Ga homeland is the Accra Plains of southeastern Ghana which extend along the Atlantic coast for about forty miles

---

12. *Religion and Medicine,* p. 16; cf. ibid., pp. 13, 18, 45n.

13. *Special Report 'E': Tribes in Ghana, 1960 Population Census of Ghana.* The Kwa languages, which J. H. Greenberg classifies as a subfamily within the Niger-Congo language family, are distributed along the West African coast from western Liberia to eastern Nigeria (Joseph H. Greenberg, *The Languages of Africa,* pp. 8, 173). Within the Kwa group, Ga is a member of "the Ga-Adangme cluster. The other dialects of this cluster are Ada, Osudoku, Krobo, Shai and the various types of Adangme spoken at Kpone, Prampram and Ningo" (Vincent Okunor, *Tone in the Ga Verb,* p. i). While Adangme speakers represent the "eastern neighbours" of the Ga people, their neighbors to the north, the Akwapim, and to the west, the Awutu, speak dialects of Twi-Fante (ibid., p. ii). Moreover, "Ga has been considerably influenced by Twi-Fante" (ibid.).

and are bounded by the Akwapim scarp on the north. The more transitory eastern and western boundaries are recognized conventionally as the Laloi Lagoon and the Densu River, respectively. Throughout Ga history, the demographic and social centers have been at the northern or southern extremities of this area. In prehistoric and early historic times, the main centers of population and authority were located on the northern littoral. As trade patterns changed from the overland gold trade to the coastal overseas gold and slave trade and as Ga lost control over hinterland trade routes, the centers of population concentration shifted to the coast.[14] For almost three centuries the Ga heartland has consisted of a series of coastal towns, each with its dependent coastal and inland villages and hamlets. These towns (Accra, Osu, Labadi, Teshi, Nungua, and Tema) are welded into a loose confederation under the Ga paramount chief (*Ga mangtsę*) in Accra, though the scope of his authority and the duration of the confederation are disputed.[15]

The most important social unit in Ga society is the cognatic family (*we*) to which members are recruited by birth and less frequently by adoption. Membership in the family is not terminated by physiological death; rather, a family comprises two categories of person: living persons and ancestral shades. The prosperity of the living is thought to depend in part upon harmonious relations between these two categories of family members. The family owns an estate consisting of

14. See Ivor Wilks, "The Rise of the Akwamu Empire, 1650-1710," *Transactions of the Historical Society of Ghana* 3:99-136; Ivor Wilks, "Some Glimpses into the Early History of Accra," and Paul Ozanne, "Notes on the Early Historic Archaeology of Accra," *Transactions of the Historical Society of Ghana* 6:51-70.

15. In Accra, it is said that the Ga paramount chief has had authority over other towns since precolonial times, and evidence presented at a government enquiry in 1907 supports this view (Ghana [Gold Coast] Government, "Proceedings Government Enquiry into Ga Constitution.") By contrast. Field, who worked primarily in the eastern towns of Tema and Nungua, presents the view that prior to the imposition of colonial rule, the *Ga mangtsę*'s authority was limited to Accra (Field, *Social Organisation*, pp. 72, 212; Field, *Religion and Medicine*, p. 85).

land, buildings, patronyms, and titles to secular and ritual office. Members of the family acquire usufruct rights to the property of an estate through the collective decision of a council of elders. This council of elders, which theoretically includes both male and female members, also selects office holders and arbitrates disputes among family members. The family is a nonresidential group whose members are dispersed in households (*shia*) not only within a town but within a number of villages. However dispersed its members, each family recognizes one building in town as the founder's house to which family members return annually to participate in the ritual feast honoring ancestral shades (*homowo*) and occasionally to observe rituals marking the fundamental biosocial transitions involving the birth and death of its members.[16]

The living members of a family reside in scattered households (*shia*). In traditional Ga society, households comprise unisexual kin groups in which adult kinswomen and children live together and adult kinsmen are coresident. The residential separation of adults of opposite sex is backed by mystical sanctions, for menstruating women are believed to contaminate ritual objects in men's compounds, thereby angering ancestral shades and divine beings. While the physical residential separation of men and women is an inviolate principle of the traditional residential system, Ga say that three types of dwelling units exist whose occupants' relationship is determined by the sex of the genealogically senior member: (1) a men's house occupied by patrilaterally related men, (2) a women's house occupied by matrilaterally related women and their children, and (3) a house with a section for patrilaterally related men and an adjacent section for women who may be either patrilaterally affiliated to the male household or wives of men living in the men's compound. In the third type of dwelling, patrilaterally related women have lifelong

16. See Marion D. de B. Kilson, "The Ga Naming Rite," *Anthropos* 63/64: 904-920.

occupancy rights, whereas affinally related women have occupancy rights only for the duration of their marriages.
Thus, in the traditional residential system, the sex of the
household head determines the relationship between the occupants of a dwelling. If the head is a man, occupants are
patrilaterally related men and women or wives and children
of these men; if the head is a woman, the occupants are matrilaterally related women and children. Thus, the traditional
residential system depends upon three structural principles:
the separation of adults of opposite sex, the sex of the household head as the determinant of the members' affiliation and
their age and sex distribution, and the superordination of
males. Although the extent to which this model of residence
was realized in practice cannot be determined, today in the
old area of Ga settlement in Accra unisexual households occur fairly infrequently; bisexual households, however, invariably involve cognates and not conjugal pairs.[17]

In order for such a residential system to work and for society to perpetuate itself, the various types of residential
units cannot be strictly autonomous. In Ga houses every
man has his own room, while several women and their children may share a single room. When a man wishes to have
sexual relations with his wife, he calls her to his room. In a
polygynous marriage, each wife in rotation has a prescribed
interval of connubial service during which it is her duty and
right to sleep with her husband and to prepare his meals. The
meals usually are prepared at the woman's house and brought
by her or by one of her children to the man's house. These
procedures imply that while men sleep in their own houses,
women may sleep elsewhere, and that the population of a
dwelling fluctuates between day and night and from one
night to another.

Contemporary Ga who reside in Accra consider their culture to have been influenced by contact with other African

17. See Marion D. de B. Kilson, "Continuity and Change in the Ga
Residential System," *Ghana Journal of Sociology* 3:81-97.

peoples. The impact of this interaction is reflected most conspicuously in Ga political and religious institutions. Ga claim that their society was initially theocratic and that secular authority associated with chieftaincy was introduced later. Whatever the historical validity of this claim, Ga consider that the nomenclature, paraphernalia, and ritual associated with chiefly institutions are based on an Akan model: Akan terms constitute the appellations associated with Ga political offices, Akan drums and music are played at Ga political ceremonies, the *asafo* military structure is thought to have been borrowed from the Fanti, and many symbolic articles associated with chieftaincy such as umbrellas, gold ornaments, and kente cloth are regarded as Akan in inspiration. With respect to religious institutions, three of the four major traditional cults practiced by contemporary Ga are non-Ga in origin: *me* is an Adangme cult, *otu* and *akọng* are Akan cults. *Kpele*, the fourth cult, is believed to be the indigenous Ga religious system. Moreover, at least at the level of linguistic usage, the *kpele* cult has been influenced by neighboring African peoples in such a way that Akan and Guang words appear frequently in the liturgy of western Ga, and Guang and Adangme words in that of eastern Ga.

Ga assume that contact with other African peoples was not limited to the exchange of ideas and customs. They believe that many "Ga" are descendants of non-Ga settlers who became assimilated to Ga cultural standards. In modern Accra, Ga distinguish between "true Ga" (*Ganyo krong*) and other Ga. The former are descendants of the Ga who in the midseventeenth century lived either on the coast or in the inland town of Ayawaso, which is known in European sources as Great Accra; the latter are descendants of later immigrant non-Ga settlers. Ga attribute the founding of the seven quarters of Accra in part to the settlement of immigrant communities and in part to the fission of established units. According to tradition, the true Ga settled in the Asere quarter. Political disputes within Asere led to the establishment of Gbese, Sempe, and Akumadze quarters. The three other quarters, however, were founded by immigrants: Otublohum by Akwamu, Abola by Fanti, and Ngleshi Alata by Nigerians. Within each of the Accra quarters today are Ga families whose ancestors are said to have been non-Ga immigrants. The differentiation between true Ga and other Ga is relevant to the practice of traditional cults, for *kpele* worship is the responsibility of true Ga families.

The culture of contemporary Ga people has been shaped not only by contact with other African peoples, but by inter-action with Europeans for more than three centuries. During the initial era of mercantile trade in gold and slaves, Ga played a decisive role as middleman between the peoples of the forest and the European traders on the coast.

> Within the northern boundary of the Accra state, near the modern Nsawam, there flourished a large market known as Abonse. Abonse was referred to as a "free market," which meant that the King of Accra permitted any traders from the interior to come there in safety to barter their goods. Such visitors, on the other hand, were not allowed to proceed beyond Abonse; from Abonse to the Accra capital, and from the capital to the beaches, trade was exclusively in the hands of the Accras.[18]

By the mid-seventeenth century, Accra had become "the greatest gold market on the Gold Coast," where five European powers (Denmark, England, Holland, Portugal, and Sweden) competed for the gold and slaves of the Ga traders.[19] The prosperity and authority of Great Accra ended abruptly with its destruction by the expanding neighboring state of Akwamu in 1677. The Akwamu succeeded in assimilating the Ga coastal territory in 1681 and maintained suzerainty over the area of the former Ga state until 1730.[20] After the Akwamu defeat of the Ga, coastal Accra began to assume its cosmopolitan character, as representatives of diverse tribal groups came there to participate in the overseas trade. Nevertheless,

18. Wilks, "Early History of Accra," p. 6.
19. Ozanne, "Early Historic Archaeology of Accra," pp. 64-65.
20. Wilks, "Rise of Akwamu Empire," pp. 106-111.

Ga people continued to play a significant role in the commercial life of Accra, which is now the major center of economic distribution in Ghana.

During the era of British colonial rule, the strategic coastal location of the Ga people facilitated their participation in Western religious, educational, and administrative institutions, especially after the transfer of the capital of the Gold Coast Colony from Cape Coast to Accra in 1876. Consequently, the proportion of Ga who are Christian, educated, and occupy skilled Western occupational categories exceeds that of other Ghanaian peoples (see Table 1). The majority of Ga, however, are not well educated by western standards

Table 1. Educational and Elite Occupational Statistics for Ghanaian and Ga Populations, 1960 (percentages)

| | *Education* | | | | | | |
| | Total over 6 years | | | Past | | Present | |
	Never	Past	Present	Middle School	Secondary School	Middle School	Secondary School
Ghana							
Males	63.4	18.1	18.5	62	6	28.2	3.6
Females	83.0	7.4	9.6	43.8	3.3	22.2	1.5
Ga							
Males	30.7	36.3	33.0	67.8	13.9	30.1	8.7
Females	60.6	16.7	22.7	65.0	4.3	30.1	3.9

Professional, Administrative, and Clerical Occupations

	Male	Female
Ghana	6.5	1.5
Ga	21.0	5.6

and participate in the national economy either as fishermen and farmers or as unskilled laborers. The differentiated socioeconomic structure of the Ga population is coordinate with variation in the cultural aspirations, values, norms, and expectations of Ga people.

The modern city of Accra, capital of Ghana, incorporates the old area of Ga settlement around the trading forts. In Central Accra there lives a stable Ga community of manual laborers, traders, and marginal elites whose more affluent kinsmen have moved away to the new suburbs ringing the city (see Table 2).[21] This community has access to and utilizes a variety of religious institutions, for within the limits

Table 2. Educational and Occupational Statistics for
Ga in Central Accra, 1960 (percentages)

	Male	Female	Number
Education (over 15 years)			
No schooling	28	72	10,307
Primary school	7	6	1,188
Middle school	52	20	5,981
Secondary school	13	2	1,149
Total	100	100	18,625
Occupation			
Professional/Administrative	8	2	567
Clerical	20	4	1,287
Sales	5	83	6,221
Fishing	21	0	1,036
Laborer	39	11	2,705
Other	7	0	365
Total	100	100	12,181

of Central Accra are located not only a large number of Christian churches, which include the edifices of established sects and indigenous "spiritual" churches, but many shrines of traditional cults. Among these cults, *kpele* occupies a dis-

21. In 1960, 91% Ga in Central Accra were born there.

tinctive position in the minds of Ga people, for *kpele* epitomizes their distinctive cultural heritage, which persists despite their assimilation of ideas from other African and Western cultures.

2 / *Kpele* Cult and Songs

Ga consider that the *kpele* cult represents the ancient religion of their forefathers. They say that the term *kpele* means "all-encompassing." The *kpele* cult is "all-encompassing" in several senses. Underlying *kpele* cult activities is a systematic conception of the ordering of the universe. This cosmology not only validates cult activities insofar as certain rituals are thought to be necessary to maintain and restore ordered relations within the universe, but it is re-created through the performance of ritual which expresses aspects of the cosmic order and the interrelations of its categories.[1] Certain periodic rites are believed necessary to ensure the reproduction and growth of plants, animals, and human beings. Such rites are performed on behalf of the entire Ga community. The aims of these rites, therefore, unite all living Ga within the *kpele* community. The community of believers, however, incorporates not only living men but ancestral shades. The latter in their lifetimes are thought to have enacted the same rites without which Ga society could not have persisted until the present; analogously, the continuity of Ga society in the future depends upon the performance of these rites by the present generation of living men. The *kpele* cult, therefore, is all-encompassing insofar as it embraces a total world view and a total community.

1. Victor W. Turner, *The Drums of Affliction*, pp. 6-8.

Nevertheless, *kpele* cult activities reaffirm the differentiation between "true Ga" and other Ga within Ga society, for true Ga families are responsible for the performance of *kpele* ritual. "True Ga" are descendants of Ga who are believed to have lived in inland towns and coastal hamlets before the late seventeenth-century movement to the coast. The present centers of *kpele* cult activities are the coastal towns in which the shrines of major deities (*dzemawǫng*, "place-god") are located. The shrines of some minor deities are located in villages, and many ritual specialists are domiciled in outlying villages from which they come to town to participate in rites.

While each true Ga family has responsibility for the cult of a particular *kpele* god, the performance of ritual is entrusted to two categories of ritual specialists: a male priest (*wulǫmǫ*) and a female medium (*wǫngtsę*). Within a cult group, the most important ascribed status is that of priest. The priesthood rotates among the component houses (*shia*) of the family (*we*). Theoretically, a family is subdivided into three houses of equivalent status which successively supply priests to serve the family god. A priest is selected from among eligible male candidates by the elders of his house. Ga say that within his house a priest can be succeeded only by his grandsons and not by his sons; available biographical evidence shows that this jural norm prevails in practice. The office of priest is a full-time and lifelong occupation. In the performance of his ritual duties, a priest is assisted by a collectivity (*agbaa*) of men and women who are recruited from the constituent houses of the family. Members of the *agbaa* perform their duties either until death or until incapacitated by old age, when they are succeeded by a younger relative, who is often an offspring of the same sex. These succession procedures to ascriptive office within cult groups differentiate subunits of equivalent status within true Ga families.

Although a priest and his ritual assistants attain office through kinship ascription, a medium achieves her position through divine intervention. Each god is thought to select (*mǫ*, "to catch") and marry (*kpe*) his medium, who serves until death. Since a marital relationship exists between medium and god, Ga expect *kpele* mediums to be women.[2] While a *kpele* medium participates in calendrical cult activities, she also performs occasional rites independently of the priest and his assistants. The medium, therefore, serves as an alternative channel to divine beings. Moreover, in certain situations, she has greater power than a priest, for only a medium can be possessed by mystical beings, which include not only divine beings, but ancestral shades and spirits of twins. Further, as an achieved status which is not restricted by kinship criteria, the office of medium constitutes a mechanism for cross-cutting and integrating cognatic units within Ga society, insofar as members of certain kin groups become involved in the cult activities of other groups.

In Accra, numerous cults, each devoted to the worship of an individual deity, perform *kpele* ritual. Six principal cults, however, are recognized. These are the cults addressed to *Nai*, god of the sea; *Sakumo*, the warrior defender of the Ga; *Naa Koole*, goddess of peace and holder of the Ga lands; *Naa Ede Oyeadu*, goddess of childbirth; *Dantu*, the time-keeping god; and *Gua*, the blacksmith god. Attached to the principal cults are subordinate cults addressed to minor deities. The relations between major and minor gods are phrased in the idiom of kinship, for the lesser deities are said to be the children (*bii*) of the major gods. Analogously, the relations between major and minor cult groups are perceived as those between senior and junior kinsmen. Representatives of the ju-

2. Ga men may become mediums for non-*kpele* cults, especially the *otu* cult addressed to warrior gods. Moreover, within the Ga area there are two or three male *kpele* mediums. Recently, various competing sociological explanations for the prevalence of female mediums in many societies have been presented in the pages of *Man* (see I. M. Lewis, "Spirit Possession and Deprivation Cults," *Man*, n.s. 1:307-329; Peter J. Wilson, "Status Ambiguity and Spirit Possession," *Man*, n.s. 2:366-378). I hope to have more information on this issue in the future; my present impression is that female mediumship in Ga society is related to status competition between the sexes on the sociological level and to the basic ambivalence of women about feminine sex identity on the psychological level.

nior cult groups participate in the calendrical rites of senior cult groups. The activities of the various cult groups, therefore, reaffirm the differentiation of subordinate and superordinate branches of true Ga families.

In summary, the organizational structure of the activities of *kpele* cult groups articulate a number of general sociological categories in Ga society. Insofar as calendrical rites are performed on behalf of the entire Ga community, *kpele* ritual differentiates the Ga from other Ghanaian peoples. The allocation of responsibility for the performance of *kpele* ritual to true Ga families serves to differentiate true Ga from other Ga within Ga society. Finally, the participation of members of minor cult groups in the rites of major cult groups distinguishes senior and junior branches within true Ga families.

Kpele cult groups perform periodic and occasional rites. In Accra, periodic or calendrical rites include weekly ritual performed by a priest on days of the week which are sacred to his family god, an annual millet (*ngmaa*) feast to celebrate each god, rites to open and close Kɔɔle Lagoon to fishing, which occur thrice during a lunar year, an annual rite to open the sea for fishing, and an annual set of rites surrounding the cultivation of millet (see Table 3).[3] While these rites vary in scale with respect to the number of participants and to the complexity of constituent ritual acts, all are system-maintaining rites, for these rites are thought to be essential for the maintenance of harmonious relations between gods and mortal men. Ga believers can scarcely contemplate failure to perform these rites, but Ga say that if these rites were not performed, the angry gods would kill human beings either directly through some cataclysmic event or indirectly by withholding sources of food.

While periodic rites recur at prescribed intervals, occasional rites occur in response to specific crises in the lives of individ-

---

3. One day of the week is sacred to each god, but ritual is performed on two additional days. Thus, *Kɔɔle*'s day is Friday, but ritual is performed on Tuesday and Sunday as well; *Nai*'s day is Tuesday, but ritual is performed on Friday and Sunday also.

Table 3. Calendar of *Kpele* Agricultural Rites in Accra*

Rite	Weekday	Interval after Dantu Shibaa	1968
Shibaa (digging ground)			
Dantu[a]	Monday		May 13
Sakumọ	Tuesday	1 day	May 14
Naa Kọọle	Friday	4 days	May 17[b]
Gua	Saturday	5 days	May 18
Naa Ede	Sunday	6 days	May 19
Nai	Tuesday	1 week, 1 day	May 21
Ngmaadumọ (planting millet)			
Dantu	Monday	1 week	May 20
Sakumọ	Tuesday	1 week, 1 day	May 21
Naa Kọọle	Friday	1 week, 4 days	May 24
Gua	Saturday	1 week, 5 days	May 25
Naa Ede	Sunday	1 week, 6 days	May 26
Nai	Tuesday	2 weeks, 1 day	May 28
Ngmaafaa (transplanting millet)			
Dantu	Monday	4 weeks	June 10
Sakumọ	Tuesday	4 weeks, 1 day	June 11
Naa Kọọle	Friday	4 weeks, 4 days	June 14[b]
Gua	Saturday	4 weeks, 5 days	June 15
Naa Ede	Sunday	4 weeks, 6 days	June 16
Nai	Tuesday	5 weeks, 1 day	June 18
Odada (welcoming gods from field)			
	Thursday	5 weeks, 3 days	June 20
Ngshọ bulemọ (opening the sea)			
	Tuesday	12 weeks, 1 day	August 6
Họmọwọ (feast for ancestors)[c]			
Lante Dzan we	Saturday	12 weeks, 5 days	August 10
Accra	Saturday	14 weeks, 5 days	August 24
Ngmaaku (reaping millet)			
Dantu	Saturday	12 weeks, 5 days	August 10
Sakumọ	Tuesday	15 weeks, 1 day	August 27
Nai	Tuesday	15 weeks, 1 day	August 27
Naa Kọọle	Friday	15 weeks, 4 days	August 30

Table 3—*Continued*

Rite	Weekday	Interval after Dantu Shibaa	1968
Ngmaayeli (millet feast)			
Dantu	Sunday	12 weeks, 6 days	August 11
Naa Koole	Friday	15 weeks, 4 days	August 30
Sakumo	Tuesday	16 weeks, 1 day	September 3
Nai	Tuesday	16 weeks, 1 day	September 3
Sakumo	Tuesday	17 weeks, 1 day	September 10
Nai	Tuesday	17 weeks, 1 day	September 10
Sakumo	Tuesday	18 weeks, 1 day	September 17
Amugi (Naibi)	Tuesday	18 weeks, 1 day	September 17
Obotu (Koolebi)	Tuesday	18 weeks, 1 day	September 17
Oyeni (Naibi)	Tuesday	18 weeks, 1 day	September 17
Nyongmotsa (Naibi)	Thursday	18 weeks, 3 days	September 19
Oshabedzi (Naibi)	Thursday	18 weeks, 3 days	September 19
Nai Afieye (Nainga)	Friday	18 weeks, 4 days	September 20
Gua	Saturday	18 weeks, 5 days	September 21
Osekan (Naibi)	Sunday	18 weeks, 6 days	September 22
Akrama (Sakumobi)	Sunday	18 weeks, 6 days	September 22
Klang	Sunday	19 weeks, 6 days	September 29
Ashiakle (Naibi)	Sunday	19 weeks, 6 days	September 29
Kpeledzoo (dance at Sakumo we)			
	Tuesday	16 weeks, 1 day	September 3
	Tuesday	17 weeks, 1 day	September 10
	Tuesday	18 weeks, 1 day	September 17
Mangnaamo (blessing town by Sakumo agbaa)			
	Wednesday	18 weeks, 2 days	September 18
Ngmaatoo (storing millet by Sakumo agbaa)			
	Tuesday	20 weeks, 1 day	October 1

*This is a partial calendar, for *ngmaayeli* dates for all Accra gods are not represented. Further, the intensity of ritual activity during the months of July through September is not represented, because the rites of non-*kpele* cults have been excluded. At least 38 additional non-*kpele* rites (yam festivals for chiefly stools and *otu* gods) are observed during this period.

a. Nine lunar months after the preceding *Lante Dzan we homowo*.

b. Opening and closing Koole Lagoon in 1968: Friday May 17, Friday June 14; Friday August 23, Friday October 4; Friday December 27; Friday February 7, 1969.

c. *Homowo* is a non-*kpele* rite performed to honor ancestral shades.

uals and groups. If, for example, a person is cursed in the name of a god, he will attempt to avert the mortal consequences of the curse by requesting the god's priest to perform ritual to appease the god. If a natural disaster such as flood, earthquake, or drought occurs, it is interpreted as a result of divine anger, and ritual will be performed to propitiate divine beings.[4] Occasional rites, therefore, are redressive rituals performed to reestablish harmonious relations between divine and mortal beings which have become disordered through both intentional and unintentional human acts.

Thus, the central aim of *kpele* ritual is to achieve ordered relations between gods and men. Calendrical rites maintain such harmonious relations, while occasional rites attempt to reestablish them. Often a redressive rite is differentiated from a system-maintaining rite not by its morphological attributes but by the context in which it is performed, for every ritual performance includes ritual acts that are formally similar to those in other rites. Among *kpele* rites, the most elaborate are the set of agricultural rites in which virtually all ritual acts performed in other contexts are enacted. In order to show the morphology of such rites, Table 4 presents an outline of the sequence of ritual acts in agricultural rites.

Kpele ritual is built upon a number of dramatic forms, including song, dance, music, prayer, and sacrifice. Probably *kpele* musical form most clearly differentiates *kpele* ritual from that of other cults. The style of instrumentation and vocalization is distinctive and readily apprehended even by untutored Western ears. *Kpele* songs integrate a distinctive musical form with textual elements. The content of *kpele* songs develops a wide range of themes, which includes cos-

4. During July 1968, unusually heavy rains resulted in serious floods throughout southern Ghana. Ga believed that the floods, which destroyed a number of riverside and seaside villages along the Densu River, were due to the anger of *Sakumo*. *Sakumo* was thought to be angry because one of the subchiefs in Accra had sold land near the mouth of the Densu River to a man who unprecedentedly began to mine salt there. In order to appease *Sakumo*, the major chiefs and priests of Accra visited the flooded areas where libations were poured, and ultimately a cow was sacrificed at the shrine of *Sakumo* in Accra.

Table 4. Morphology of *Kpele* Agricultural Rites

Epi-sode	Universal Elements	Unique Elements Shibaa	Ngmaadumọ	Ngmaafaa	Ngmaaku
1	Ritual at the shrine				
	preparation of water bowl				
	purification of participants				
	libation				
	formation of procession				
2	Procession to the sacred field				
3	Ritual in the sacred field				
	libation				
	performance of agricultural task	digging ground	planting seed	transplanting shoots	harvesting plants
4	Recession to the shrine			possession dancing by mediums	
5	Ritual at the shrine		dance by *agbaa*		dance by *agbaa*
	greeting				
					distribution of plants
	presentation of drink by secular authorities				
	libation				
	serving drink to participants				

mogony, relations between gods and men, the attributes of natural phenomena and moral beings, the performance of ritual, the nature of Ga society, and events in Ga history.

Ga believe that *kpele* songs are the product of divine revelation. The *Olila* medium, whom Ga recognize as one of the foremost authorities on *kpele* ritual symbolism, said, "They are gods' songs. When they [the gods] sing, from their songs we get our speech and our humility." It is heretical to suggest that a person might create a song, though informants have conceded that a god might reveal a hitherto unknown song to his medium. *Kpele* songs, therefore, are believed to be ancient songs revealed by gods to their mediums.

Although Ga believe that all *kpele* songs originated in this way, the singing of *kpele* songs is not restricted to mediums. Singers are cult members, most of whom learn songs informally by attending *kpele* song performances. Their repertoire depends primarily on personal interest, for only a few songs form integral parts of the liturgy of certain periodic rites. Two categories of performers are recognized for their proficiency in singing *kpele* songs: mediums and *olai*. Mediums learn to sing songs during their professional training, which usually continues for several years under the tutelage of an older medium. *Olai* are men who have learned *kpele* songs informally but whose proficiency has elevated them to the status of interpreters for mediums when they utilize occult language. An ability to sing a *kpele* song, however, is not synonymous with either an understanding of the text, which frequently incorporates non-Ga words, or an appreciation of the symbolic significance of the song. Such linguistic and exegetical understanding is limited to a small proportion of *kpele* mediums and an even smaller fraction of all *kpele* singers.

Kpele songs may be sung as part of the liturgy of agricultural rites, as informal greetings between ritual specialists, as preludes to dancing at *kpele* dances, and as authoritative validations of an argument. Although *kpele* songs may be sung by those who know them on a variety of ritual and secular occasions, the archetypal *kpele* song performance is the solo of a possessed medium at a *kpele* dance which integrates vocal singing with percussive instrumentation and dancing. On such occasions, the dancing area is a large cleared space, approximately 20 yards by 40 yards. At one end of this area sit the musicians, under the shade of a large tree: three drummers sit behind their drums on the edge of the dancing area; behind them sit two gong players and several other men who may be called upon to relieve tired musicians. Around the remaining sides of the dancing area sit mediums who are not possessed, *agbaa* members who may act as a chorus for certain familiar songs, and spectators who may number several hundred. As each medium arrives, she greets first the drummers and then the mediums who have preceded her before taking her place on the sidelines. The spatial positions of the participants at *kpele* dances are determined by the musicians sitting under the tree. It is the availability of a large tree, surrounded by a sufficient clear and flat area for dancing, that determines the spatial orientations of a dancing area, rather than compass directions.[5]

The dance begins with drumming and gong playing. When a medium wishes to dance, she approaches the drums, stands before them, and places her ritual broom on the middle drum to silence the musicians and to entreat the gods that "there may be peace in the dance." She then sings a song, which is usually in the form of a couplet. Her singing informs the drummers of the rhythm they are to beat while she dances. After she finishes singing, she dances away from the drummers towards the opposite end of the dancing area and ultimately dances back to the drums where she again silences the musicians by laying her ritual broom on the middle drum to indicate that she has finished her performance. During the medium's dance, the musicians observe her movements as cues to alterations in the rhythmic patterns which they produce, for the movements of the medium control the form of instrumental accompaniment throughout the dance. The only difference between the performance of a medium who is

5. I have attended three *kpele* dances. At each of these dances, the directional orientation of the drummers was different. On one occasion, the drummers sat on the west side of the dancing area; on the second, they sat on the east side; and on the third, they sat on the north side.

A *Kpele* Dance
  Drummers and Gong Players
  Group of Mediums Dance

possessed and that of one who is not possessed at such dances is that an unpossessed medium will rise from and return to her stool on the sidelines, while a possessed medium will step aside and remain constantly jigging on the edge of the dancing area until she decides to dance again. Although as many as twenty mediums may sing and dance in this way at *kpele* dances, rarely do all of them become possessed, and few are possessed throughout the entire dance, which continues for several hours. In addition to the solo song and dance of mediums, mediums may sing without dancing and dance without singing at *kpele* dances. Occasionally two possessed mediums may engage in a song duel on one side of the dancing area without regard either to the drumming and gong playing or to the dancing that may be taking place in the center of the dancing area. When a respected older medium who is not possessed dances, she often is accompanied by several younger mediums who dance behind her and pattern their movements on hers. At any given time during a *kpele* dance, only one person or one group dances to the accompaniment of the musicians. The musicians, however, play incessantly throughout the period of the dance, whether or not anyone is dancing.

While the solo singing of possessed mediums at *kpele* dances represents the most dramatic *kpele* song performance, through its integration of song, dance, and instrumental accompaniment, more restrained song performances may be given by individuals and groups on other occasions. Some songs form integral parts of agricultural rites. These songs are sung by the *agbaa* either in unison or in two-part harmony as they process between the shrine and the sacred field. On such occasions, one song, which is usually in the form of a couplet or a quatrain and which is not accompanied by instrumentation, is sung repeatedly until the procession arrives at its destination. A more complex form of group song performance is represented by a group of singers who come together in order to sing *kpele* songs either for their own enjoyment or to honor some person. The singers are led by one singer, who introduces each song either on his own initiative or at the suggestion of one of the group members. The singing, which is unaccompanied except for handclapping or gong playing, may continue without interruption for several hours. The texts of the songs tend to be longer and the singing more harmonically complex than on the other occasions which have been described. As the singers experiment with line patterns and harmonies, it is clear that they derive great enjoyment from singing familiar songs and learning new ones on such occasions.

Kpele songs not only constitute sources of enjoyment for their singers, but are symbols of the *kpele* religion for their audiences. Ga say that *kpele* worship is "a form of prayer, a kind of dance, a style of music." The distinctive musical form of *kpele* songs immediately identifies them as part of *kpele* ritual to their hearers. For Ga people, this cult connotes the continuity and integrity of their culture and society.

3 / Singing *Kpele* Songs

The singing of a *kpele* song is a performance involving the integration of musical, textual, and often dance forms. Such a performance depends upon permutation of four variables: occasion, choice of song, performers, and audience (see Table 5). Since the audience of a *kpele* song performance rarely is restricted in any formal way, song performances are invariably public. *Kpele* songs are sung by those who know them on ritual and secular occasions. These occasions include periodic and occasional rites as well as informal meetings and discussions between ritual specialists. While certain songs form integral parts of processions during agricultural rites of different cult groups, the choice of song is otherwise unrestricted and depends on the preference and knowledge of the singer. When the occasion for singing *kpele* songs prescribes ritual dancing by mediums, such as at *kpeledzoo*, at the annual rite of a god (*ngmaayeli*), and at status transition rites, the performers of a song include not only singers but musicians (*fifianku*) who are members of the *agbaa* of the officiating cult group.

Although the archetypal *kpele* song performance is the solo of a possessed medium, *kpele* songs often are sung by groups in which one singer leads the songs while the others respond as a chorus. J. H. K. Nketia, the foremost authority on Ghanaian music, has observed that the *kpele* singing style has an "open voice quality and an evenness or gradual decrease in

Table 5: *Kpele* Song Performances

Occasion	Choice of Song	Performers		Audience
		Singers	Musicians	
Periodic Ritual				
Agricultural rites	prescribed	*agbaa*	——	unrestricted
Ngmaafaa	unrestricted	possessed medium	——	unrestricted
Kpeledzoo	prescribed	*agbaa*	drummers and gong players	unrestricted
	unrestricted	mediums	drummers and gong players	unrestricted
Annual rite of god	unrestricted	mediums	drummers and gong players	unrestricted
Occasional Ritual				
Funeral (medium, priest, etc.)	unrestricted	mediums	drummers and gong players	unrestricted
Initiation (medium, priest, etc.)	unrestricted	mediums	drummers and gong players	unrestricted
Secular Occasions				
Formal: to honor chief	unrestricted	mediums	——	restricted
Informal:				
Greeting	unrestricted	unrestricted	——	unrestricted
Discussion	unrestricted	unrestricted	——	unrestricted
Spontaneous possession	unrestricted	medium	——	unrestricted

breath force towards the end of long musical sentences."[1] According to Nketia, *kpele* music is based on an anhemitonic pentatonic scale.[2] Group singing utilizes a wide range of harmonic intervals, and "harmonising parts . . . move in all direc-

1. J. H. K. Nketia, *African Music in Ghana*, pp. 31-32.
2. Ibid., p. 64.

tions. . . . [In group songs] choral endings are quite common and are realised in thirds. Occasionally a full triad is used."[3] The complexity of *kpele* harmony is matched by the intricacy of its rhythmic patterns. Percussion instruments may contribute two patterns and choral singers one to produce a triple rhythm. The performance of a *kpele* song, therefore, constitutes a richly diverse musical experience for performers and audience alike.

Kpele song performances are public, but the multilingual nature of many texts, quite apart from the din of drumming and gong playing, raises the issue of the intelligibility of texts for audiences. As M. J. Field noted thirty years ago, a *kpele* song line frequently contains words from a number of languages.[4] Nevertheless, as Nketia has observed, the Ga intonation which is given to non-Ga words means that Ga is "an important unifying factor in the language of *kpele* as it is heard when sung."[5] The problem of intelligibility is complicated further by the frequent elision of words to fit the metrical requirements of a song. While it is true that many singers do not know the meaning of the words which they sing, expert singers not only can translate the texts of songs into Ga but can provide exegeses of them. In fact, these songs are rich "storehouses" of Ga cosmological notions.[6] Nevertheless, the occult language of many songs means that knowledge of the ideas which they contain is restricted to students of *kpele* song, who are invariably ritual specialists.

The texts of the songs presented in Part II were recorded by singers who belonged to different *kpele* cult groups in Accra. While some songs were recorded during *kpele* rites, others were collected from singers either during interviews on other topics or at sessions organized expressly for the purpose

3. J. H. K. Nketia, "Traditional Music of the Ga People," *Universitas* 3:80.

4. M. J. Field, *Religion and Medicine of the Ga People*, p. 16.

5. J. H. K. Nketia, "Historical Evidence in Ga Religious Music," in *The Historian in Tropical Africa*, ed. J. Vansina, R. Mauny, and L. V. Thomas, p. 273.

6. Victor W. Turner, *The Drums of Affliction*, p. 2.

of recording *kpele* songs. At recording sessions, singers were asked to repeat the text and to explain the meaning of every song which they sang. This proved to be an exceptionally difficult task, as singers often were unable to repeat the texts slowly or to provide exegeses of them. Consequently, the *Olila* medium, who has an unparalleled knowledge of *kpele* songs, checked and emended many song texts recorded by other singers.

Ga believe that each *kpele* song originated through divine inspiration. The form of a *kpele* song, therefore, is thought to be immutable. An examination of recorded texts shows that not only do singers freely elaborate the line patterns of texts, but substantively different versions of songs exist. Although the Ga belief in the immutability of divinely inspired song texts may contribute to the persistence of a recognizable *kpele* song tradition in Ga culture, singers exercise considerable freedom in the manipulation of the form and content of songs in practice.

Line Patterns

An analysis of recorded *kpele* song texts shows that singers elaborate the line patterns of song texts in several ways. The number of substantive lines in *kpele* songs varies. In the songs in Part II, the number of lines in a text ranges from one to twenty-eight. Approximately one-third of the texts are couplets and another third either triplets or quatrains.[7] Whatever the number of substantive lines in a song text, singers rarely sing the text through once; rather, the singing of a song involves conceptual and formal elaboration. At times the focus of elaboration is on the content of the song, and an analysis of the recorded text does not disclose a formal line pattern. Often, however, the elaboration emphasizes repetition of lines and produces a recurrent line pattern. When a song is sung, the order of the formal line pattern is varied through a

7. Number of lines/number of songs: 1/8, 2/109, 3/73, 4/48, 5/18, 6/10, 7/10, 8/6, 9/5, 10/3, 11-28/10.

nonrepetitive introductory phrase, the inversion of the order of lines, the successive repetition of lines, or the changing of a word in a line without altering the substantive meaning of the line. A recorded song text, therefore, rarely accords precisely with the formal model of line pattern to which it corresponds. Further, when several songs are sung on the same occasion, the set includes some texts that are based primarily on the elaboration of conceptual content and others that are developed through the formal repetition of lines.

The following text (song 62-2) exemplifies a song in which the focus of elaboration is on content, rather than on a formal repetition of lines.[8]

A Ataa Naa Nyọngmọ.
B Naibi Aklẹ ha wọ ngọngọi enyọ.
B Naibi Aklẹ ha wọ ngọngọi enyọ.
B Naibi Aklẹ ha wọ ngọngọi enyọ.
C Akẹẹ ehii kwraa.
C Akẹẹ ehii kwraa.
B Naibi Aklẹ ha wọ ngọngọi enyọ.
B Naibi Aklẹ ha wọ ngọngọi enyọ.
D Akẹẹ ehii, shi ehi nọngng;
D Akẹẹ ehii, shi ehi nọngng;
D Akẹẹ ehii, shi ehi nọngng.
E Kingbi Aklẹ ehi nọngng;
E Kingbi Aklẹ ehi nọngng.
F Aklẹ ehi nọngng.
E Kingbi Aklẹ ehi nọngng;
E Kingbi Aklẹ ehi nọngng.
F Aklẹ ehi nọngng.
D Akẹẹ ehii, shi ehi nọngng.
B Naibi Aklẹ ha wọ ngọngọi enyọ.
D Akẹẹ ehii, shi ehi nọngng.
C Akẹẹ ehii kwraa.
G Gomua ngshra wọ, wọyẹ okuntshẹrẹfo bọ ntsirima;
G Gomua ngshra wọ, wọyẹ okuntshẹrẹfo bọ ntsirima;

8. Song numbers refer to the texts in Part II.

G   Gomua ngshra wọ, wọyẹ okuntshẹrẹfo bọ ntsirima;
G   Gomua ngshra wọ, wọyẹ okuntshẹrẹfo bọ ntsirima.
H   Aklẹ Dede, Gomua ngshra wọ ekuntebi anọ;
H   Aklẹ Dede, Gomua ngshra wọ ekuntebi anọ.
G   Gomua ngshra wọ. wọyẹ okuntshẹrẹfo bọ ntsirima.
I   Gomua tsẹrẹa okuntebi anọ.
H   Aklẹ Dede, Gomua ngshra wọ ekuntebi anọ.

A   God
B   Nai's child Ashiaklẹ gave us two gongs.
C   They said that she is not good at all.
D   They said that she is not good, but she is good.
E   The king's child Ashiaklẹ is good.
F   Ashiaklẹ is good.
G   The Gomua surround us, beat the military drums.
H   Ashiaklẹ, the Gomua surround us, turn into little
    stones.
I   The Gomua surround us, turn into little stones.

The song opens with a nonrepetitive introductory line (A).
Conceptually, the remainder of the song is divided into two
parts, which are related only by the fact that they concern
the same deity, *Ashiaklẹ*. The first part consists of lines B-F;
lines G-I constitute the second part. Although within each
part lines are repeated successively (BB) and alternately (BCB
DEFEFDBDC), there is not any consistent order of alteration
or succession. Nevertheless, each part is conceptually coherent, because it repeats a single conceptual theme. The theme
of the first part is conveyed in lines B and D; that of the second part is expressed in lines G and H. The remaining lines
merely restate parts of the theme in slightly different words.
The coherence of each part of the song and of the song as a
whole, therefore, depends on a conceptual form rather than
on a formal patterning of lines.

The elaboration of songs through the repetition of lines
rather than concepts produces a variety of line patterns. Analysis of recorded texts, however, shows that these various

line patterns derive from the interaction of a limited number of principles. Central to the understanding of the operation of these principles is the notion of the repetitive unit. The form of the repetitive unit in *kpele* songs is usually either a couplet or a triplet. The simplest form of repetition is the successive repetition of a single unit, which may be expressed formally as UN, in which U represents unit and N represents repetition. More complex forms of repetition are produced by the repetition of more than one unit, such as two couplets, two triplets, or one couplet and one triplet. In *kpele* songs based upon multiple repetitive units, the form of line pattern derives from the interaction of two sets of variables: the form of unit repetition and the form of unit construction.

The form of unit repetition in *kpele* songs is either successive or alternating. That is, the component repetitive units of a song may be sung successively or they may be sung alternately. For example, if a song is based upon two couplets, either the first couplet may be repeated several times before the second couplet is sung repeatedly, or the singing of the second couplet may follow the first singing of the initial couplet and the pair of couplets then are repeated several times. These two forms of unit repetition may be expressed formally as (1) $U_1 N + U_2 N$ and (2) $(U_1 + U_2)N$, in which U represents unit, N represents repetition, and subscripts refer to the initial ordering of units.

The second set of variables contributing to the elaboration of line patterns in songs based upon multiple repetitive units is the form of unit construction. The constituents of units may be independent or partially constant. That is, in a song based upon multiple repetitive units, all the unit constituents may be different, or some of the unit constituents may be different and others may be the same. For example, if a song is based upon two couplets, the lines in each couplet may be different, or one line in each couplet may be the same. These two forms of unit construction may be represented schematically as (1) $U_1 = I_1 + I_2$ and $U_2 = I_3 + I_4$ and (2) $U_1 = I_1 + S$ and $U_2 = I_2 + S$, in which U represents unit, I represents independent constituent, and S represents constant constituent.

Theoretically, the two forms of repetition and the two forms of unit construction should interact to produce four types of line patterns for multiple repetitive units: (1) independent units repeated successively, (2) constant units repeated successively, (3) independent units repeated alternately, and (4) constant units repeated alternately. In my collection of *kpele* songs, however, there are examples of types 1, 2, and 4, but none of type 3. Table 6 presents formal models of the types of line patterns represented in my collection of *kpele* songs.

Table 6. Line Pattern Models

Repetitive Unit	Type	Model	Componential Form	Formal Line Pattern
Single	SR	CN	$(I_1 + I_2)N$	$L_1+L_2+L_1+L_2\bar{}...$
		TN	$(I_1 + I_2 + I_3)N$	$L_1+L_2+L_3+L_1+$ $L_2+L_3 \ldots$
Multiple	I-SR	$C_1N + C_2N$	$(I_1+I_2)N + (I_3+I_4)N$	$L_1+L_2+L_1+L_2$ $\ldots +L_3+L_4+L_3$ $+L_4 \ldots$
		$CN + TN$	$(I_1+I_2)N + (I_3+I_4+I_5)N$	$L_1+L_2+L_1+L_2$ $\ldots +L_3+L_4+L_5+$ $L_3+L_4+L_5. \ldots$
	S-SR	$C^S_1N+C^S_2N$	$(S+I_1)N + (S+I_2)N$	$L_1+L_2+L_1+L_2$ $\ldots +L_1+L_3+L_1+$ $L_3 \ldots$
		$T^S_1N+T^S_2N$	$(S_1+I_1+S_2)N + (S_1+I_2+S_2)N$	$L_1+L_2+L_3+L_1+$ $L_2+L_3. \ldots L_1+$ $L_4+L_3+L_1+L_4+$ $L_3 \ldots$

Table 6—*Continued*

Repetitive Type Unit	Model	Componential Form	Formal Line Pattern
S-A	$(C_1^S+C_2^S)N$	$(S+I_1 + S+I_2)N$	$L_1+L_2+L_1+L_3+$
			$L_1+L_2+L_1+L_3$
			...
	$(C^S+T^S)N$	$(I_{1-n}+S_1 + I_{1-n}+S_1+S_2)N$	$L_1+L_2+L_1+L_2+$
			$L_3+L_4+L_2+L_4+$
			$L_2+L_3+L_5+L_2+$
			$L_5+L_2+L_3+L_6+$
			$L_2+L_3 \ldots +L_n$
			$+L_2+L_n+L_2+L_3$

SR: Successive repetition
I-SR: Independent unit successive repetition
S-SR: Constant unit successive repetition
S-A: Constant unit alternating repetition
Subscripts refer to ordering of units.
Superscripts refer to presence of constant unit.

C: Couplet
T: Triplet
I: Independent unit
S: Constant unit
N: Repetition
L: Line as sung

In order to clarify this discussion of formal line-pattern models, I wish to illustrate the models with textual examples. The simplest line pattern is produced by the repetition of a single couplet (C) or a single triplet (T) in which the constituents of the unit are independent. This line pattern, which may be represented as CN or TN, is exemplified by the following texts:

Song 10: $CN = L_1 + L_2 + L_1 + L_2$

Akọkọ nu nsu fatrẹ Nyame;
Nyampong dzi onukpa.

Akọkọ nu nsu fatrẹ Nyame;
Nyampong dzi onukpa.

Song 179-1: TN = $L_1 + L_2 + L_3 + L_1 + L_2 + L_3$

Dǫde Akabi,
Miba oye;
Oma ntęm anto.

Dǫde Akabi,
Miba oye;
Oma ntęm anto.

With respect to the various line patterns produced by multiple repetitive units, the first type is based upon the successive repetition of units composed of independent constituents. In the *kpele* songs in this collection, this type of line pattern involves either two couplets or a couplet and a triplet. These two line patterns, which may be represented as $C_1N + C_2N$ and as CN + TN respectively, are illustrated by the texts of songs 216 and 173:

Song 216: $C_1N+C_2N = L_1+L_2+L_1+L_2 \ldots +L_3+L_4+L_3+L_4 \ldots$

Patu su mi hu ade;
Mihu ade.

Patu su mi hu ade;
Mihu ade.

Shwila tee bahere omang;
Oshwila Adu Kǫme bahere omang.

Shwila tee bahere omang;
Oshwila Adu Kǫme bahere omang.

Song 173: CN + TN = $L_1+L_2+L_1+L_2 \ldots +L_3+L_4+L_5+L_3+L_4+L_5 \ldots$

Atsę mi Ganyo krong,
Atsę mi Ganyo Ayite.

Atsę mi Ganyo krong,
Atsę mi Ganyo Ayite.

Afutu kẹẹ enyangta;
Ayigbe kẹẹ egblẹ;
Gamẹi kẹẹ ehii.

Afutu kẹẹ enyangta;
Ayigbe kẹẹ egblẹ;
Gamẹi kẹẹ ehii.

The second type of line pattern produced by multiple units involves the successive repetition of units composed of some constant components. In this collection of *kpele* songs this form of line pattern derives either from two couplets that share a common line or from two triplets that share two component lines. These line patterns are represented by the formal models $C^s_1N + C^s_2N$ and $T^s_1N + T^s_2N$. Further, these line patterns may be expanded to incorporate additional units, such as a third or fourth couplet; the formal model for such an expanded form is $C^s_1N + C^s_2N + C^s_3N + C^s_4N$. The basic form of this type of line pattern is illustrated by the accompanying texts:

Song 60: $C^s_1N + C^s_2N = L_1 + L_2 + L_1 + L_2 \ldots + L_1 + L_3 + L_1 + L_3 \ldots$

Mangọ tsẹrẹpọng ngkẹẹ bu nyẹ Ga abẹ;
Shi miwie Ga, onu.

Mangọ tsẹrẹpọng ngkẹẹ bu nyẹ Ga abẹ;
Shi miwie Ga, onu.

Mangọ tsẹrẹpọng ngkẹẹ bu nyẹ Ga abẹ;
Mabu nyẹ abẹ wudzii.

Mangọ tsẹrẹpọng ngkẹẹ bu nyẹ Ga abẹ;
Mabu nyẹ abẹ wudzii.

Song 217: $T^s_1N + T^s_2N = L_1 + L_2 + L_3 + L_1 + L_2 + L_3 \ldots + L_1 + L_4 + L_3 + L_1 + L_4 + L_3 \ldots$

Kọkọbi Dene
Mahi faahe,
Manu wọlọmọ.

Kɔkɔbi Dene
Mahi faahe,
Manu wɔlɔmɔ.

Kɔkɔbi Dene
Mahi dzɔɔhe,
Manu wɔlɔmɔ.

Kɔkɔbi Dene
Mahi dzɔɔhe,
Manu wɔlɔmɔ.

The final type of line pattern represented in this set of *kpele* songs is produced by the alternating repetition of multiple units involving constant constituents. The multiple units may be couplets or triplets. Although the basic forms of this type are two couplets, which may be represented by $(C^S_1 + C^S_2)N$, and one couplet and one triplet, which may be diagrammed as $(C^S + T^S)N$, this pattern may be expanded to incorporate additional units such as the alternating repetition of three couplets or the alternating repetition of one triplet and three couplets. The basic form of this type of line pattern is illustrated by the texts of songs 51 and 15-2.

Song 51: $(C^S_1 + C^S_2)N = L_1 + L_2 + L_1 + L_3 + L_1 + L_2 + L_1 + L_3 \ldots$

Kɔme, midzara omani;
Miti ade mproobi.

Kɔme, midzara omani;
Mihu ade mproobi.

Kɔme, midzara omani;
Miti ade mproobi.

Kɔme, midzara omani;
Mihu ade mproobi.

Song 15-2: $(C^s + T^s)N = L_1 + L_2 + L_1 + L_2 + L_3 \ldots + L_n + L_2 + L_n + L_2 + L_3$

Awi Tẹte ngkẹ dzeng ba
Awi lo, ngkẹ dzeng ba.

Awi Tẹte ngkẹ dzeng ba
Awi lo, ngkẹ dzeng ba,
Ngkẹ dzeng ba.

Awi Tẹte ngkẹ nu ba
Awi lo, ngkẹ dzeng ba.

Awi Tẹte ngkẹ nu ba
Awi lo, ngkẹ dzeng ba,
Ngkẹ dzeng ba.

Awi Tẹte ngkẹ ngmaa ba
Awi lo, ngkẹ dzeng ba.

Awi Tẹte ngkẹ ngmaa ba
Awi lo, ngkẹ dzeng ba,
Ngkẹ dzeng ba.

The line patterns described as models rarely correspond precisely with song texts as they are sung. When a song is sung, variation within these patterns is introduced in several ways. These include introductory phrases, the successive repetition of single lines or couplets, the inversion of line order, the deletion of lines, and the utilization of connective words. The recorded text of song 217, which illustrated the successive repetition of two triplets with constant constituents ($T^s_1 N + T^s_2 N$), exemplifies many of these sources of variation. The following text reproduces the song as it was recorded:

1	Olai	4	Mahi faahe
2	Moomo	5	Manu wọlọmọ
3	Kọkọbi Dene	6	Kọkọbi Dene

7 Manu wǫlǫmǫ	23 Kǫkǫbi Dene
8 Manu wǫlǫmǫ	24 Olai
9 Kǫkǫbi Dene	25 Manu wǫlǫmǫ
10 Oshwila	26 Kǫkǫbi Dene
11 Kǫkǫbi Dene	27 Mahi dzǫǫhe
12 Mahi faahe	28 Manu wǫlǫmǫ
13 Manu wǫlǫmǫ	29 Kǫkǫbi Dene
14 Kǫkǫbi Dene	30 Mahi dzǫǫhe
15 Kǫkǫbi Dene	31 Manu wǫlǫmǫ
16 Olai	32 Kǫkǫbi Dene
17 Kǫkǫbi Dene	33 Mahi dzǫǫhe
18 Mahi dzǫǫhe	34 Manu wǫlǫmǫ
19 Manu wǫlǫmǫ	35 Kǫkǫbi Dene
20 Kǫkǫbi Dene	36 Mahi dzǫǫhe
21 Mahi dzǫǫhe	37 Manu wǫlǫmǫ
22 Manu wǫlǫmǫ	

The recorded song text comprises thirty-seven lines; twenty-four, or two-thirds, of these lines accord exactly with the line pattern model, $T^s_1 N + T^s_2 N$. These consistent lines are 3-5 and 11-13 for T^s_1 and 17-22 and 26-37 for T^s_2. The remaining recorded lines divert from the model. The modes of diversion include introductory phrases (1,2), connective words (10,16, 24), successive repetition of lines (14,15), inversion of lines (8,9), deletion of lines (6,7) or a combination of these modes of variation (e.g., 6-9, 23-25). Although the recorded text diverts from the model, the formal line pattern is recognizable, and the forms of variation are distinct from those in texts which emphasize the elaboration of conceptual content.

Observation of *kpele* singers indicates that the more accomplished and confident a singer, the greater line-pattern variation he introduces into his song. This correlation between freedom of expression in line pattern and expertise of singer, however, pertains only to *kpele* song performances by unpossessed singers. By contrast, in the archetypal *kpele* song performance in which a possessed medium sings before the drums, she rarely sings more than an unelaborated song text.

Versional Variation

Another stylistic issue relating to the manipulation of texts is the problem of versional variation. Although only one version was obtained for most songs included in Part II, multiple texts were recorded for 49 of the 243 songs. Two texts were collected for 42 songs, three texts for 6 songs, and four texts for 1 song. Of these multiple texts, eight (14%) were identical, but only two of these eight were sung by the same singer on different occasions. An analysis of the variant versions of other song texts discloses several forms of textual variation. These include multilingual confusion, incorporation, variant expression of similar ideas, and variant meanings that are either closely affiliated or disparate. Table 7 summarizes the frequency of various forms of textual variation.

Table 7. Forms of Textual Variation (percentages)

Songs	N	Without Variation	With Multilingual Confusion	With Incorporation	With Variant Expression	With Variant Meaning	
						close	disparate
2 texts	42	17	19	19	26	9.5	9.5
3 texts	6	8	8	17	0	50	17
4 texts	1	0	0	33	67	0	0
All texts	57	14	16	19	23	17.5	10.5

In nine cases (16%) textual variation was due to multilingual confusion; that is, the text was distorted, because part of the text was in a non-Ga language unfamiliar to the singer, who consequently garbled the text. Multilingual confusion in texts for which alternative versions are not available led to the rejection of forty additional texts from the collection presented in this book.

In eleven cases (19%) versional variation resulted from incorporation; that is, one short text was included within another longer version. This form of versional variation is illustrated by the following texts for song 9:

Version 1

Okposansa—	Spadefish—
Nyame ni bǫǫ;	God created;
Minim pong;	My face is swollen;
Mitsi pong;	My back is swollen;
Mi hiẹ kpǫ.	My face is swollen.

Version 2

Okposansa—	Spadefish—
Nyame ni bǫǫ mi;	God created me;
Minim pong;	My face is swollen;
Mitsi pong.	My back is swollen.
Nyame bǫǫ mi sa;	God created me so;
Mi hiẹ kpǫ;	My face is swollen;
Mi sẹẹ kpǫ.	My back is swollen.
Nyǫngmǫ ni bǫǫ mi.	God created me.

This form of textual variation may be attributed to a variety of factors, including differences in the knowledge of singers and the exigences of the song performance. Whereas certain singers may be familiar with only the abbreviated text, other singers may sing an abbreviated version on one occasion and a longer version on another (see Table 8). In the latter instance, various perceptions of the singer concerning the situation of the song performance may be relevant, such as a sense of a time limit or a wish to withhold information.

Table 8. Forms of Textual Variation in One Singer's Songs

Texts Recorded	Without Variation	With Incorporation	With Variant Expression
One year	1	2	0
Different years	2	0	1
Total songs	3	2	1

Textual variation based upon incorporation and multilingual confusion cannot be assessed as versional variation. That is to say, these forms of textual variation are more likely to be due to the proficiency of the singer than to the existence of different versions of the same song within the established *kpele* song repertoire. Versional variation in this latter sense is suggested by the remaining forms of textual variation.

One form of versional variation which pertains to 13 cases (23%) is the variant expression of consistently similar ideas; that is, different words are utilized to convey the same notions. This form of variation is exemplified by the following texts for song 21:

Version 1

Nyǫngmǫ kplę huu;	The sky roars;
Asase ni ano,	The earth does not have a mouth,
Asase kantobi;	The earth cannot speak;
Asase ni ano,	The earth does not have a mouth,
Masa ni anu.	It cannot speak but it hears.

Version 2

Asase nyanii, ngkasabi;	The earth is silent, it cannot speak;
Nyǫngmǫ kplęǫ huu.	The sky roars.
Shikpong bę naabu ni ekę wie Ga.	The earth does not have a mouth with which to speak Ga.
Nyǫngmǫ kplęǫ huu.	The sky roars,
Ni ekplę huu.	And it roars.
Nyǫngmǫ, Nyampong kplęǫ huu.	The sky, God roars.

The remaining textual versions differ not only in words but in the ideas which they convey. Nevertheless, ten cases (17.5%) involve the expression of closely related ideas, whereas six (10.5%) convey disparate notions. These two forms of versional variation are illustrated by the accompanying texts.

Song 152: variant meaning, closely related ideas

Version 1

Wǫdzę Ga mli;	We came among Ga people;
Wǫhi Ga mli;	We live among Ga people;
Wǫdzę wuoyi;	We came from the south;
Wǫdzęę kooyi.	We did not come from the north.

Version 2

Wǫdzę Ga mli;	We came among Ga people;
Wǫya nina Gamęi.	We met Ga people.

Song 62: variant meaning, disparate ideas

Version 1

Ashiaklę dzę wuoyi ta lęlę mli;
Bosobrobi dzę wuoyi ta lęlę mli;
Akrę Kripo dzę wuoyi ta lęlę mli.
Akrę, bo mpabi.
Aklę, akęę ehii.
Ekęę ehi.
"Mi amralobi, mi kingbi, mi Bosobi, mi mangshǫbi;
"Mina ngǫngǫ enyǫ kęha bo."

Ashiaklę came from the south sitting in a canoe;
Nai's child came from the south sitting in a canoe;
Ashiaklę came from the south sitting in a canoe.
Ashiaklę, you are a quarrelsome person.
Ashiaklę, they said that she is not good;
She said that she is good.
"I am the lord's child, I am the king's child, I am Nai's
child, I am the sea's child;
"I have two gongs to give you."

Version 2

Naibi Aklę ha wǫ ngǫngǫi enyǫ.
Akęę ehii kwraa.

Naibi Aklę ha wǫ ngǫngǫi enyǫ.
Akęę ehii, shi ehi nǫngng:
Kingbi Aklę ehi nǫngng;
Aklę ehi nǫngng.
Gomua ngshra wǫ, wǫyę okuntshęręfo bǫ ntsirima;
Aklę Dede, Gomua ngshra wǫ, ekuntebi anǫ;
Gomua tsęręa, okuntebi anǫ.

Nai's child Ashiaklę gave us two gongs.
They said that she is not good at all.
Nai's child Ashiaklę gave us two gongs.
They said that she is not good, but she is good;
The king's child Ashiaklę is good.
Ashiaklę is good.
The Gomua surround us, beat the military drums;
Ashiaklę, the Gomua surround us, turn into little stones;
The Gomua surround us, turn into little stones.

The forms of textual variation for songs with multiple texts in this collection suggest that singers may manipulate the content of *kpele* songs. This hypothesis is supported by the variant texts of songs sung by one singer (Table 8) and by four cases in which one line forms part of the text of two different songs. Certain forms of textual variation, especially incorporation and multilingual confusion, may result from differences in the proficiency of singers. The other forms of textual variation may be due either to the existence of alternative versions of *kpele* songs or to the innovation of singers. Both sources of versional variation, however, contradict the Ga belief that the content of *kpele* songs is immutable. Rather, perhaps unconsciously, *kpele* singers exercise considerable control over the content as well as the form of *kpele* songs.

Structure of Song Sets

A *kpele* singer has considerable freedom not only in the way he sings a song but in the choice of song. Several factors influence the selection of songs, when a number of songs are sung on one occasion.

An examination of the themes of fourteen song sets discloses three thematic categories by which song sets may be classified (apart from a set of songs sung for the Ga paramount chief, *Ga mangtsẹ*, the songs sets were sung specifically for recording purposes). These classificatory categories are (1) disconnected themes, (2) sequential themes, and (3) recurrent themes (see Table 9). Within the category of disconnected themes are placed song sets in which the content of songs is unrelated, though occasionally consecutive songs may deal with similar conceptions. The thematic pattern for such song sets may be diagrammed as: $H_1 + H_2 \ldots + H_n$ in which H represents theme and subscripts represent the order in which themes are introduced. The seven sets which make up this category were sung by three different singers. Within the second category of sequential themes are song sets in which a number of themes are developed successively in such a way that contiguous themes are more closely related than distal themes. The basic thematic pattern for this category may be expressed as: $NH_1 + NH_2 \ldots + NH_n$, in which N refers to repetition, H to theme, and subscripts to the order in which the themes are introduced. Two song sets by one singer are classified within this category. The third category of song sets, recurrent themes, involves the repetition of a number of themes within the set. The basic thematic pattern for this category may be represented schematically as: $(NH_1 + NH_2 \ldots + NH_n)N$, in which N pertains to repetition, H to theme, and subscripts to the order in which themes are introduced. Among the five song sets sung by three different singers within this category is the set sung for the Ga paramount chief. In one sense, this form of song set is less orderly than the progression of themes within the second category, that of sequential themes; in another sense, however, the conceptual coherence of the entire set is greater than in the second category.

As an example of a song set with recurrent themes, I consider the set sung for the Ga paramount chief by the *Olila* medium. After the enstoolment of the chief in 1965, he was confined for several weeks to his house. During this period,

Table 9. Thematic Sequences within Song Sets

Song Sets	Number of songs	Thematic Sequence
Disconnected themes		
1	3	$H_1 + H_2 + H_3$
2	6	$H_1 + H_2 + H_3 + 3H_2$
3	4	$2H_1 + H_2 + H_3$
4	5	$2H_1 + H_2 + H_3 + H_4$
5	8	$H_1 + 2H_2 + H_3 + H_4 + H_5 + H_6 + H_7$
6	15	$H_1 + H_2 + H_3 + H_4 + 3H_5 + H_6 + 2H_5 + H_4 + H_7 + H_8 + H_9 + H_{10}$
7	24	$H_1 + 3H_2 + H_3 + 3H_4 + H_5 + H_6 + 2H_7 + H_2 + H_8 + 2H_9 + 3H_{10} + H_{11} + 2H_{12} + H_{13} + H_{14}$
Sequential themes		
8	12	$2H_1 + 3H_2 + 7H_3$
9	21	$11H_1 + 2H_2 + 3H_3 + 3H_4 + H_5 + H_6$
Recurrent themes		
10*	20	$H_1 + H_2 + H_3 + H_2 + 2H_4 + H_5 + H_4 + H_1 + 2H_4 + 3H_3 + H_4 + 3H_6 + H_4 + H_6$
11	14	$4H_1 + 4H_2 + 3H_1 + 2H_3 + H_4$
12	32	$5H_1 + 5\frac{1}{2}H_2 + 4\frac{1}{2}H_3 + 2H_2 + 2H_1 + 7H_3 + H_4 + H_5 + H_6 + 4H_7$
13	17	$H_1 + 2H_2 + 7H_3 + H_1 + H_4 + H_3 + H_1 + H_4 + 2H_3$
14	9	$3H_1 + H_2 + 2H_3 + H_4 + H_1 + H_5$

H: Theme
* Song set for Ga chief

elders of the royal family instructed him in his official duties before publicly introducing him to his subjects. Every evening during the third week of the chief's confinement, the *Olila* medium sang for him. His paternal grandfather, a noted *Nai olai*, had helped to instruct the medium during her training. She, therefore, wished to honor both the memory of the grandfather and the new status of the grandson. I attended the final song performance at the medium's invitation. On that occasion, the *Olila* medium came to the chief's house with ten women. They sat in a room adjoining the chief's audience chamber; throughout the evening the door between the rooms remained closed. Apart from a Ga friend, my husband, and myself, only a few men from the chief's household were present in the room with the singers. The women sang continuously without instrumental accompaniment for two hours; as the evening progressed the *Olila* medium did not permit hand-clapping, for she was on the verge of possession and did not wish to go into trance. Under the leadership of the *Olila* medium, the women sang twenty songs. The order of the songs corresponds to the following texts in Part II: 62-2, 176, 196, 177, 46, 160, 166, 185, 2, 154, 126, 187, 163, 64, 202, 130, 128, 129, 214, and 131. An examination of the song texts and their exegeses, which were obtained on other occasions from the *Olila olai* or the *Olila* medium, discloses six principal themes: H_1: relations between divine and mortal beings, H_2: military exploits, H_3: human nature, H_4: Ga society and institutions, H_5: role of the Ga chief, and H_6: ritual performance. The sequence of these exegetical themes in the song set is $H_1 + H_2 + H_3 + H_2 + 2H_4 + H_5 + H_4 + H_1 + 2H_4 + H_3 + 2H_2 + H_4 + 3H_6 + H_4 + H_6$.

The occasion for singing this song set clearly influenced the selection of songs. Some songs allude to the personal situation of the new chief; others instruct him in the nature of Ga culture and society and in the conduct of chiefly office; and several pertain to the structure of the song set itself. Three songs refer directly to the *Ga mangtsę*, Nii Amugi II. The young chief is a member of *Amugi we*, a house which may provide not only Ga paramount chiefs but also *Nai* priests. *Nai* is the god of the sea; one of *Nai*'s children is *Ashiaklẹ*. The first song (62-2), which at the exegetical level of meaning refers to the relations between gods and men in general and to those between *Ashiaklẹ* and *Nai we* in particular, is therefore an allusion to the kinship affiliations of the confined chief for whom the songs are sung. The second song that refers directly to Nii Amugi II is the fifteenth (song 202), which exegetically refers to the Ga custom of expressing sincerity of intention through a dual handclasp. On this occasion, it refers to the welcoming of Nii Amgui II as Ga paramount chief, which is the teleological meaning of the entire song set. Finally, the nineteenth song (214), describing the dependence of a student on the training of his teacher, refers to the situation of the confined chief who is dependent upon the instruction of his tutors for the successful fulfillment of his future duties.

Apart from four songs that refer explicitly to the conclusion of the song set or perhaps even to the conclusion of the set of song sets that has been performed on successive evenings (songs 130, 128, 129, 131), the songs instruct the confined chief either in the conduct of political office or in the nature of Ga society. Thus, the two songs pertaining to human nature (songs 196, 187) at the exegetical level are warnings about people who may cause trouble during his reign. The first of these songs is followed by four songs relating to the appropriate conduct of a paramount chief: one emphasizes the importance of adhering to traditional precedent and of acting unobtrusively but purposefully (song 177), two stress reciprocity in human relations (songs 46, 160), and the fourth exhorts the chief to act well (song 166). These four songs are followed by four additional songs instructing the new chief in Ga history (song 185), belief (song 2), and institutions (songs 154, 126). These songs are followed by the second warning about human nature (song 187) which precedes two more didactic songs concerning Ga history and society (songs 163, 164). A consideration of the influence of the occasion for the song set on the selection of songs, therefore, suggests a didactic contextual configuration for the song set which is not apparent from a consideration of the sequence of themes at an exegetical level alone.

Two song sets sung by the *Ashiakle* priest exemplify a distinctive thematic pattern in which the set develops several nonrepetitive themes in such a way that successive themes are more closely related than discontinuous themes. The first song set, which the *Ashiakle* priest sang, illustrates this pattern of sequential development of themes. On this occasion, the priest, who is acclaimed as an expert *kpele* singer, came with two men to sing for me at the house of a Ga friend. Since I expressed an interest in cosmogonic beliefs, the priest introduced the song set with a lengthy statement concerning the creation of the world, the historical relations between his forefathers of *Nai we* living on the beach and other true Ga at Great Accra, and the ritual duties of his family. He concluded by saying, "We will sing about our house" (*wobaala kedze woshia le mli*). The priest and his associates, who were silent except for choral contributions, sang twelve songs in the following order: 141, 142, 153, 191, 226, 39, 235, 97, 98, 65, 66, 62-1. The song set develops three themes sequentially: H_1: ritual structures, H_2: attributes of *Nai we*, and H_3: *Nai* and his children. The ordering of these themes is $2H_1 + 3H_2 + 7H_3$. Thus, the priest began by singing two songs about the shrine of a god which were followed by three songs concerning the relations between *Nai we* and other families. The basic conceptual motif of these three songs is that a superior does not visit an inferior. The remaining songs concern *Nai*, the god of the sea, or his children, which include both fish and gods. Not only is the thematic sequence of the entire song set orderly, but the arrangement of successive songs within each thematic unit is exceptionally systematic. For example, within the third and largest thematic unit, the first song describes the action of the sea on the beach; the second describes fish, who are children of the sea, hitting stones near the beach; the third and fourth refer explicitly to *Nai's* procreative powers, and the three remaining songs deal with two of *Nai's* divine children, *Totroe and Ashiakle*. Within this thematic unit, therefore, the conceptual focus of the songs progresses from natural phenomena, through relations between natural phenomena and gods to gods. The transitions between units, therefore, are as orderly as those within thematic units. The entire song set forms a neat conceptual entity concerning the human, animal, and divine members of *Nai we*.

A set of six songs sung by the *Akumadze Afieye* medium exemplifies a song set with disconnected themes. Thrice this medium recorded songs for me in her room at the *Akumadze mangtse*'s residence. The song set discussed was the second of the three sets; at the time of the recording the only other person present was a Ga interpreter. The order of songs corresponds to the following texts in Part II: 89-1, 209, 15-1, 210, 211, 95-2. At the topical level, three themes are expressed in this song set: H_1: gods, H_2: birds, and H_3: cosmogony. The ordering of these themes within the song set is $H_1 + H_2 + H_3 + 3H_2$. Although four of the songs concern birds, their content is otherwise unrelated; consequently, I consider that the set as a unit represents a set of disconnected themes. Within the song set, however, there is a recurrent stylistic pattern involving the enumeration of items. The first, third, and fifth songs in the set deal with different conceptual themes but treat them in the same way. In each song various items are enumerated: articles of clothing in the first song (song 89-1), subsistence items in the third song (song 15-1), and body parts in the fifth song (song 211). The songs that succeed each of the enumerative songs are different in stylistic pattern both from the enumerative songs and from one another. In this song set, the stylistic line pattern integrates the set more systematically than the thematic component.

Consideration of *kpele* song sets suggests three principal factors underlying the grouping of songs: the occasion for singing, the structure of the performance, and the effect of preceding songs. The occasion for singing songs provides a conceptual focus for the song set, which influences the selection of songs. The song set sung to honor the new *Ga mangtse* implicitly revolves around this fact, for while various recurrent themes are expressed, all relate to aspects of the chief's role and situation. Apart from the song set sung to honor and instruct the *Ga mangtsẹ*, the song sets were sung to instruct me in *kpele* songs. With one exception, therefore, the analyzed song sets lacked an occasional focus that would assist in determining the choice of songs. The lack of occasional focus for all but one song set may help to account for the fact that 50% of the sets are thematically disconnected. In the remaining song sets, the singer consciously or unconsciously imposed a conceptual focus on the situation. As I have noted, the *Ashiaklẹ* priest explicitly stated that he would sing about his house, *Nai we*, which he did in an exceptionally systematic fashion on two occasions. Although none of the other singers explicitly defined their aims, their song sets concern a limited number of recurrent themes from which a general conceptual focus can be deduced.

The structure of the performance may also influence the choice of songs. Any song set necessarily begins and ends with some song. Although these song sets do not have standardized introductions and conclusions, evidence suggests that many song set performances do. A number of song sets in this collection begin with the *kpele* song (song 4) which is sung on all ritual occasions. The song set sung for the *Ga mangtsẹ* concludes with four songs which convey the notion that the song performance is ending. I suggest that under less contrived conditions than those in which most of these song sets were obtained, the approaching conclusion of a song performance would be expressed through the content of final songs. Thus, the structure of the song performance itself would determine the selection of songs to convey to the chorus and to the audience that the principal singer wishes to finish his performance.

Finally, within a song set the content and the style of a song may influence succeeding songs. This form of stimulus is evident within song sets based on thematic patterns and within song sets without obvious thematic interconnections. The stylistic regularities in one song set sung by the *Akumadze Afieye* medium have been discussed already. Although this is the only song set in the collection in which this form of stylistic stimulation is evident, it probably occurs on other occasions. More frequently, the content of a song influences succeeding songs at a subthematic level. An activity or an object in one song may recur in successive songs which are thematically disconnected. In a long song set sung by *Kle agbaayoo*, for example, the motif of seeing is conveyed in seven songs. This motif is introduced in the sense of observation in the sixth song of the set (song 230), in which a whale comes to see what is happening in the town. The two succeeding songs also convey the notion of observation; the first (song 193) concerns Ga who go to see the incomprehensible letter of the European, and the second (song 7) concerns observations of divine beings. The motif recurs in the twelfth, thirteenth, and fifteenth songs of the set. In the twelfth song, the observations of the owl are discredited (song 215-2); in the thirteenth song, someone announces that he is crossing the Volta River to see what is happening (song 106-2); and in the fifteenth song, a ruler is instructed to watch over the town (song 168-2). Similarly, in one short song set, the *Akumadze Afieye* medium utilizes the motif of speaking. In the first of four songs, a god tells a medium to come so that he may speak (song 120); in the third, a bird cries and attracts someone's attention (song 212). Analogously, creatures or deities may appear in successive songs which are otherwise conceptually unrelated. For example, another long song set sung by *Kle agbaayoo* concluded with two pairs of songs. The initial pair (songs 206, 10) concerns the cock; the second pair (songs 124, 54) is coupled by its reference to the god, *Sakumo*. The first song states that when you hear a cock crow, you know that it is morning; the second says that when a cock drinks water, he shows it to God. The final pair of songs refer to *Sakumo*; in the first song, Sakumo says that he will possess some medium, and in the second song, human beings ask him what fish they can eat. Within thematically disconnected song sets, this form of transition between songs predominates, whereas within thematically coherent song sets, this form of song stimulus serves to integrate more fully the basic thematic unity of the song set.

4 / The World of *Kpele* Songs

A conception of the ordering of the world underlies *kpele* ritual. This world view is a system of classification that isolates, differentiates, and relates cognitive categories. This system of ideas not only classifies cosmological categories, but explains the vicissitudes and continuities of human experience insofar as these are believed to depend on the relations between members of different categories. Aspects of the cognitive system are expressed and recreated through the performance of ritual. Among the diverse sources of ritual symbols, the content of *kpele* songs constitutes a particularly rich source of *kpele* cosmological conceptions. Since any song, motif of ritual action, or ritual object reveals only fragmentary evidence of the cosmological system, it is only by integrating evidence from a variety of sources that the underlying cosmological model can be constructed. As Mary Douglas has observed, "The primitive world view . . . is rarely itself an object of contemplation and speculation in the primitive culture."[1] While such a system of thought may not be a conscious unity for its adherents, they utilize aspects of it to classify and explain their experience.

At the core of *kpele* cosmology is a conception of a hierarchy of beings comprising five classes: a supreme being, divine beings, human beings, animals, and plants. The differentiation and ranking of classes is based on four existential distinctions: creative/created, immortal/mortal, rational/non-

1. Mary Douglas, *Purity and Danger*, p. 91.

rational, and mobile/immobile. The creative power of the supreme being differentiates it from all other classes of being; the immortality of gods distinguishes them from all other forms of created life; the rationality of human beings differentiates them from animals and plants; the mobility of animals distinguishes them from plants. The value of an existential attribute that differentiates a superordinate class of being from a subordinate class not only characterizes that class but all superior classes in the hierarchy; conversely, the attribute that distinguishes the subordinate class pertains not only to that class but to all lower classes within the hierarchy. The assignment of these variant existential attributes to classes of being may be expressed schematically as:

class	*existential attributes*			
supreme being	creative	immortal	rational	mobile
divine beings	created	immortal	rational	mobile
human beings	created	mortal	rational	mobile
animals	created	mortal	nonrational	mobile
plants	created	mortal	nonrational	immobile

At the apex of the hierarchy of beings is the supreme being, a personified creative life force, whom Ga call *Ataa Naa Nyɔngmɔ*. Ga interpretations of the name express important attributes of this personified force. In everyday usage, *ataa* is a term of address for father, but in this context some Ga suggest that it may mean *taolɔ*, seeker or person who cares for, thereby implying that *Ataa Naa Nyɔngmɔ* has concern for the well-being of the universe of his creation and of human beings within it. This nurturant connotation, which is consistent with the Ga concept of father (*ataa*), is expressed in the *kpele* song line: "and he looks after us" (*ni ekwraa wɔ*; song 3). While *naa* usually is utilized as a term of address or reference for a grandmother, in this context *naa* is said to be a contraction of *naanɔ*, which means eternal or everlasting. Similarly, *nyɔngmɔ* in everyday parlance means rain; informants, however, suggest that in this context it may mean *nyɔɔngmɔ*, night person or nocturnal being. This notion is consistent with the Ga belief that the night is the time of activity for divine beings. In several *kpele* songs (e.g., songs 17, 18, 110), *nyongmo* is used as a synonym for sky, which is believed to be the locus of divine presence. Indigenous exegeses of the name *Ataa Naa Nyongmo*, therefore, suggest that the supreme being is a nurturant, eternal, nocturnal being associated with the sky.

Further attributes of the supreme being are suggested by the *Olila* medium's statement that while Ga call the supreme being *nyongmo*, gods use the Akan word *nyampong*, and Guang speakers say *nyebo*, which means "able to create." Her statement alludes to the creative capacity of the supreme being. Ga consider that *Ataa Naa Nyongmo* created the universe; this conception is expressed in the following *kpele* song (song 1):

Nyongmo Adu Akwa,	God,
Le dzi okua agbo le.	He is the great farmer.
Le ebo dzeng	He created the world
Ni eha anyieo mli ahi.	And he gave it to them to live in.

Although cosmogonic notions are not elaborated by *kpele* believers (see songs 13, 14), it is thought that the supreme being created first the physical world, then gods, animals, plants, and ultimately human beings. The *Ashiakle* priest described the creation of the physical world in the following words:

Creation, how they told us is: the sky [was first], the next was the earth and on it all the rivers were created and ran down on this earth and they all gathered together and they made the sea. And so after the sky is the earth and the sea, three things. And so then at creation these three things [were], and so then I know that they hold all the power in the world.

Just as primogeniture establishes precedence in human society, so in the physical world the sky is superordinate to land and sea. Ga also say that the universe is round and that it is shaped like a cylinder which moves or is moved forward and backward (song 16). *Ataa Naa Nyongmo* is believed to be the source of life in general and of specific forms of life. In one *kpele* song, a fish rationalizes his ugly appearance by saying that God created him that way (song 9); in another a plant says that its red color came from God and not from the earth (song 11). In *kpele* thought, the supreme being not only created the universe in the distant past, but continues to be the source of all forms of life at the present time.

A final attribute of *Ataa Naa Nyǫngmǫ* is his infinite nature. This aspect of the supreme being is suggested by one *kpele* song (song 2):

Wǫyaahu Nyǫngmǫ ngmǫ,	We will go to cultivate God's field,
Dzenamǫ hu wǫyę mli;	The whole night we are in it;
Ataa Naa Nyǫngmǫ ngmǫ ahuu kę gbeenaa.	One does not finish the cultivation of God's field.

The supreme being of the *kpele* world, therefore, is a personified life force without spatial or temporal limitations.

Ataa Naa Nyǫngmǫ not only created the universe and its creatures but controls cosmic processes and thereby the lives of mortal creatures. The supreme being controls the falling of the rain and the shining of the sun, which in turn determine the growth of plants on which animals and human beings depend for subsistence. Human beings, therefore, depend upon *Ataa Naa Nyǫngmǫ* not only for existence but for the means of perpetuating life. In prayer, Ga appeal to the supreme being through gods and ancestral shades for blessing for the living and unborn Ga, for increase in the population, for abundant food, for rain to nurture plants, for success in human endeavors, and for peace among Ga. If men anger the supreme being by failing to perform certain rites or by violating divine injunctions, *Ataa Naa Nyǫngmǫ* may punish men by witholding the means of perpetuating life or by causing calamitous events, such as epidemics and earthquakes. The maintenance and restoration of order in the relations between the supreme being and mortal men depend on the performance of ritual. Although the supreme being is the ultimate source and controller of life, human beings cannot achieve contact with him directly; rather relations between the supreme being and men are mediated by gods and ancestral shades.

The immortality of gods (*dzemawǫdzii*) differentiates them from other classes of being that *Ataa Naa Nyǫngmǫ* created. Gods are immortal, sky-dwelling spirits. Although the locus of their activity is thought to be the sky, gods may descend to earth. Certain gods are associated with specific topographical features, such as lagoons, mountains, and rivers, which are thought to be their customary places of descent. Not only may gods descend to particular terrestrial locations, but they may manifest themselves as moral beings of other classes and may speak directly to men through mediums (*wǫngtsęmęi*).

Men, on the other hand, may appeal directly to gods and thereby to the supreme being through either female mediums or male priests. Although gods are the most important mediators between *Ataa Naa Nyǫngmǫ* and living men, ancestral shades may act as intermediaries between their descendants and divine beings. An understanding of the ancestral role necessitates a brief explication of Ga notions of person. Ga believe that a person (*adesa*) has two aspects: one corporeal, the other spiritual. During mortal life, the soul (*susuma*) inhabits the body (*gbomǫtso*, person tree) except during sleep, when it may leave the body to travel without limitations of time or space. At physiological death, the soul is thought to continue to inhabit the body for three days, after which it leaves the body to wander until the final funerary rites (*faafo*) are performed a year or more later. At these rites, the soul "crosses the river" (*faa-fo*) and achieves its ultimate social status as an ancestral shade (*sisa*). Although the world of the shades (*gbohiiadzeng*, "dead persons' world") is not sharply defined by Ga, they believe that a person has the same social status in death as in life: a chief is a chief, a priest is a priest, and a commoner is a commoner.

Ga believe that ancestral shades continue to be involved and concerned with the affairs of living men. Ancestral shades may manifest themselves to the living in human form or in dreams, and their spiritual presence may be invoked to assist the living. Men appeal to ancestral shades to intercede with divine beings or to act in their own right on behalf of their living descendants. While the soul is the immortal aspect of a person, the body involves the soul in certain inextricable relations. The blood (*la*) which a person derives from both parents affiliates him with individuals and groups in Ga society during his lifetime, and after death his soul continues to be concerned with the affairs of these same social units.

Although men die, like animals and plants, men are differentiated from animals by their capacity to reason. Ga say that "the mind is the person" (*dzengmọ dzi gbomọ*). The rationality of human beings enables them to order their existence, especially their sexuality, on which orderly social relations depend.

The mobility of animals differentiates this class of being from that of plants. Ga distinguish three categories of animals on the basis of their natural habitat: animals of the sea (*ngshọloo*), animals of the forest (*kooloo*), and domestic animals (*shialoo*). Within each of these categories a distinction is made between winged (*looflọ*) and wingless (*loo*) creatures. The primary significance of both animals and plants to Ga is as sources of food.

Ga utilize two conceptual models to characterize relations within the hierarchy of beings. The anthropomorphic model involves associations drawn from human society and experience to describe nonhuman classes of being; the physical model utilizes physical phenomena and attributes to characterize relations within the hierarchy. While motifs of ritual action frequently convey physical associations, the richest source of anthropomorphic imagery is *kpele* song.

Anthropomorphic models of nonhuman reality are variously expressed in *kpele* songs. Not only do many songs describe nonhuman beings in human terms, but singers sometimes interpret songs as analogues of human life. Such analogues are exemplified by indigenous exegeses of songs. One song states that a domestic fowl does not understand a wild bird (song 214), just as members of one society do not comprehend the customs of another society. Another text says that fowls which do not have an appropriate sleeping place lay anywhere (song 207), just as children who are not well-reared behave antisocially. Another song describes the control of the sea over the movement of shells on the beach (song 233-2), just as a master controls his servant or a man his money. In these analogies, as in social relations, behavior, and appearance, members of nonhuman classes are characterized in anthropomorphic imagery.

Anthropomorphic visual, behavioral, and psychological attributes of nonhuman classes of being in *kpele* songs can be summarized briefly. With respect to the appearance of members of these classes, human physiognomic attributes and dress are described. The goddess *Kǫǫle* is said to have an ugly neck (*ekuę tangtang*, song 85); the penis of *Nai* is mentioned (song 97); a bird describes his body parts from head to toe, and the parts he enumerates are human not avian body parts (song 211); the goddess *Afieye* and her son *Odame* describe their clothing, which in one case is the dress of a *kpele* medium and in the other that of a *kpele* priest (song 89-1, -2). Not only do members of nonhuman classes look like human beings, they behave like human beings. Fish sleep on mats (song 243); a goddess braids her hair (song 89); one god eats only blue shark (song 101), another eats any creature (song 81); a god strolls through the town (song 137); the supreme being is a farmer (song 1). Nonhuman beings are described as having human personality attributes as well. One goddess is said to be a quarrelsome person (*mpabi*, song 62-1), while a tortoise is called meddlesome (*sasaplęfo*, song 219).

The anthropomorphic model persists in the names given to certain nonhuman beings. Apart from patronymic birth-order names for each sex, Ga also have sets of names for males and females that denote the weekday of birth and express birth order among full siblings of the same sex. In *kpele* songs, day and birth-order names are given to certain gods and animals. Birth-order names are used for the goddess *Ashiaklę Dede* (*Ashiaklę*, first-born daughter, song 62-2), for crabs *Somo Dede* and *Somo Kǫkǫ* (fiddler crab first-born female, and fiddler crab second-born female, song 228), for a fish *Tęte* (first-born male, song 235). Day names are assigned to a snake,

Lomo Aku blika (Lord Wednesday-born male puff adder, song 221) and to several species of fish which include *Potsiri Kofi* (eagle ray Friday-born male, song 237), *Oşęrę Kofi* (guitar fish Friday-born male, song 237), *Bonso Aku* (whale Wednesday-born male, song 230), and *Odoi Kǫbla* (barracuda Tuesday-born male, song 242). In human society, Ga use these nonpatronymic names to differentiate persons with the same patronyms from one another. I suggest that a similar differentiation between members of the same category is expressed in the utilization of day and birth-order names for gods and animals in *kpele* songs.

A final use of anthropomorphism in *kpele* songs is the description of social ties for both divine beings and animals in the idiom of human kinship. At least four sets of relations are mentioned in the song texts: parent/child, sibling/sibling, husband/wife, and co-wife/co-wife. For example, one god is said to have begotten two daughters (song 45); a goddess berates her unruly children (song 82); a god boasts that he has many children (song 96); sexual relations between divine spouses are the theme of two texts (songs 83, 84), and two divine co-wives hurl insults at one another in a trio of songs (songs 85, 86, 87). In one song a fish maintains that he and another had the same mother, but different fathers (song 241); Western science also classifies these two species as members of the same family.[2] Social relations within divine and animals classes of being, therefore, are modeled on human kinship. I think that there are a number of reasons why this should be so. First, Ga are thought to have significant relations with both classes of beings. Gods are thought to control the course of human social life in a number of important respects (see Chapter 5). Not only are animals sources of food, but the spirits of some animals are believed to possess certain human beings. Human beings, therefore, may communicate directly with nonhuman beings, especially on ritual occasions. I suggest that such interaction is possible only be-

2. F. R. Irvine, *The Fishes and Fisheries of the Gold Coast*, pp. 140, 145.

tween similar kinds of being. Second, Ga believe that both classes of being are differentiated from human beings by only one existential attribute. The immortality of gods differentiates them from mortal human beings, while the rationality of men distinguishes them from nonrational animals. Third, by generalizing similarities with other aspects of nonhuman existence through analogic processes, the behavior and relations of nonhuman classes of being become intelligible, predictable, and ultimately controllable.

It is significant that the social relations within nonhuman classes of beings suggested in *kpele* songs are relations at the domestic level of social integration and not relations pertaining to some other societal level. As I have noted, in Ga society kinship is cognatic and relations between cognates are conceptualized in the idiom of blood (*la*). By birth to a particular pair of parents, an individual achieves membership in cognatic kin groups through which he acquires access to important statuses and resources in traditional Ga society. While divine beings necessarily exist only in the minds of men, the physiological limits and necessities of animal life are empirically similar to those of human beings. Through analogical processes, other aspects of animal life can be readily assimilated to human categories, especially those categories which are thought to have a physiological foundation, namely kinship. Such an explanation, of course, cannot apply to divine beings who have only an ideological reality. Rather, the most parsimonious explanation for the form of social relations within divine and animal classes is the Durkheimian hypothesis that Ga notions about the ordering of human society are the most readily available model for interrelations among nonhuman beings.

I suggest, therefore, that an anthropomorphic model of social relations within nonhuman classes of being not only makes relations within these classes intelligible to men, but creates the ideological basis for orderly interaction between members of these classes and human beings. Through the assimilation of the existence of nonhuman beings to human categories, interrelations between nonhuman beings and human beings become possible.

Anthropomorphic models, however, represent only one mode through which relations within the hierarchy of beings are conveyed. Another conceptual mode is the physical model. Physical models have a consistent formal structure in which two physical phenomena or properties are conceptualized as polar categories. The complementary asymmetrical relationship between these two physical entities connotes a series of paired associations of moral and physical categories. Within this series or set, the relationship between members of each pair is analogous to the relationship between the initial primary pair. The bases of analogy include spatial, physiological, and sensory perceptions, which, in turn, frequently constitute the basis for the expression of the primary opposition in ritual acts and objects. Before examining specific physical models of moral relations, two further attributes of such models should be noted. In different conceptual contexts, one set of physical relations may connote variant sets of associations, and, conversely, one association may be conveyed by different physical relations. As Turner has suggested, the activation of one set of associations in a particular context implies the possibility of generating other sets, and this multireferential potential of physical polarities contributes to their symbolic richness.[3]

Two sets of associations are based on the conception of an asymmetrical complementarity between sky and earth. One set pertains to the location of classes of being; the other relates to notions of sexuality. With respect to the locations of classes of being, the sky is the abode of immortal beings, the earth and sea of mortal beings. The notion of sky and earth as parallel planes of existence for different classes of being is implied by a *kpele* song which states that "the earth is flat, the sky is flat" (*shikpọng tẹtrẹ nyọngmọ tẹtrẹ*, song 18). As I have noted, divine beings are immortal spirits who are taxonomically intermediate between the supreme being and human beings and who mediate relations between the supreme being and mortal men. While the locus of divine activity is

3. Victor W. Turner, *Chihamba, The White Spirit*, pp. 69-81.

thought to be the sky, gods have the capacity to descend to earth. Further, individual divine beings are associated with specific topographical features, such as bodies of water, hills, and rocks. *Nai* is associated with the sea, *Sakumo* with the Densu River, *Koole* with the Koole Lagoon, *Ogbede* with the Kpeshi Lagoon, *Opoku* with a mountain, and *Totroe* with a rock on the beach. The generic term for *kpele* gods, moreover, means "place god" (*dzema-wong*). When informants were asked to explain the association between a divine being and a topographical feature, most replied that a particular divine being was both a god and a topographical feature. For example, one informant said, "*Nai* is the sea, but he is a god" (*Nai te ngsho shi dzemawong*), and "*Sakumo* also is a river and he is a god" (*Sakumo hu te faa ni te dzemawong*). The *Olila* medium, however, gave a more sophisticated explanation for the association between divine beings and natural features. She said that the gods are stars in the sky; when a star falls to earth, the place where it falls becomes associated with the god, and there the god descends to earth when he wishes. Her explanation is consistent with the view of the sky as the locus of gods and with the notion that particular terrestrial locations are associated with individual divine beings. Divine beings, therefore, may be localized in natural features.

The significance of such localization of spirit is suggested by Robin Horton's analysis of Kalabari sculpture. Horton demonstrates that "Kalabari sculpture is first and always an instrument for localizing the spirit it represents."[4] By localizing a spirit in a sculpture, it becomes controllable, and "by giving a sculpture the name of a spirit, and so making it into a name in its own right, Kalabari convert a transitory form of the name into one which is fixed and enduring; and in so doing, they convert a less efficacious form of name into one which is more efficacious."[5] Although Ga are less explicit than Kalabari about the relations between physical form and

4. Robin Horton, *Kalabari Sculpture,* p. 15. I am endebted to T. O. Beidelman for calling my attention to this monograph.
5. Ibid., pp. 8, 10.

human control over spirits, it seems probable that an analogous process is operative in the association between *kpele*
gods and topographical features. This hypothesis is supported
by certain Ga beliefs about relations between immortal beings
and human beings. Ga believe that human beings can achieve
contact with gods, and through this interconnection men may
succeed in achieving goals through these same spirits who
have some natural form. By contrast, Ga do not believe that
it is possible to achieve such contact with the supreme being,
who is without spatial or temporal limitations. Although the
localization of *kpele* gods in natural features seems to be analogous to the localization of Kalabari spirits in sculpture, an
explicit analogue to the Kalabari procedure exists in *kpele*
ritual. In the shrine (*gbatsu*) that a *kpele* priest tends and the
room (*wɔngtsu*) that a *kpele* medium uses for invocations is a
pot (*kulo*) of water which is said to symbolize the god.[6]
When a medium invokes spiritual beings, which include not
only gods but ancestral shades and spirits of twins, these beings become localized in the pot of water and reveal their
messages from the pot to the medium and through her to
other mortals. *Kpele* water pots, therefore, are the analogues
of Kalabari sculpture in which spirits take form and through
which human beings may exert control over spiritual beings.
The use of *kpele* water pots differs from the use of Kalabari
sculpture in that the identity of the localized spirit may
change in the former case but not in the latter. The enduring
association between god and form in *kpele* ritual is the association between a god and a topographical feature.

6. In my paper, "Libation in Ga Ritual" (*Journal of Religion in Africa* 2:161-178), I discuss the significance of water (*nu*) in *kpele* ritual.
I suggest that water relates to the conception of rain (*nu*) as the mediating substance between the world of divinity (*Nyɔngmɔmang*, "God's
town") and the world of men (*hulumang*, "sun's town") in general, and
between the supreme being and human beings in particular. The supreme being, who is associated with the sky, sends rain to earth as a sign
of his concern for men and his approval of their actions. Ga, therefore,
regard rain as a propitious omen for any undertaking, as it is a sign of
divine approval. Since the gods are considered to be intermediaries between the supreme being and mortal men, it is appropriate that they
should be identified with water, the natural phenomenon that mediates
between sky and earth.

In one conceptual context, therefore, the differentiation between sky and earth connotes the differentiation between a class of immortal beings and one of mortal beings. This association is symbolized in the ritual motif of upward and downward movement. When *kpele* mediums wish to become possessed at ritual dances, they make downward pulling movements with their arms which are known as "sky" (*ngwęi*) and by which they express their intention to bring divine beings from sky to earth so that they may speak through mediums to other mortals. When sacrificial animals are offered to divine beings, they are raised and lowered in order to show the beasts to gods in the sky. The first set of associations which the complementary relationship between sky and earth connotes includes the following polarities.

sky	earth
immortal being	mortal being
up	down
superior	inferior

An asymmetrical relation between sky and earth is relevant not only to ideas concerning the physical location of different classes of being, but also to notions of sexuality within taxonomic classes. In this context, sky represents active seminal masculinity and earth connotes passive fecund femininity. These notions are suggested by a constantly reiterated theme in prayer during the annual *kpele* agricultural rites, "May rain fall that the earth may be moist, that mushroom may grow" (*bleku aka ni shikpǫng nǫ adzǫ ni mlę akwę*), and by a *kpele* song which describes the thundering articulateness of sky and the dumbness of earth (song 21). This differentiation between masculine sky and feminine earth also pertains to differentiations within divine and human communities. Ga consider that there are two categories of divine beings: male sky divinities and female earth divinities (*afieye*). The earth goddesses are wives of the sky gods. Analogously, within the religious community of mortal men, priests have ritual wives

A *Kpele* Dance
Oliila Medium Invokes the God
Possessed *Oliila* Medium Sings

who are also called *afieye*. Ga recognize the analogy between divine and mortal spouses. Thus, the *Olila* medium said that the priests' wives are called *afieye*, "because the gods' wives are *Afieye*. And so when they install a priest, they will give him a wife; they call her *Afieye*" (*te wodzii ni amẹ ngamẹi dzi Afieye. Nohewo kẹ ato wulọmọ ni abaaha lẹ nga; Afieye atsẹọ lẹ*). With respect to sexuality, therefore, the set of dualistic oppositions relevant to the notion of masculine sky and feminine earth include the following oppositions:

sky	earth
male	female
god	god's wife (*afieye*)
priest	priest's wife (*afieye*)
active	passive
seminal	fecund
articulate	dumb
superior	inferior

Another physical model that expresses significant relations among mortal Ga is based on a primary differentiation between sea and land. The sea is associated with the south, the land with the north. The first Ga on the coast are said to have been members of *Nai we*, who came from the south (songs 152, 153, 191); there is some evidence of maritime trade between the Bights of Benin and this part of the Ghanaian coast in pre-European times.[7] The coastal-dwelling *Nai we* people are distinguished from Ga who in historic times fled from the inland town of Great Accra to the coast. Since the first settlers of any Ga community are superordinate to subsequent settlers, members of *Nai we* consider themselves and their god, *Nai*, to be superior to all other Ga and their gods in Accra. The superiority of *Nai we* is conveyed in various ways. One mode of expressing asymmetrical status relations is that persons of subordinate rank visit persons of superordinate rank. It will be recalled that three songs sung by the *Ashiaklẹ*

7. Paul Ozanne, "Notes on the Early Historic Archaeology of Accra," *Transactions of the Historical Society of Ghana* 6:67.

priest, a member of *Nai we*, assert that members of *Nai we* refuse to visit other Ga (songs 153, 191, 226). Another mode of expressing status differentiation is through color symbolism. As I discuss later, white connotes superiority in several different senses. The ritual use of white clay (*ayilɔ*) for body markings by *Nai* worshippers and of red clay (*tung*) by worshippers of other major gods in Accra is both an assertion of the superiority of *Nai* and his cult and a means of maintaining the distinction between early settlers who came from the sea and later immigrants who came from the hinterland.[8] A final mode of expressing the differentiation and superiority of *Nai* over other gods is through the pouring of libation. When libation is poured on ritual occasions, the officiant faces first seaward and southward to invoke *Nai* and his children, and then inland and northward to call other gods. In Ga thought, the sea and the south also connote civilized and superior life styles in contrast to the land and the north, which are associated with rustic and inferior cultural patterns. Thus, the associations connoted by the asymmetrical relation between sea and land include:

sea	land
south	north
Nai we	other Ga
sea gods	other gods
white clay	red clay
superior	inferior

A number of spatial orientations are germane to relations within the hierarchy of beings. The most important of these spatial conceptions is that of the five, sometimes seven, corners of the world. In one *kpele* song (song 178), people come from the seven corners of the world to witness an event. The seven corners of the world (*dzeng kodzii kpawo*) consist of the four compass directions, and sea, land, and sky. More often reference is made to the five corners of the world

---

8. The only other god whose celebrants use white clay for ritual body markings is *Naa Kɔɔle*, who is said to be a daughter of *Nai*.

(*dzeng kodzii enumo̧*) which are the compass directions and the middle of the world (*dzeng teng*). The *Olila* medium explained the five and seven corners of the world in the following words:

> You see how this place is; you see that this is north [*koogbȩ,* "forest way"], this is south [*ngshoģbȩ,* "sea way"], you see this is east, this is west, you see that the fifth is the middle exactly. And so that is how the world lies; five corners, so it is our Ga gods' world, they [the gods] carry the world, their five corners of the world, but they [people] say seven corners of the world—so one speaks, but it is the five corners of the world which they carry.

> We have a certain star, they call it the seven corners of the world . . . seven corners of the world and one says seven shrines [*gbatsui kpawo*]. And so it was already in the sky before they created the name.

In these exegetical comments, the distinction between the sky, the abode of immortal beings, and the earth, that of mortal men, is maintained, but their interpenetration also is acknowledged, especially in the notion of the middle of the world.

The middle of the world is a significant conception in *kpele* thought. One song (song 20) states that "the middle of the world guides us." The middle of the world is life-sustaining air, the abode of the gods. As I have noted, in *kpele* cosmology, the world has five corners: the compass directions and the air between sky and earth which sustains life and in which gods exist as intermediaries between the personified life force and human beings. The notion of the five corners of the world is represented in two ritual symbols. The first is the distinctive ritual hair style (*kukuru*) of *kpele* mediums, in which the hair is braided into five cones arranged to represent the compass directions and the middle of the world; the second is the ritual broom of *kpele* priests and mediums, in which five bunches of twigs are arranged in a similar pattern.[9] A further spatial orientation that conveys social values is laterality. In the *kpele* songs in this collection, however, not only is laterality mentioned infrequently (only in songs 202, 203), but these references do not connote the significance of this distinction in ritual action. Laterality is utilized in ritual action to connote status differentiations among human beings. A fundamental polarity conveyed by laterality is the association of right with masculinity and left with femininity, which is consistent with the general association of superordinate status with right and subordinate status with left. In the context of ritual action, right is associated with ritual office and left with secular office, for, as I discuss in the following chapter, secular authority is subordinate to ritual authority in relation to divinity. Thus, the physical model based on laterality includes the following set of associations:

right	left
superordinate status	subordinate status
male	female
ritual office	secular office
superior	inferior

Apart from physical phenomena and spatial orientations, a variety of other sensory phenomena are utilized to convey social values. Among these are patterns of color and light and analogies of size and weight. Although analogies of size and weight are not mentioned explicitly in any of the *kpele* songs, they are implicit in a few (e.g., songs 68, 96). Size and weight

9. The broom, which constitutes part of the paraphernalia of mediums and priests, is a symbol of the purificatory functions of ritual office. At *kpele* rites, all priests and mediums carry brooms. Occasionally a possessed medium uses her broom to sweep the bodies of other ritual performers, thereby removing any mystical pollution that may surround them. These are the only utilizations of the broom which I have observed. I also noted that a number of brooms are stored with other ritual objects in the god's room (*woŋgtsu*) of a medium.

are used as analogies for relative status between and within classes of being. Greater magnitude in either of these physical dimensions implies relatively senior status. Divine beings, therefore, are heavier than mortal men. When gods descend to earth, whatever objects they contact become heavy (*tsii*), not merely figuratively but literally. For example, E. A. Ammah recorded in his 1937 field notes the difficulty with which a bowl of water was thrown away after a rite.

> After the prayers and blessing the Ashiakele [*Ashiaklε*] priestess took the tsese [bowl] to throw the water away; it was with great difficulty that she was able to do this water throwing away ceremony. The vessel seemed so heavy in her hand, for the gods have touched it. . . .[10]

Analogously, greater physical size implies greater social status. In the natural sphere, the sea is vaster than any other physical entity. In Accra, the god of the sea, *Nai*, outranks all other divine beings. Among the creatures of the sea, the whale (*bonso*) is largest in size and consequently senior in status. Among the priests in Accra, the *Nai* priest, who is theoretically superordinate to all other *kpele* priests, often is referred to as whale (*bonso*). The relative ranking of *Nai* and his priest in relation to other beings within the same classes is symbolized by the brim on the ritual hat of the *Nai* priest; the hats of other priests are brimless. The set of associations connoted by relative physical size, therefore, includes:

larger size	smaller size
senior status	junior status
sea	other topographical phenomena
whale	other sea animals
Nai	other gods
Nai priest	other priests
brimmed hat	brimless hat
superior	inferior

10. E. A. Ammah, "Field Notebooks, 1937," p. 3.

As a final physical model of moral categories, certain patterns of color and light which are noted in *kpele* song texts may be mentioned briefly. These references fall into two main categories: phenomenological and analogical. Within the phenomenological category are included such references as a dark cloud (song 29), gold is like sunshine (song 25), the leaves of a plant and the skin of a god are red (songs 11, 73), a star shines brightly (song 27). Such colorative attributes are more relevant to cosmogonic and anthropomorphic considerations than to moral categories. The analogical category, however, is of considerable interest, though it falls somewhat outside the present line of analysis. In a number of songs, there are reference to whiteness and brightness and to blackness and darkness. These two colors are used in the songs as analogies for certain abstract conceptions about the quality of human life. White color or white clay (*ayilǫ*) connotes positive conceptions such as peace, success, blessing, prosperity (songs 203, 204, 205) and black is associated with negative notions such as difficulty and impediment (song 203). In *kpele* thought these connotations are generalized to an association of white with life, divine beings, sky, and purity, and black with death, mortal beings, earth, and impurity.

Since white is associated with *kpele* gods, ritual objects are invariably white. The robes of mediums and priests are white, the pots in shrines are white, the bracelets, anklets, and necklaces of ritual specialists are white, and sacrificial animals are completely or partially white. White is both a symbol of purity and a symbol of divinity. Objects or person who mediate relations between mortal men and immortal gods must be purer than other members of their class in order to achieve contact with still purer deities. The set of associations based on a polar opposition between white and black includes:

white	black
light	dark
life	death
immortal beings	mortal beings
sky	earth
ritual objects	secular objects

order	disorder
success	failure
purity	impurity
superior	inferior

In *kpele* thought, physical models represent one mode through which differentiation within the hierarchy of beings is conveyed. Each model is based on a primary opposition between two physical entities; this initial polarity connotes a set of paired associations in which the relations between members of each pair are analogous to the relations between the primary pair. The content of certain sets pertain to relations between categories within the same taxonomic class, others to relations between classes, and still others to a combination of categorical and interclass relations. Flexibility exists not only in the taxonomic status of the complementary asymmetrical relations within sets, but in the utilization of pairs in different sets. One dualistic pair may form part of different physical models; for example, the differentiation between masculinity and femininity enters sets of associations based both on laterality and on the differentiation between sky and earth; similarly, the differentiation between gods and men is relevant not only to a set based on a primary opposition between sky and earth but to one based on the differentiation between black and white. The fact that one pair may form part of variant physical models accounts for the multireferential potential of such models. Although the content of physical models varies, the form is invariant. Moreover, the invariant form of physical models facilitates the interchange of cognitive categories between sets.

This discussion of *kpele* taxonomy has been based primarily on the content of *kpele* song texts. The system of ideas which orders the *kpele* world, however, is not only a system of classification but an explanatory model of human experiences, for success and failure in human society depend fundamentally on the quality of relations between different classes of being. Such relations are effected by the performance of ritual.

5 / Metaphors in *Kpele* Ritual

Throughout the year, *kpele* cult groups perform ritual in order to achieve contact with immortal spirits and to realize various goals through this contact. Through the performance of periodic calendrical rites, men aspire to maintain existing harmonious relations with immortal gods; through the enactment of occasional rites, they aim to restore orderly relations with immortal spirits when those relations have become disordered through intentional or involuntary human acts. Although ritual is addressed to immortal spirits, only certain categories of men are allowed to engage in the performance of ritual. Consequently, *kpele* ritual performances involve two sets of relations: one between immortal spirits and mortal men, the other between mortal men with respect to immortal spirits. Certain ideas about these relations recurrently find symbolic expression in *kpele* ritual. Since I am concerned with the ritual expression of these relations in general terms, I do not present extended analyses of specific rites.

Consideration of *kpele* songs, prayers, and ritual acts and of indigenous exegetical statements about these acts reveals that several premises about relations between classes of being underlie the performance of *kpele* ritual. These premises are: (1) the supreme being is the creator and controller of the universe, (2) human beings can achieve interconnection with the supreme being only indirectly through gods, and (3) gods are responsive to human action. Although the supreme being represents the personified life force which controls cosmic processes and existence in the universe of his creation, human beings cannot achieve contact with him directly. Relations between the supreme being and human beings are mediated by gods, who constitute the taxonomically intermediate class of being within the hierarchy of beings. Since gods are the channels through which messages between the supreme being and mortal men must pass, they are the focus of ritual activity. As I have described, the *kpele* religious system consists of a series of cults; each cult is devoted to the worship of a single deity. By addressing ritual to gods, men aspire to find favor with the supreme being which will produce beneficial results for human society.

As instruments of the will of the supreme being, the gods are regarded as givers and takers of life. As one aspect of their life-giving powers, gods are believed to control natural processes. In prayer and song, gods are supplicated for rain which will enable plants to grow, for fish and other forms of food (songs 66, 67, 76, 103). Gods sustain human life not only by providing sources of subsistence, but by protecting Ga in battle (songs 62-2, 64, 55), making barren women fertile, and healing the sick. While gods, as agents of the supreme being, are givers of life, they may be takers of life, for if angered they may cause death either directly or indirectly through natural disasters, such as floods and epidemics. Ga, therefore, fear and respect the powers of their gods (song 40):

Wọwọi lo, wọhię amẹ;	The gods lo, we hold them;
Wọngshẹ amẹ.	We fear them.
Kọme, wọngshẹ amẹ,	Sakumọ, we fear them,
Yibumẹ.	Protect us.

The idea of divine wrath and retribution suggests the final premise underlying *kpele* ritual, namely, that the gods are responsive to human action. The deeds of men may please or displease gods. The affective consequences of human deeds have cosmic repercussions, for gods through the supreme being control cosmic order. Order within the universe, which is reflected in the regular passage of seasons, the growth of plants, increase in human and animal populations, depends upon harmonious relations between divine and mortal beings.

Human action in the form of periodic rites is thought to be necessary to maintain such amicable relations. Nevertheless, human action irrespective of the actor's intentions can disturb the relations between gods and men. When relations between gods and men are disordered, disorder in the natural world resulting from divine intervention is to be anticipated. Cosmic disorder is reflected in unusual natural events, such as floods, droughts, earthquakes, and epidemics, which have dire consequences for human society. To prevent or alleviate cosmic disorder, redressive ritual must be performed so that harmonious relations between immortal gods and mortal men may be reestablished. Relations between mortal men and immortal gods, therefore, are the metaphor in which adversity and prosperity in human society are explained. If these relations are amicable, men prosper; if they are disordered, men suffer. When natural calamities occur, the relations between gods and men must be disordered; the cause must be sought in prior social events and the disorder redressed through appropriate ritual. Ritual, therefore, is performed by cult groups in order to restore or to maintain harmonious relations between gods and men for the benefit of human society or of individuals and groups within society.

These premises are fundamental to an understanding of *kpele* ritual performances. Such performances further elaborate conceptions concerning relations between gods and men and those between human beings with respect to divinity. These structural notions are conveyed through words, gestures, temporal sequences, and spatial orientations in ritual. Many symbolic modes of expressing structural relations recur in all *kpele* rites, whether or not the rite is system-maintaining or redressive.

The essential statement of *kpele* ritual concerning the relationship between divine beings and human beings is simple: divine beings are superordinate to human beings. In the preceding chapter, I noted that within the hierarchy of beings, the immortality of gods differentiates them from mortal men. Otherwise these classes of being are existentially undifferentiated, for both classes were created by the supreme being and both classes comprise rational and mobile beings. The differentiation between these classes is conveyed through the association of gods with the sky and men with the earth. Not only are gods existentially similar to men, except for their longevity, but, as I have described, the patterns of relations and activities within each of these classes are analogous. Divine activity in the sky is analogous to human activity on earth. This notion of parallel planes of divine and mortal activity, which is implied by one song (song 18), is developed in indigenous exegetical statements about ritual performances. Ga say that the calendrical agricultural rites which men perform on earth are performed first by gods in the sky. Perhaps the most vivid exposition of this notion is the *Olila* medium's statement that when possessed mediums dance, it looks as though women are dancing on the ground, but in actuality gods are dancing in the sky. Thus, within divine and human classes relations between members are analogous.

While relations within the class of divine beings and within that of human beings are analogous, the relations between these classes are asymmetrical. The structural asymmetry is expressed through cosmic metaphors, which, in turn, are conveyed through modes of ritual symbolism. The cosmic associations for divine beings have been outlined previously. Divine beings are immortal, nocturnal, sky beings; human beings are mortal, diurnal, earth beings. These cosmic associations convey the complementarity of the opposition between gods and men. In *kpele* ritual, the complementary opposition between immortality and mortality is conveyed through color symbols. White is associated with immortality, black with mortality. Ritual objects, including dress, ornaments, sacrificial objects, and utensils, are white. The color white symbolizes divinity and the positive connotations of divine munificence for human society. By contrast, black connotes mortality, death, and adversity in human experience. Analogously, the timing of certain activities conveys the complementary notions of nocturnal gods and diurnal men. Ga say that the "day" of divine beings begins at sundown, while that of human beings begins at dawn. Consistent with this conception is the fact that important rites frequently are preceded by nocturnal vigils. Priests and mediums, who intercede with divine beings on behalf of other human beings, are required to observe certain dietary and sexual prescriptions during sacred days; the period of abstinence begins on the eve of the sacred day and terminates at sundown on that day. While the association of gods with night may be partially related to the conception of night as a time of darkness and mystery, I think that fundamentally this association of night with gods and day with men is an expression of the complementary differentiation of divine beings and human beings. Finally, the variant physical locations of these classes of being is conveyed through the motif of upward and downward movement in ritual action. Whenever mediums wish to become possessed during *kpele* dances, they make downward pulling motions with their arms, called "sky" (*ngwẹi*), by which they symbolize their intention to bring gods to earth. Similar movements are utilized in the presentation of sacrificial objects to divine beings. Whenever human beings offer a sacrificial object to gods, they thrice raise the object to show it to gods in the sky and lower it to earth to entreat divinities to accept its life. Sacrificial objects include libations, fowl, sheep, and occasionally cattle. Libations are poured on all ritual occasions; sacrificial animals are used on the occasion of major calendrical rites, such as the opening of the sea (*ngshọ bulemọ*) and the millet feast (*ngmaayeli*) of a god, and frequently are demanded by gods through their mediums before redressive ritual can be performed. Each conceptual element within the set of cosmic associations has a primary mode of ritual expression. The complementary opposition between immortality and mortality is conveyed through patterns of color; that between divine and human activities through the timing of rites; that between physical locations through a motif of ritual action. These symbolic modes convey classificatory differentiation and complementary asymmetry between gods and men.

Other symbolic modes convey dynamic aspects of the relationship between gods and men. As agents of the supreme being, gods are believed to regulate cosmic processes. The control of gods over cosmic processes is mimed in certain collective dances at the planting rite (*ngmaadumǫ*) of the *Dantu* and *Sakumǫ* cults and at the transplanting (*ngmaafaa*) and reaping (*ngmaaku*) rites of the *Sakumǫ* cult. On these occasions, when the celebrants return to the shrine from the sacred field, they form a circle in single file outside the shrine and dance counterclockwise to symbolize the shining of the sun and then clockwise to symbolize the falling of rain. These alternating dance progressions, which are repeated thrice, not only symbolize the control of divine beings over cosmic processes, but express the aims of the ritual actors. By performing these acts human beings seek to influence divine beings to utilize their regulatory powers over natural processes in ways which will be beneficial to human society. The miming of cosmic processes, therefore, conveys both the powers of the gods and the aims of men.

Analogous utilization of the concept of straightness is made in *kpele* ritual in which straightness is a metaphor for order. This directional concept has two basic referents: one pertains to human activities, the other to divine activities. The Ga word for worship (*dzamǫ*) means "to straighten" which conveys the underlying aim of ritual, namely, to order relations between gods and men. In prayer, gods are implored to straighten crooked humanity. One or both connotations of straightness may be conveyed in the utilization of linear ritual motifs. Priests and mediums sometimes use linear gestures. For example, a ritual specialist may pass his hand in a vertical line over the belly of a pregnant woman, thereby symbolizing his desire for her safe delivery. Whether or not her confinement is without hazard depends on the will of the gods as agents of the supreme being. Through this linear gesture, however, the powers of divine beings and the aims of human beings are conveyed simultaneously. Similarly, on ritual occasions the bodies of priests and mediums are marked in clay with two parallel lines, while those of *agbaa* members and uninitiated mediums are dotted with clay. The linear markings of priests and mediums symbolize both their roles as representatives of human beings to the gods who order human existence and their wish to establish harmonious relations between gods and men through ritual performances.

Apart from cosmic and linear metaphors, the asymmetrical relationship between divine beings and mortal men is expressed by images of human subordination. These images include the partial nakedness of ritual performers and the use of two hands, which are placed parallel, to make offerings to divine beings. In Ga society, when a subordinate addresses a superior, he drops his cloth to his waist as a sign of respect. In *kpele* rites, priests, mediums, and *agbaa* members also convey their inferiority in relation to divine beings by performing ritual acts bare-breasted. In Ga society, when a person wishes to express the sincerity with which he performs an act, he uses both hands or proffers two gifts (see song 102). A warm greeting, therefore, is symbolized by a dual handclasp, a sincere gift by the presentation of two similar objects. Analogously, in *kpele* ritual, the respectful sincerity of the intentions of ritual performers is expressed by the use of two hands in pouring libations, in offering sacrificial animals, in bathing, and by double prestations of drink and fowl in sacrifice.

Hitherto I have considered a number of ritual metaphors which express the superordination of divine beings and the subordination of human beings. The aim of ritual performance is to bring these two classes of being into contact. In order to facilitate the achievement of this goal and to ensure its propitious outcome for human beings, the constituents of the ritual field, which include performers, objects, and places, must be isolated from mundane society. These constituents of the ritual field must be set apart from those aspects of human society which might affect negatively their capacity to achieve contact with divine beings. Because the mortality of human beings differentiates them from divine beings, ritual performers must be isolated from the physiological processes and acts associated most intimately with human mortality, namely, death and sexual acts. Human beings who mediate between divine beings and other mortals must avoid contact

Double Prestations
  Nai Wulọmọ Libates
  Nai Wulọmọ Offers Sacrificial Fowl

with such polluting situations during ritual periods. More-over, while sexual restrictions for priests and mediums are limited to ritual occasions, prohibitions on contact with death are perpetual, for priests and mediums may neither attend funerary rites nor mourn their dead.[1] During the annual agri-cultural rites, *agbaa* members also are forbidden to participate in funerals; this prohibition is extended to the entire com-munity during the uncertain period of seed germination be-tween the rites of planting and transplanting. Such sexual and mortuary prescriptions serve to isolate ritual performers from human society and to prepare them for contact with immortal spirits.

Apart from such restrictions on the behavior of ritual per-formers, the constituents of the ritual field are set apart through various purificatory procedures, such as fumigating, bathing, and sweeping. At periodic rites, shrines, processional routes, fields, and participants are fumigated with incense (see song 143). Mediums brush the bodies of other participants with ritual brooms. Aside from the pouring of libation, bath-ing is probably the most frequently performed ritual act. The priest's preparation of a bowl (*tsɛsɛ*) of sacred water in which worshippers bathe constitutes the central ritual act of weekly worship and the initial ritual act of agricultural rites. When participants in agricultural rites enter the courtyard of a shrine, they first bathe in the sacred water before their bodies are decorated with clay markings and before greeting the assembled participants. The aims of such cleansing pro-cedures are not only to remove the contamination of mortal existence from the ritual field but to achieve positive goals which human beings aspire to attain through contact with di-vine beings on ritual occasions. The gods, as agents of the su-preme being, are believed to be able to heal the sick, to make barren women fertile, to ensure the successful realization of human goals whether these pertain to economic, domestic, or political aspects of human life. When individuals bathe in

---

1. In 1968, the death of one *kpele* priest in Accra was attributed to breaking this prescription, for he died after he wept at the suicide of a beloved son-in-law.

ritually prepared water, fumigate ritual spaces, sweep with ritual brooms, they seek not only to remove mystical pollution from themselves and their surroundings but to achieve some positive goal for themselves or for others through contact with divine beings.

Men attempt to establish contact with divine beings primarily through prayer and sacrificial acts, for gods are thought to respond to human words and deeds. The prayers which priests and mediums offer on ritual occasions set the terms of the contract between gods and men which subsequent sacrificial acts attempt to establish. *Kpele* prayers have three component parts: invocation, exegesis, and supplication. In prayer, divine beings are invoked and thereby isolated as a class of being in relation to mortal men. The aim of invocation is to lessen the distance between divine and mortal beings by bringing gods temporarily closer to men through ritual acts. After gods have been invoked, the officiant explains why they have been summoned by stating the rite which is being performed, its appropriateness with reference to preceding ritual or social events, and the role of gods in ensuring the success of the rite. These exegetical statements articulate the dependence of human beings upon divine beings. Finally, the gods are supplicated. The central themes of supplication are that the gods should reward the faithful who worship them and that they should punish the enemies of the community of believers. Supplication, therefore, sets the reciprocal basis of the relationship between immortal gods and mortal men. Essentially, this relationship is a contractual one founded on moral reciprocity. Through prayer, human beings state the nature of the contract between gods and men which subsequent sacrificial acts attempt to effect. Interconnection is achieved through sacrificial acts in the form of food offerings, libation, and bloody sacrifice. Through the offering of prayer and sacrificial objects, men aspire to bring divinity to man and to bind these classes of being together through reciprocal moral obligations. Although the underlying notions concerning interconnection between gods and men are constant, the aims of sacrificial acts may vary. The variant goals of sacrifice are expressed not only in prayer but sometimes in ritual action. Thus, in libation when separation of gods from men through redressive ritual is desired, the liquid of libation is poured away from the officiant; whereas when continued connection between gods and men through periodic rites is wanted, the liquid is poured toward the officiant. The interconnection which men aspire to achieve through ritual is symbolized by the sharing of food or drink among gods and men. Since divine beings are superior to mortal beings, food and drink are offered to them before they are served to human beings. Through commensuality, interconnection between gods and men is realized.

Since ritual performances are predicated on the notion that gods respond to human supplication, invocation necessarily implies the diversion of divine beings from their customary autonomous activities. Sometimes the autonomous work of divine beings assumes precedence over the desires of human beings; at such times, human beings should not attempt to invoke them. During the uncertain period of seed germination between the rites of planting and transplanting, the gods are believed to be watching over the seed in the sacred fields and thereby ensuring its successful growth. During this period not only is weeping and wailing for the dead prohibited, but all forms of unnecessary noise, such as clapping, whistling, drumming, and singing, are restricted. Recently Needham has hypothesized a connection between percussion and transition.[2] If, as is true for Ga, human beings attempt to achieve contact with transcendental beings through percussive instrumentation and analogous devices such as clapping, and if the achievement of such interconnection necessarily implies a disruption of divine activity, the imposition of a ban on percus-

2. Rodney Needham, "Percussion and Transition," *Man*, n.s. 2:606-614. In subsequent issues of *Man*, several contributors have responded to Needham's article in ways not directly relevant to my current discussion (William C. Sturtevant, "Correspondence: Categories, Percussion and Physiology," n.s. 3:133-134 [1968]; Anthony Jackson, "Sound and Ritual," n.s. 3:293-299 [1968]; John Blacking, "Correspondence: Percussion and Transition," n.s. 3:313-314 [1968]; C. R. Hallpike, "Correspondence: Percussion and Transition," n.s. 3:314 [1968]).

sive modes of behavior implies an interdiction on the disruption of the work of the gods by diverting their attention to other human requests. The imposition of a period of silence between the rites of planting and transplanting, therefore, suggests that the important work of divine beings should not be interrupted.

Table 10. Relations between Gods and Men

Conception		Ritual Expression of Conception	
Divine Being	*Human Being*		
immortal	mortal	white	black
nocturnal	diurnal	nocturnal vigil	diurnal rite
sky	earth	upward movement	downward movement
control cosmic processes	subject to cosmic processes		
shining of sun	—	counterclockwise movement	—
falling of rain	—	clockwise movement	—
control life	—		
straight	crooked	linear motifs	—
pure	impure	—	purificatory procedures
superior	inferior	—	nakedness two hands two prestations

Thus far, I have considered some ritual metaphors of the asymmetrical relationship between divine beings and human beings (see Table 10). A ritual performance, however, is a statement not only about relations between gods and men but about status differentiations among human beings in relation to divinity, for the role of mediation between these classes is reserved for certain categories of human beings. Several sets of social relations are symbolized in *kpele* rites, through nonverbal symbolic modes such as the spatial orientation of ritual performers and the sequence of ritual acts. The sets of relations which I discuss are relations between ritual and secular authority, relations between male and female, and medial status relations. This analysis is restricted to agricultural rites, as within the context of these rites, these relations are expressed most clearly and fully.

The differentiation between secular authority and ritual authority is conveyed through patterns of color, spatial orientations, and temporal sequences in *kpele* ritual. In relation to divine beings, secular authority is subordinate to ritual authority, for chiefs can approach divine beings only through mediums and priests. The three senior chiefs in Accra, Nii Ga, Nii Gbese, and Nii Asere, participate in the agricultural rites of the *Sakumọ* cult and *kpeledzoo*. The differentiation of secular and ritual officials is conveyed through color symbolism. As I have noted, white is associated with divine beings and through them with ritual office, for it connotes the mediating role of priests and mediums between gods and men. White is associated with ritual office, red is associated with chieftaincy. Red connotes the martial role of chiefs as defenders of the integrity of the Ga polity, as well as the bloodshed of war. At *kpeledzoo*, the cloths of the chiefs are red, those of priests and mediums are white. At the funerals of these officials, mourners wear red clothing for dead chiefs and white for deceased priests. The association of red with secular office and white with ritual office is constant and conveys both status differentiation and asymmetry insofar as white symbolizes superior status through its associations with immortal gods and red connotes inferior status through its associations with the physiological processes of mortal men. The relative inferiority of chiefs to ritual officials in relation to divinity is represented through spatial orientations and in the performance of ritual acts. The seating of chiefs on ritual occasions reflects their subordinate status, for in the courtyard of a shrine, they sit on the left and inferior side of the entrance to the shrine, while male members of the *agbaa* sit on the right and superior side. Analogously, at *kpeledzoo* the *agbaa* sit behind the drums or near the area of divine activity, while the chiefs sit at the opposite end of the dancing area. The relative inferiority of chiefs is represented not only in seating positions, but also in the performance of ritual acts. At agricultural rites, chiefs remain in the courtyard of the shrine while the *agbaa* go to the sacred field; when drink is served, mediums and male members of the *agbaa* are served before chiefs; every year the three senior chiefs present cere-monial logs to each of the three senior priests in Accra, who are *Nai, Sakumǫ*, and *Kǫǫle* priests, just as each year women present firewood to their mothers-in-law during *homǫwǫ*. Such acts are symbolic not only of the relative status of priests and chiefs but of the interdependence of secular and ritual authority, for while priests are responsible for ordering relations between gods and men, chiefs are responsible for or-dering relations among men. The interdependence of secular and ritual authority is symbolized further by the division of millet after the rite of reaping (*ngmaaku*) of the *Sakumǫ* cult. On this occasion three millet stalks and three ears of maize are presented not only to the elders of the house of *Sakumǫ we* but to the three senior chiefs. Since agricultural rites are performed for the benefit of the entire community, the chiefs as representatives of the community should share in the pro-duce of the ritual field. The various values by which the dif-ferentiation between secular and ritual authority is expressed are summarized in the following set of complementary oppo-sitions:

ritual office	secular office
white	red
right	left
near	far
first served	second served
superior	inferior

Another important set of social relations expressed in *kpele* ritual is the differentiation between male and female. In secu-lar society, women are called "left-handed people" (*abekulǫi*) and are thought to be incapable of rational thought, which is the characteristic of men. The relative inferiority of women in relation to men within the ritual community is expressed in various ways. In the courtyard of a shrine, women sit apart from men. At *Sakumo*'s shrine, the women of the *agbaa* sit on the left behind the chiefs, while the men of the *agbaa* sit opposite them on the right of the entrance to the shrine. When the *agbaa* walks to and from either the sacred field or the beach, men precede women. Men and women go together to the sacred field on all ritual occasions except *Sakumo* and *Koole* rites of reaping (*ngmaaku*). On the latter occasions, the women of *Koole agbaa* do not go to the field and those of *Sakumo agbaa* go after the men have completed their ritual tasks in the field. When drinks are served to the *agbaa*, male members are served before female members. The values associated with men and women within the ritual community reproduce those associated with male and female in secular society, and their expression in spatial orientations is summarized in the following set of complementary oppositions:

male	female
agbaa male	*agbaa* female
right	left
ahead	behind
before	after
superior	inferior

Finally, the notion of the mediating status as it is expressed in ritual illuminates a very important motif of *kpele* ritual action, the triple performance of a ritual act. Among hereditary ritual statuses within a cult association, the office of priest is senior. The priest represents human beings to divine beings and, therefore, mediates between these two classes of being. In performing ritual acts, such as libation at the shrine or agricultural tasks in the field, the position of the priest in relation to other participants symbolizes his mediating role. The priest stands not only in front of the other celebrants, but in the center of the group. At the shrine, the central position of the priest, who stands facing the shrine to libate, divides the congregation into male members of the religious community,

The Priest's Mediating Status
   Koole Agbaamẹi Enter the Sacred Field
   Sakumọ Agbaamẹi Divide the Harvest

who stand on his right, and male members of the secular community and women, who stand on his left. The notion of the priest as mediator between sky-dwelling divinity and earth-dwelling humanity is symbolized by the elevated seat on which priests sit whether in the courtyards of their gods' shrines or in other locations. At *kpeledzoo,* which is performed "under the dancing tree" *(kpeletsoshishi)* outside the *Sakumǫ* shrine, the *Sakumǫ* priest sits in an elevated position, at a height considerably above the heads of all other participants.

Although the priest is the highest ranking person among hereditary ritual practitioners, he always occupies a medial position. When he walks in procession, he walks in the middle of his male ritual assistants. In fact, the association of highest rank with medial spatial position is constant in Ga symbolism; on this person's right or in front of him is stationed the second-ranking person in the group, and on his left or directly behind him is placed the third-ranking person. When the Ga paramount chief goes in procession, he walks between his two senior subchiefs; at the infant-naming ceremony, the baby who unites two unrelated kin units is laid between his patrikinsmen and his matrikinsmen; at *kpele* dances, three drums are utilized and the largest pace-setting drum is placed in the center. All these examples suggest the association of medial spatial position with highest status; such a status mediates whatever sets of relations may be involved in these contexts.

right side	medial position	left side
front	center	behind
below	above	below
medial rank	highest rank	lowest rank
superior	intermediary	inferior
senior *agbaa* male	priest	junior *agbaa* male
small *kpele* drum	big *kpele* drum	smallest *kpele* drum
senior subchief	chief	junior subchief
patrikin	infant	matrikin

The notion of medial status or position implies a notion of things mediated, or minimally two elements which are brought into connection through a third element. I suggest that this dialectical notion underlies the triple motif which is the hallmark of Ga ritual action in general and *kpele* ritual in particular. Many examples of this triple motif in *kpele* ritual can be enumerated: libation is poured on the ground three times; celebrants sip a ritual drink three times; nonpossession dances are performed thrice; each god is worshipped on three days of every seven-day week; the incense carrier fumigates the gateway to a sacred field three times before entering; inside the field the priest fumigates the field three times before beginning to pray; sacrificial animals are raised and lowered three times before they are slaughtered; three ringlets of *nyanyara* leaves and three sponges are put into all bowls of ritual bath water; three ritual drums are used in *kpele* dances.

Ga exegetical statements concerning this pervasive ritual motif are not particularly enlightening. Informants have said: (1) that when a person goes to a house, he first knocks, then he is asked to enter, and finally he states his case; (2) that there are three senior gods in Accra, and one asks blessing from these three by performing a ritual act thrice; (3) that gods will be sure to hear or to see the third time that they are supplicated.

I suggest that two ideas underlie the triple motif in Ga ritual action. The first is that power is augmented through a repetition of similar units, whether these units be symbolic actions or symbolic objects.[3] I further suggest that there are three units and not some other number, because three is the smallest number within which the notion of mediation can be contained. This notion of mediation is central to Ga cosmological conceptions of a hierarchy of beings and to the aims which men attempt to achieve by interconnection between classes within this hierarchy through the performance of ritual. Although this is a deductive explanation of the

3. Cf. E. R. Leach, "Lévi-Strauss in the Garden of Eden," *Transactions of the New York Academy of Sciences* 23:386-396.

triple motif in *kpele* ritual which is not verbalized by even the most thoughtful of *kpele* authorities, it is consistent with the ideas which they articulate and those which they enact in ritual.

Ultimately, the notion of mediation is central to the notion of *kpele* ritual performance. Ritual is the means by which men attempt to mediate relations between divine and mortal beings and to achieve certain benefits from this interconnection. Only certain human beings may perform this mediating role. Because divine beings are superordinate to human beings, the people who mediate between gods and men must be superior to other men. Gods themselves, however, have a taxonomically medial status, for they are intermediate between the supreme being and mortal men, and have a medial role as the channels through which messages between the supreme being and men must pass. *Kpele* ritual, therefore, revolves around the notion of mediation as it pertains to different sets of structural relations within the *kpele* world.[4]

4. My analysis suggests that metaphors of status differentiation are expressed most frequently in patterns of color, spatial orientations, and temporal sequences in *kpele* ritual. While this is likely to be true of all ritual, the values attached to positions in space or sequences of acts in time depend on a particular culture. For a discussion of some rather different values attached to similar spatial and temporal orientations, see Renato I. Rosaldo, Jr., "Metaphors of Hierarchy in a Mayan Ritual," *American Anthropologist* 70:524-536.

6 / The *Kpele* Community

The *kpele* religious system incorporates not only a system of belief and practice, but a community of believers. Within the contemporary Ga population, two sets of factors influence membership in the *kpele* community of believers. Traditional ideology restricts membership to certain categories of Ga. Theoretically, membership in the *kpele* community of believers depends upon membership in true Ga families. This potential community of believers has been reduced by the loss of eligible members to Christianity. The loss of *kpele* adherents to Christianity, however, is less than demographic statistics suggest, for most Christian Ga also participate at some level in traditional religious systems.

Although Ga ideology restricts membership in the *kpele* community to true Ga families, family membership is not limited to mortal life. A family comprises both living and dead members. Ga consider, therefore, that the *kpele* community comprises living and dead true Ga (*Ganyo krong*).

Ga believe that ancestral shades are involved and concerned with the affairs of living men. Ancestral shades play a dual role, for they act as guardians of the interests of living kinsmen and as custodians of Ga culture. As guardians of living kinsmen, ancestral shades may be called upon to intercede with the gods or to act in their own capacity to achieve goals which living men desire. The dead are believed to participate with their living kinsmen in religious and life-crisis rites. On these ritual occasions, the souls of the dead are invoked and propitiated with sacrificial acts of libation or bloody sacrifice. Moreover, annually ancestral shades are celebrated in the *homowo* rite in which living members of family units (*we*) gather to commemorate their dead and to share a festal meal of *kpekpei* with these ancestral shades.

Although Ga believe that interaction with the dead can be beneficial to the living, they regard the relationship between living and dead with ambivalence. Both categories of men are thought to be able to initiate interaction. When living men initiate and control interconnection with the dead, it is welcomed and desired. When, however, ancestral shades initiate interaction with the living to achieve their own goals, the living attempt to achieve separation from the dead as rapidly as possible. Ancestral shades may manifest themselves to the living either at night in dreams or as human apparitions or by possessing the body of a living person. On such occasions, they make known their desires to the living, who attempt to fulfill these wishes and thereby to turn the dead away from the living. Ga informants have said that a person does not fear the appearance of a dead kinsman, but that the sight of a dead nonkinsman is dreadful, for it implies that the shade is an agent of another person's malevolence. Ancestral shades, therefore, are feared in proportion to the control which the living are thought to exercise over them. Nonkinsmen over whom a person has least control are most feared; dead kinsmen who are invoked for limited purposes are least feared.

Ancestral shades not only act as guardians of the welfare of their living kin but serve as custodians of Ga culture of which distant ancestors were founders. This latter aspect of the role of ancestral shades is particularly relevant to *kpele* religion. To its adherents, this religious system is the embodiment of Ga tradition and achieves its authority through the enactment of custom established in the distant past. The role of the ancestral shades as founders of Ga culture in general and *kpele* religion in particular is expressed in *kpele* prayers and songs. The opening of every *kpele* prayer includes the phrase: "What is today? Today is this weekday, grandfathers' day, grandmothers' day" (*Ngmene ashi me? Ngmene ashi hogba* [Friday], *niimẹi ahọgba, naamẹi ahọgba*). This phrase recalls the naming of the days of the week by the ancestral shades during their mortal lives. Among the songs which concern the precedent for *kpele* ritual in ancestral times and the related notion of cultural continuity which is embodied in the performance of *kpele* rites (e.g., songs 126, 148-151, 154-157), none is more explicit than the following song (song 149):

> Ataamẹi shi ha wọ;   Fathers left it to us;
> Tsẹmẹi shi ha wọ.   Fathers left it to us.

The singer interpreted this song as referring directly to the annual performance of agricultural rites and indirectly to all other customary cultural practices. For *kpele* believers, the time of the founding ancestors represents a golden age of which the present constitutes an imperfect reflection. This notion of adverse cultural change is conveyed in song 150:

> Dzeng bọ ade wọyẹ mli;   The created world we are in;
> Tsutsu blema bẹ nẹkẹ.   Former times were not like
> these.

The authority for contemporary *kpele* rites, therefore, is the precedent of the ancestral shades in the distant past.

While the verification of such a belief is neither possible nor sociologically relevant, a number of *kpele* songs refer to ancient "historical" events and personages (e.g., songs 108, 152, 153, 177-185). Recent archaeological and historical research in Ghana permits the dating of some of these events in Ga traditional history and some insight, therefore, into the chronological span of *kpele* time. It is known from early historic records that the seat of Ga authority in the early seventeenth century was the inland town of Great Accra at Ayawaso from which the Ga controlled the lucrative gold trade between the hinterland and the coast. This town was destroyed in 1677 by the expanding Akwamu state which incorporated the Ga coastal territory three years later and maintained suzerainty over the area of the former Ga state for the next fifty years.[1]

1. Ivor Wilks, "The Rise of the Akwamu Empire, 1650-1710," *Transactions of the Historical Society of Ghana* 3:106-111.

Many of the references to personalities and events in this collection of *kpele* songs pertain to the turbulent seventeenth-century period. According to Ga tradition, the first chief at Great Accra was Ayi Kushi (song 108), whose death probably occurred in 1614.[2] His grandson, Chief Mampong Okai, who was murdered in 1642 or 1643, was the husband of the tyrannical regent Dǫde Akabi whose death is the subject of two songs (songs 178, 179).[3] Their son, Chief Okai Koi, was killed during the sack of Great Accra in 1677 by the Akwamu (song 180) whose capital had been established nearby at Nyanao (song 177) before the turn of the seventeenth century.[4] After the destruction of Great Accra (song 151), Okai Koi's son Ofori escaped to coastal Accra (song 133) where he ruled until 1681, when he fled from the invading Akwamu to Little Popo (song 184).[5] Some additional *kpele* songs refer to persons who are believed to have lived before the sack of Great Accra, such as Ayi Anafo, the "first" *kpele* drummer at Great Accra (songs 115-119), and Lakote Adu Awushi, the founder of *Nai we* at coastal Accra (songs 181, 182); other songs refer to later historical personages who include Boi Tono (song 108) of *Nai we* to whom the Dutch trading company gave an engraved staff in 1734, which is still part of the ritual paraphernalia of the *Nai* cult, and the prophet Lomoko, who died in 1866 (songs 120, 185). The internal evidence of the songs, considered in conjunction with archaeological and historical data, therefore, suggests that *kpele* time begins in the late sixteenth century.

In presenting the hypothesis that *kpele* time begins in the late sixteenth century, I do not intend to imply that the *kpele* religious system has persisted without modification through four centuries. I merely wish to indicate the probable chronological limits of the age of the founding ancestors. The

2. Paul Ozanne, "Notes on the Early Historic Archaeology of Accra," *Transactions of the Historical Society of Ghana* 6:69.
3. Ivor Wilks, "Some Glimpses into the Early History of Accra," p. 4.
4. Wilks, "Rise of Akwamu Empire," p. 106; Ozanne, "Early Historic Archaeology of Accra," p. 69.
5. Wilks, "Rise of Akwamu Empire," p. 111.

discrepancy between chronology and structural time and the sociological significance of this discrepancy have been appreciated for some time.[6] For contemporary *kpele* adherents, the chronology of traditional events is not as important as their belief that in performing *kpele* ritual, living men enact their forefathers' ancient rites and that the prosperity of both the *kpele* community and the entire Ga community depends upon the performance of calendrical rites.

While the *kpele* community of believers theoretically comprises all living and dead true Ga, the transfer of adherents from the traditional cult to Christian sects during the past two hundred years has diminished the size of the community. The extent to which the potential community of believers has been reduced in this way cannot be assessed definitively, for evidence suggests that many Ga participate in both traditional and Christian religious communities. Despite these problems in evaluating the numerical strength of the *kpele* community, the general sociological parameters of the traditional religious community can be defined.

This discussion of the boundaries of the contemporary *kpele* community of believers is based primarily upon data from Central Accra. Central Accra incorporates the old Ga coastal settlement around the forts and its northern extensions. Before the development of a retail center north of the railway depot after World War II and the opening of the port at Tema in 1959, Central Accra was the center of commercial life in Accra. Today Central Accra is primarily an African residential and trading center.

Central Accra has been the site of a growing Ga community for more than three hundred years. In 1960, Ga constituted 58% (36,239) of the total population of Central Accra and almost all of these Ga (91%) had been born there. Within this unusually stable urban population, there is considerable difference between the educational and occupational profiles of

6. E.g., E. E. Evans-Pritchard, *The Nuer*, chapter 3; Ian Cunnison, "History and Genealogies in a Conquest State," *American Anthropologist* 59:20-31.

men and women (see Table 2). Whereas the majority of men
have had at least a middle school education, only a fifth of
the women have enjoyed corresponding educational opportunities. Slightly more than a quarter of the male population is
engaged in some white collar occupation; a fifth pursue the
traditional coastal occupation of fisherman; and the remainder are engaged in some manual occupation. By contrast, the
overwhelming proportion of Ga women are engaged in trading (83%) and only 6% in white collar occupations.[7] Essentially, therefore, the Ga population of Central Accra constitutes a stable community of manual laborers, traders, and
marginal elites.

Within Central Accra are located not only many shrines of
traditional cults but a large number of Christian churches
which include the imposing edifices of established sects and
rooms which have been transformed from residences into
meeting places for indigenous "spiritual" churches. The Ga
who reside in Central Accra, therefore, have access to a variety of religious institutions.

The numerical limits of the traditional religious community,
which includes not only *kpele* adherents but members of
other indigenous cults, can be approximated from a consideration of certain statistical data. According to the 1960 Ghana
census, 69% of Ghana Ga classified themselves as Christian; a
survey of a limited sample of Central Accra Ga in 1965
showed that 80% considered themselves Christian.[8] The lower
limit of the traditional religious community in Central Accra,
therefore, may be placed at 20% of the Ga population. Nevertheless, the 1965 survey showed both that 68% of the Ga respondents knew the name of their family deity, and that
95% of the respondents had participated in the traditional
homowo rite during the preceding year.[9] On the basis of these

7. These figures are from M. D. de B. Kilson, "Ga and Non-Ga Populations of Central Accra," *Ghana Journal of Sociology* 2:18-25.
8. M. D. de B. Kilson, "Variations in Ga Culture in Central Accra,"
Ghana Journal of Sociology 3:33-54.
9. The correlation between Christianity and ignorance of the identity
of family god was statistically insignificant: $X^2 2.74$, p. 0.10.

data, the upper limit on membership in the traditional religious community may be placed at 95%. The tremendous range (20%-95%) encompassed by these limits makes a numerical assessment of the traditional religious community futile. Rather, these data suggest not only that Central Accra Ga participate in different religious systems for variant purposes but that they do not perceive participation in variant religious systems to be intrinsically contradictory.

If systematic statistical data were available, they probably would demonstrate that a relatively small proportion—no more than one-third—of the Central Accra Ga population participate exclusively in either a traditional cult or an established Christian sect and that the majority of Ga participate in both systems to achieve variant goals. Participation in the Christian religion may be utilized primarily to symbolize status within the modern industrial stratification system. For example, although within contemporary Ga society a betrothal ceremony legalizes marriage, persons who aspire to elite status as well as those of established elite status have church weddings. By contrast, recourse to traditional religious institutions is likely to occur in times of personal and community crisis. Such crises include illness, infertility, theft accusations, employment problems, unseasonal floods or droughts. When these crises occur, individuals appeal to ritual specialists to intercede with traditional deities on their behalf. Observational and interview data suggest that the relative importance of traditional or Christian religious participation is correlated with socioeconomic factors, in such a way that higher levels of Western educational and occupational status are associated with Christianity and, conversely, lower ranking educational and occupational categories are associated with traditional religion.

Nevertheless, whatever the quantifiable strength of traditional religious adherence among the Ga population in Central Accra, the cults persist as viable institutions. Periodic rites are performed, ritual offices are filled when vacancies occur, shrines are maintained, communal ritual prescriptions are respected. When a ritual procession approaches, people flee from its path into their houses and motor traffic stops to permit the unhindered passage of the *agbaa* and the unseen gods who are believed to accompany them. Similarly, during the three weeks which intervene between the rites of planting and transplanting, cafe owners who play their victrolas or radios are summoned before a court of *kpele* priests and enjoined to observe the communal ban on noise. Thus, believers and nonbelievers alike are required to respect the tenets of *kpele* worship.

I turn now to a consideration of factors that facilitate the continuity of traditional cults in Central Accra. Two interrelated social facts are significant in this regard: the stability of the Ga population and the socioeconomic structure of the community. The temporal continuity of the Central Accra Ga population has permitted the persistence of a personalistic community in which many social relations are defined by ascriptive kinship criteria and controlled by informal sanctions. Moreover, the members of the community are predominantly lower class, for relatively few men and fewer women have the requisite educational skills to participate effectively in the industrialized sector of Ghanaian society except in unskilled or semiskilled occupational categories. Individuals who acquire such skills and achieve elite occupations and status usually leave the community. The population which remains, therefore, is a residual community of traders, laborers, and marginal elites. For occupants of marginal elite categories within the industrial stratification system, high status within the traditional religious and political system competes effectively with medial social status in the modern sector. Two of the three senior *kpele* priests and at least four of the eight chiefs in Accra relinquished positions as clerks or teachers to assume their current positions in the traditional status hierarchy. Trading is the usual occupation of illiterate and semiliterate women for whom the achievement of the status of medium in a traditional cult is more prestigious and often more lucrative than trading. The socioeconomic structure of the Ga population, therefore, facilitates the persistence of traditional cults that compete effectively as a prestige system within the contemporary Ga community in Central Accra. Demographic stability and socioeconomic immobility, therefore, interact to produce a social milieu in which traditional cults may persist, "spiritual" churches may flourish, and established sects may be maintained.

The relevance of these conclusions to the total Ga population may be inferred from the socioeconomic characteristics of communities in which Ga reside. These communities fall into three main categories: (1) racially and ethnically integrated communities of professional and administrative elites. (2) predominantly Ga communities of marginal elites, and semiskilled and unskilled laborers, and (3) Ga communities of laborers, fishermen, and farmers. The first category is represented by some residential neighborhoods on the periphery of Accra, the second by Central Accra, Osu, and Labadi, and the third by Nungua, Teshi, old Tema, and villages on the Accra Plains. While the first category includes only a very small proportion of the Ga population, the second and third categories are roughly equivalent numerically. The Central Accra data suggest a correlation between religious participation and socioeconomic criteria, and religious participation in the three types of communities probably ranges from very little participation in traditional cults to exclusive participation in traditional cults. Thus, while the theoretical *kpele* community of living members is undoubtedly greater than the actual community of participants, the great majority of eligible members are involved with traditional cults at some level of belief and practice.

Part II / *Kpele* Song Texts

Introductory Note

The ordering of this collection of *kpele* songs is based upon the *kpele* taxonomy of beings. The four basic differentiations of the supreme being, divine beings, human beings, and animals have been elaborated into nine topical categories: (1) the supreme being, (2) cosmogony, (3) cosmos, (4) divine beings, (5) ritual performance, (6) human society, (7) Ga polity, (8) Ga culture, and (9) animals. The songs presented in the following pages are grouped under these nine topical categories. Each topical category is introduced by a brief statement that indicates thematic subgroups of songs.

For each song, *kpele* and English texts are presented. Although these texts represent the basic pattern of recorded song lines, they rarely reproduce the full recorded text (see Chapter 3). When multiple versions of a song contain significant conceptual differences, two texts are provided for the song. The texts of each song are supplemented by notes that identify the singer and the occasion for recording the text and provide indigenous exegeses and ethnographic commentary whenever possible or relevant. The exegeses are either translations or paraphrases of singers' comments.

The ethnographic commentary for each song text includes limited information about the lexical provenience of the *kpele* text insofar as it indicates whether or not the words are Ga. The provenience of the non-Ga words is not designated, because my information about such words is not reliable. Nevertheless, probably most of the non-Ga lexemes are Twi.

Singers who are Twi-speakers readily provided Ga translations of non-Ga phrases and words; whereas, informants who did not speak some Twi language frequently both distorted *kpele* texts and could not provide Ga translations of *kpele* texts. Moreover, the Ga intonation given to non-Ga words in *kpele* texts (see Chapter 3) made it difficult for Ghanaian informants whose natal language is Twi to identify non-Ga lexemes. Consequently, I have identified only Ga words within the *kpele* texts.

The collection of 243 songs is based on 300 recorded texts. Slightly more than a fifth of these texts were recorded under natural conditions: during the discussion of other issues (25), at the Ga paramount chief's residence (20), during rites (15), and during conversations between ritual specialists (6). The great majority (243) of the texts, however, were collected from eight singers at sessions organized specifically for the recording of *kpele* songs. With two exceptions, each singer participated in at least two recording sessions.

Nevertheless, as will be apparent from a brief glance at the following pages, a very large proportion of the songs were sung by the *Olila* medium (*Olila wɔngtsɛ*). Her disproportionate contribution reflects her incomparable knowledge of *kpele* song and my more intimate association with her than with any of the other singers. She recorded nearly one hundred songs for me in 1965. Although we did not organize any formal recording sessions in 1968, I had numerous opportunities to record her songs. Sometimes she sang songs to answer a question or to develop a point which she wished to make. For example, she sang songs 13 and 14 in response to a query about the creation of the world. I accompanied her to a number of ritual events which often provided an opportunity for recording songs either at the time or during subsequent discussion of the event. Once when we went to a remote Ga village where she was to perform a rite, an old woman hobbled over to greet her and began to sing song 180, to which the *Olila* medium responded with song 183. I also relied upon the *Olila* medium to clarify textual problems in the songs of other singers and this frequently led her to sing another song with a related theme. Thus, after reviewing another singer's version of song 85, she proceeded to sing songs 86 and 87, which also concern the relationship between *Naa Kǫǫle* and her co-wife *Ogbede*. The results of such formal and informal procedures explain the contribution of the *Olila* medium to this collection of *kpele* songs.

The other singers who have contributed to this collection of *kpele* songs are identified as *Abudu wulǫmǫ, Ashiaklẹ wulǫmǫ, Ashadu wǫngtsẹ, Akumadze Afieye wǫngtsẹ, Kle agbaayoo, Kǫǫle agbaayoo,* and *Olila agbaanuu* (see Table 11). Apart from the *Abudu wulǫmǫ,* whom I visited in the village of Oblogo in 1965 and who died in 1968 before my second visit to Accra, these singers recorded songs for me in 1968 either at their residences or at Mr. E. A. Ammah's house in Mataheko, a suburb of Accra. All seven singers live either in Central Accra or its adjacent suburbs, except for *Abudu wulǫmǫ.* Although none of the singers is under thirty years of age, there is considerable variation in their ages, which may be classified into a younger (30-45 years) category and an older (55-65 years) category. The younger category includes *Ashiaklẹ wulǫmǫ, Akumadze Afieye wǫngtsẹ,* and *Olila agbaanuu;* the older category includes *Abudu wulǫmǫ, Ashadu wǫngtsẹ, Kǫǫle agbaayoo,* and *Kle agbaayoo.* While *Ashadu wǫngtsẹ* and *Akumadze Afieye wǫngtsẹ* learned *kpele* songs during their vocational training, the other singers developed their interest in *kpele* songs from a relative who was an expert singer. Thus, *Ashiaklẹ wulǫmǫ's* father had been *Nai olai, Kǫǫle agbaayoo's* mother had been the *Koole wǫngtsẹ, Kle agbaayoo's* sister's daughter is the present *Kle wǫngtsẹ,* and *Olila agbaanuu* is a cognate of the *Olila wǫngtsẹ.*

Although each of the eight individuals from whom I collected texts during recording sessions clearly enjoyed singing *kpele* songs, they varied greatly in their proficiency as singers, in the scope of their repertoires, and in their understanding of the content of the songs. Although the *Olila* medium has an unparalleled knowledge and exegetical understanding of *kpele* songs, the quality of her voice is not as rich as it probably was

Table 11. *Kpele* Singers and Locations of Recording Sessions

Singer	Ritual Status	Age	Residence	Location of Recording Session
Abudu wulọmọ	priest	ca. 64	Oblogo	his residence
Akumadze Afieye wọngtsẹ	medium	ca. 30	Central Accra	her residence
Ashadu wọngtsẹ	medium	ca. 63	Central Accra	her residence
Ashiaklẹ wulọmọ	priest	ca. 40	Chorkor	E. A. Ammah's residence
Kle agbaayoo	female member of *agbaa*	ca. 55	Mataheko	E. A. Ammah's residence
Kọọle agbaayoo	female member of *agbaa*	ca. 55	Kaneshi	her residence
Olila agbaanuu	male member of *agbaa*	ca. 40	Central Accra	E. A. Ammah's residence
Olila wọngtsẹ	medium	ca. 60	Ofankor and Central Accra	her husband's residence at Bubuashi and *Ga mangtsẹ*'s residence

in her youth. The best performer among my informants was the *Ashiaklẹ* priest, who has a rich full voice. While his repertoire is not as extensive nor his exegetical understanding as profound as the *Olila* medium's, his abilities exceed those of my other informants with the possible exceptions of the *Akumadze Afieye* medium and *Olila agbaanuu*. The remaining informants (*Abudu wulọmọ*, *Kle agbaayoo*, *Kọọle agbaayoo*, and *Ashadu wọngtsẹ*) showed enthusiasm for singing *kpele* songs but were indifferent singers and had very little understanding of the meaning of the song texts which they sang either at the level of Ga translation or at the level of exegetical interpretation. Their attitude toward the songs is summarized by *Kle agbaayoo*'s proverbial response to exegetical inquiry: "that is the way *kpele* people sing" (*kpele-tsẹmẹi la*).

Finally, I wish to mention the methodology utilized in collecting song texts. Each text was recorded on tape. The situation in which a text was recorded determined in part the form of preliminary transcription and translation. If a song text was recorded under "natural conditions," I transcribed the *kpele* text and translated the text into English with the assistance of E. A. Ammah. If Mr. Ammah and I were uncertain about lexical elements, we consulted the *Olila* medium. If the recording of a text was made during a song session, a more elaborate preliminary transcription and translation procedure was followed. After the singer had sung a song, he was asked to repeat the words of the *kpele* text and to provide a Ga translation of ambiguous words. As the singer repeated the text, I made both a preliminary transcription and a rough English translation of the *kpele* text with the assistance of either E. A. Ammah or Henry A. Adjei. After the form of the text was established, the singer was asked to elaborate on its meaning. This procedure proved difficult and tedious for some informants, especially *Kọọle agbaayoo* and *Ashadu wọngtsẹ*. The interview session (i.e., texts and exegeses of a song session) was transcribed from tape and translated into English by a Ga research assistant, Gladys Adjei. The transcribed *kpele* song text and its English translation then were reviewed by E. A. Ammah. If further doubts concerning *kpele* transcription or English translation of a text remained, Mr. Ammah and I consulted the *Olila* medium. Since we failed to consult her about all the collected texts, approximately forty additional texts which contain lexical ambiguities have been deleted from the corpus of songs presented in this book.

The Supreme Being

This group of songs relates to *Ataa Naa Nyɔngmɔ*, the personified creative life force in the *kpele* universe, whom I term God in the English texts. In Chapters 4 and 5, I discussed various Ga beliefs concerning the nature of the supreme being and the relations between this being and human beings. A number of these beliefs are expressed in this group of songs. The first two songs emphasize God's infinite and creative nature; others stress his role as the ultimate source of human prosperity (songs 3-7); others concern various creative acts of the supreme being (songs 8-11); and the final song relates to the supreme being's control of cosmic processes.

[1]   Nyɔngmɔ Adu Akwa,
      Lɛ dzi okua agbo lɛ.
      Lɛ ebɔ dzeng
      Ni eha anyiɛɔ mli ahi.

      God,
      He is the great farmer.
      He created the world
      And he gave it to them to live in.

Singer: Olila wɔngtsɛ
Occasion: Discussion of *kpele* ritual, 1968.
Exegesis: Then God is the big farmer; God is the senior farmer. God created the world and God gave it to human beings to live in.

114

Commentary: This song expresses the Ga belief that the supreme being created the physical world so that human beings might live in it. The image of the supreme being as a farmer connotes the nurturant aspect of the supreme being's nature and exemplifies the utilization of personal models in *kpele* thought.

The words of the *kpele* text are Ga, with the exception of *adu, akwa,* and *okua.*

[2] Wọyaahu Nyọngmọ ngmọ,
   Dzenamọ hu wọyẹ mli.

   Wọyaahu Nyọngmọ ngmọ,
   Ataa Naa Nyọngmọ ngmọ ahuu kẹ gbeenaa.

   We will go to cultivate God's field,
   The whole night we are in it.

   We will go to cultivate God's field,
   One does not finish the cultivation of God's field.

Singer: Olila wọngtsẹ.
Occasion: Singing for the *Ga mangtsẹ,* 1965.
Exegesis: This is God's world; no human being can encompass the world, for God's field is boundless.
Commentary: This song, which conveys the notion of the infinite nature of the supreme being in contrast to the finite nature of human beings, is based on an agricultural metaphor. Farming and fishing constitute the two traditional subsistence activities of men in Ga culture. In this song the conception of the supreme being as a farmer is expressed again. The utilization of anthropomorphic imagery, which assimilates the experience of nonhuman beings to human categories through analogic processes, creates the preconditions for interaction between different classes of being (see Chapter 4).

The words of the *kpele* text are Ga.

[3] Nyampong dzi onukpa,
Okrẹmaduamọ lẹ ekwraa wọ,
Ni ekwraa wọ.

Nyọngmọ dzi onukpa,
Okrẹmaduamọ lẹ ekwraa wọ,
Ni ekwraa wọ.

God is senior,
God looks after us,
And he looks after us.

God is senior,
God looks after us,
And he looks after us.

Singer: Olila wọngtsẹ.
Occasion: Recording *kpele* songs, 1965.
Exegesis: The *Olila* medium said that *Okrẹmaduamọ* is a *kpele* word for God, but E. A. Ammah said that it meant the earth, the earth is energy.

Although three additional versions of the song vary only with respect to expression and not concepts, the exegetical comments for these versions are noteworthy. (1) Alternate version 1: *Olila agbaanuu,* 1968. The stream from which we drink is a god's river. When the god descends on someone, she [the medium] will first call God who looks after all of us. And so if any spirit [*susuma*] descends on a person, God knows about it before it occurs. (2) Alternate version 2: *Kle agbaayoo,* 1968. The meaning is like someone ruling the town, he looks after the people. (3) Alternate version 3: *Olila wọngtsẹ,* 1968. Lo, we are calling God, we are calling the earth. A medium will stand to call them; when they are called, the song becomes beautiful.
Commentary: The notion of the supreme being as an omniscient guardian of human welfare is conveyed in this song and its exegeses.

The words of the *kpele* text are Ga, with the exception of *Nyampong* and *Okrẹmaduamọ.*

[4]   Awo, Awo, Awo;
      Awo;
      Awo, agbai breku tsǫǫ.
      Awo;
      Awo, agbai breku tsǫǫ.
      Awo;
      Awo, nu.
      Awo;
      Awo, nu.
      Nsu, nsu;
      Nsu, nsu;
      Nsu, nsu.
      Ngmaa, ngmaa;
      Omanye, manyo-a;
      Adiba kpǫtǫ.

      God, God, God;
      God;
      God, the congregation calls for abundant rain.
      God;
      God, the congregation calls for abundant rain.
      God;
      God, water.
      God;
      God, water.
      Water, water;
      Water, water;
      Water, water.
      Millet, millet;
      Peace, peace;
      Abundant food.

Singer: Olila wǫngtsẹ.
Occasion: Recording songs, 1965.
Commentary: This song, which is sung by *agbaa* members at every *kpele* rite, is the only song performed by all *kpele* cult groups. During agricultural rites it is sung in the courtyard of the god's shrine, in procession, and at the sacred field. The

text expresses the aims men seek to achieve through the performance of ritual: contact with the supreme being, who will cause rain to fall, which will germinate the seed so that men may reap an abundant harvest and be at peace with one another. The text also conveys the related beliefs that God controls cosmic processes and that mortal existence depends upon the will of the supreme being.

The words of the *kpele* text are Ga with the exception of *nsu, breku, adiba, kpoto.*

[5]   Ope tere omanye;
      Manye shra;
      Manye ba.

      God carries peace;
      Peace encircles us;
      Peace comes.

Singers: Nai agbaa; Sakumo agbaa.
Occasion: Procession *Nai ngmaafaa*, 1968; recession *Sakumo ngmaafaa*, 1965.
Commentary: In commenting on this song, E. A. Ammah writes, "Besides God being the source of life and light, He is also the very embodiment of peace" (Ammah, "Ghanaian Philosophy," January 1962, p. 18).

Nai wulomo, who acknowledged that he did not know the meaning of the song, provided another text that exemplified versional variation arising from multilingual confusion.

The Ga words in the *kpele* text are *manye* and *ba.*

[6]   Sha Awo miba;
      Sha Awo, Awo,
      Awo, Awo miba.

      In stately procession God is coming;
      In stately procession God, God,
      God, God is coming.

Singer: *Ashiaklẹ wulọmọ.*
Occasion: Recording songs, 1968.
Exegesis: It means may someone have a blessing.
Commentary: This song and the preceding one exemplify a slightly different utilization of anthropomorphic imagery to characterize the actions of the supreme being. In this song, the movements of the supreme being are analogous to those of a chief in procession who moves slowly with regal bearing.

Another shorter version was recorded by *Kle agbaayoo* in 1968.

The words of the *kpele* text are Ga, with the exception of *sha.*

[7]   Atẹ Nyampong baana;
      Klewi baana.

      Father God will see;
      Klewi will see.

Singer: Kle agbaayoo.
Occasion: Recording songs, 1968.
Commentary: The singer could not offer an interpretation of the song, although the words of the *kpele* text are Ga, with the exception of *Nyampong.*

I have been unable to identify *klewi* except as a species of bird, but E. A. Ammah's commentary on another song is pertinent.

> *Klewi* (a bird of the swallow family), an angel or sage, promised to unfold the mystery or the Being and the beginning of God. He entered space *en route* to God's 'dwelling place', he flew so many, many millions of miles into space, the further he flew, so an unaccountable distance receded. . . . So *Klewi*, the Angel/Sage returned to earth, without finding or reaching the abode of God. The outcome of the intrepid, but fruitful adventure [in] to space is the following hymn: *God great God,/God most great,/Klewi goes to call God and come* [Ammah, "Ghanaian Philosophy," February 1962, p. 8].

Ammah's comments suggest either that *klewi*, the bird, may act as a messenger for the supreme being who informs him of events occurring in human society, or that whatever birds observe is also observed by the supreme being. Although Ga consider that birds may be simply a category within the animal class, they also believe that gods, who mediate between the supreme being and human beings, may descend and take form in animal species. A possible interpretation for this song, therefore, is that a god who manifests himself through *klewi* will observe human activities and relate his observations to the supreme being.

[8]   Opete Kpaakpo,
      Mi ngto le̩.

      God's lake,
      I myself made it.

Singer: Possessed medium.
Occasion: Nai ngmaafaa, 1968.
Commentary: This song conveys the notion of the supreme being as the creator of the physical world in general and of particular topographical features. Opete Kpaakpo (lit., "God's lake") is the marshy area to the west of Ko̩o̩le Lagoon; it and the Od̩o̩ River feed the lagoon. In this song, the supreme being states that he created the marsh.

The wording of the text also exemplifies the utilization of anthropomorphism in *kpele* thought.

The words of the *kpele* text are Ga, with the exception of *Opete.*

[9]   Okposansa—
      Nyame ni bo̩o̩ mi;
      Minim pong,
      Mitsi pong.

      Nyame bo̩o̩ mi sa.

Mi hiẹ kpọ,
Mi sẹẹ kpọ;
Nyame ni bọọ mi.

Spadefish—[1]
God created me;
My face is swollen,
My back is swollen.

God created me so.

My face is swollen,
My back is swollen;
God created me.

1. *Okposansa,* spadefish (*Drepano punctata*).

Singer: Olila wọngtsẹ.
Occasion: Checking *kpele* songs, 1968.
Commentary: Two shorter versions with non-Ga words were
recorded in 1968 by *Ashiaklẹ wulọmọ* and *Kle agbaayoo.* Although the priest was unable to translate the non-Ga words
into Ga, he knew the general sense of the song.

The basic notion conveyed by this song is that the supreme
being determines the physical attributes of creatures. The
spadefish cannot change his ugly bulbous appearance, for God
gave him this form.

The words of the *kpele* text are Ga, with the exception of
Nyame, minim, mitsi, and *pong.*

[10]   Akọkọ nu nsu fatrẹ Nyame;
        Nyampong dzi onukpa.

        When a fowl drinks water, it shows it to God;
        God is senior.

Singer: Olila wọngtsẹ.
Occasion: Recording songs, 1965.

Exegesis: Every time a fowl drinks water, she lifts her head, which means that she thanks God.

Commentary: Kle agbaayoo sang an identical version of this song in 1968.

This song exemplifies another form of anthropomorphism, whereby an instinctive reaction of an animal species is interpreted in human terms. When fowls drink, they lift their heads to swallow; this movement is interpreted as an acknowledgment of the life-sustaining role of the supreme being.

The Ga words in the *kpele* text are *nu, dzi,* and *onukpa.*

[11]   Tifiamlẹ:
         Midi mi kọkọ fri ase,
         Midi fri Nyame.

         Tifiamle:
         I did not get my red color from the earth,
         I got my color from God.[1]

1. Lit., I did not get red from the earth, I got it from God.

Singer: Olila wọngtsẹ.
Occasion: Recording songs, 1965.
Exegesis: Tifiamlẹ, a plant with red leaves, is singing that it got its red color from the sky and not from the earth. If a plant grows with red leaves, it is its nature, which cannot be changed. One cannot change one's nature, which comes from God.

Commentary: I have been unable to identify *tifiamlẹ* further.

The text and the *Olila* medium's exegesis convey the same conception concerning the supreme being as the determiner of physical attributes as expressed in song 9.

The words of the *kpele* text are non-Ga.

[12]   Awi, lo,
         Sanaa ma Awi, lo;
         Pompompọ.

Awi sanaa ma, Ankrama;
Pompompǫ.

Awi hi ni,
Sanaa ma Awi, lo;
Pompompǫ.

Sun, lo,
Obstruct the heat of the sun;
May abundant rain fall.

God, obstruct the heat of the sun;
May abundant rain fall.

Sun do not shine too strongly,
Obstruct the heat of the sun;
May abundant rain fall.

Singer: Olila wǫngtse.
Occasion: Recording songs, 1965.
Exegesis: Dantu agbaa invoke God to bless the millet seed
which is sown at *ngmaadumǫ.*
Commentary: After the millet seed has been sown in the sacred field, *Dantu agbaa* sing this song as they go from house
to house in Central Accra to announce the imposition of the
ban on noise (see Chapter 5). In order for the seed to grow,
there must be sufficient rain and sunshine. The supreme being regulates the falling of rain and the shining of the sun; the
basic theme of the song, therefore, is the supreme being's control over cosmic processes.

See songs 15 and 83 for notes on *Awi* and *Dantu,* respectively.

The words of the *kpele* text are non-Ga.

Cosmogony

The three songs in this group (songs 13-15) concern *kpele* cosmogonic notions. While the texts emphasize human ignorance concerning the origins of the physical universe, divine beings, and social institutions, the enumeration of the lacunae in human knowledge actually recapitulates basic cosmogonic concepts and cosmological categories of *kpele* thought.

[13]   Obi nni Nyampong ase,
         Obi nni tente wǫakong,
         Obi nni dada wǫ aye,
         Obi nni me wǫ aye,
         Obi nni Nyampong ase daa.

         No one knows God's origin,
         No one knows the origin of *kpele*, our sacred dance,
         No one knows the ancient origin of what we do,
         No one knows the origin of *me* that we do,
         No one knows God's origin ever.

Singer: Olila wǫngtsę.
Occasion: Discussion of *kpele* cosmogony, 1968.
Exegesis: How was the world created? Because the world was created before human beings were created, no one knows God's origin.
Commentary: The song mentions three of the four tradition-

124

al cults which Ga practice. *Tente* is another term for *kpele*, particularly for *kpele* dance and music. *Akǫng* is an Akan cult which Ga practice; sometimes the term is used as a synonym for ritual dance, as it is in the second line of the *kpele* text. *Me* is an Adangme cult which Ga describe as a "sibling" (*nyẹmi*) of *kpele*. Moreover, Nketia's comparative analysis of *me* and *kpele* music shows the distinctive stylistic affinities between the two musical traditions (Nketia, "Historical Evidence in Ga Religious Music," pp. 276-278). Of course, the close linguistic ties between Ga and Adangme have been appreciated by scholars for some time.

The words of the *kpele* text are non-Ga.

[14]   Oshi Adu Kǫme,

   Moko lee Nyǫngmǫ shishi kǫkǫǫkǫ.
   Namǫ le Nyǫngmǫ shishi?
   Moko lee Nyǫngmǫ shishi kǫkǫǫkǫ.

   Moko lee shikpǫng shishi dzee.
   Namǫ le shikpǫng shishi momo?
   Moko lee shikpǫng shishi dzee.

   Namǫ etsǫ wǫwǫi ashishi?
   Moko etsǫǫ Buadza shishi,
   Moko etsǫǫ Kǫme shishi,
   Moko etsǫǫ Kǫǫle shishi.

   Moko etsǫǫ lomo shishi-e.
   Moko etsǫǫ Nkran pong shishi.

   Sakumǫ who is feared,

   No one knows God's origin ever.
   Who knows God's origin?
   No one knows God's origin ever.

   No one knows the origin of the earth.
   Who knows the origin of the earth long ago?
   No one knows the origin of the earth.

Who teaches the origin of the gods?
No one teaches Olila's origin,
No one teaches Sakumǫ's origin,
No one teaches Kǫǫle's origin.

No one teaches the origin of chieftaincy.
No one teaches the origin of Great Accra.

Singer: Olila wǫngtsę.
Occasion: Discussion of *kpele* cosmogony, 1968.
Commentary: Buadza is a synonym for *Olila.* The *Olila* medium said, "Then *Olila* shakes as the wind is blowing now, then everything shakes [*ngwoso*], then it is shaking us [*elilawǫ*]. The name is *Buadza.* You see sky, earth, and sea, but *Buadza* covers the sky [*eha ngwęi hię*] and so he holds the power; all the power that exists, all these many people he holds them, because he covers the face of God and the sky [*eha Nyǫngmǫ hię kę atatu*]. He is the wind, he holds all the world, there is nowhere that you may reach in the world and not see him. He is everywhere. *Oboadza,* maybe someone will say that it is a stone, but it is not a stone; *abǫ bo* means 'they created you' and he is good [*edza*]; God created him and he is good. One says *Ataa Boadza,* but *Boadza* is difficult to say, and so they call him by the name of his work, *Olila.* Nothing can compare with *Boadza.*"

According to the *Olila* medium, Ayi Kushi, whom tradition recognizes as the first *Ga mangtsę* at Great Accra, was the first person to worship *Olila.* She said that before the Ga left Great Accra for the coast, *Olila* was the senior god. The *Olila* medium, therefore, considers that all *kpele* gods who are associated with inland natural features, such as rivers, mountains, and rocks, are subordinate to *Olila.* These subordinate gods include *Omanye, Sakumǫ, Nsaki, Asafoa, Kpla, Osu Ablekuma, Nyęngtalębi, Baawale, Opobi, Opoku, Klang, Oshilike, Oshra Yengke, Adǫdǫi,* and *Abęka.* In contemporary Accra, however, the cult of *Olila* has been superseded by that of *Sakumǫ.*

Sakumǫ (Kǫme, Odai): There are two *Sakumǫ* cults associated with different rivers and lagoons. The senior cult at Tema is associated with the nearby Sakumǫ Lagoon; the junior cult at Accra is associated with the Densu River. *Sakumǫ* is known as the warrior guardian of the Ga people. His martial role is symbolized by the arrow atop both his shrine (*gbatsu*) and his priest's hat (*koto*) in Accra. *Sakumǫ*'s role as the impartial defender of the Ga is the theme of most of his appellations, which his priest invariably recites in the following order: Grandfather/Old man *Sakumǫ* (*Nii/Nuumǫ Sakumǫ*); Great, great *Sakumǫ* (*Klǫǫte kotobridza akotobri*); *Sakumǫ*, it is good when you are present (*Odai womu oye*); You destroy and you repair (*ofite osaa*); When *Sakumǫ* is called, he answers (*abuǫ Tete kę tsei*); One on whom one leans in danger (*onyanku afle*); You kill for Ga (*Oku ama Nkran*); *Sakumǫ* senior yes, *Sakumǫ* junior yes (*Tęte yee, Tętę yee*); Ewe fear you, Ashanti fear you (*Angula sro, Ashanti sro*). In Accra, *Sakumǫ*, who ranks second to *Nai*, has a number of wives and children. Among the former are *Naa Kǫǫle*, the third ranking god in Accra, and *Ogbede* at Labadi. *Sakumǫ*'s children (*bii*), who have cult groups but whose priests participate in the agricultural rites of *Sakumǫ*'s cult, include *Abudu, Kǫǫna, Tętę Ogbu, Oku, Kle*, and *Laculǫ*.

Naa Kǫǫle, the third-ranking deity in Accra, is said "to hold" the Accra lands and is a goddess of peace. It is believed that she once saved the Ga from defeat at the hands of the Ashanti by cooking a meal which satiated the Ashanti and enabled the Ga to vanquish them. Her appellations include Lady *Naa Kǫǫle* (*Naa Kǫǫle Abooyoo*); Flowing like water (*Oshanka*); Truthful (*Oshi du ɛdu*); Woman warrior (*Oma*); Omnipresent mother (*Dzengkrę awo*); Grandmother, Ashanti shall never succeed (*Naa, Ashanti ngkǫwie daa*); It is woman that cools things (i.e., peacemaker; *Yoo dzoo nii ahe*). She is said to be the daughter of *Nai*, the god of the sea, and the wife of *Sakumǫ*. She has a number of children, among whom are *Onya Kǫbla, Onya Kwashi, Ahumaha, Tętę Klu, Akpadokwei, Kane, Katra, Oblipong Koto, Osukwa Adoa, Oshidzeng, Oyaadzo*, and *Afieye*. She is associated with Kǫǫle Lagoon, which forms the western boundary of Central Accra.

This song recapitulates certain cosmogonic and taxonomic conceptions of *kpele* thought. Although I translate *nyǫngmǫ* as "God," an alternative and appropriate translation is "the sky." According to *kpele* cosmogony, the sky, which is associated with the supreme being, existed before the creation of the earth. The ordering of the text both suggests the cosmogonic and taxonomic precedence of the sky to the earth and differentiates the supreme being from subordinate classes of being: gods and men. Within the text there is a significant shift in the verbs utilized to discuss the origins of different orders. While no one *knows* the origins of God/sky and earth, no one *teaches* the origins of gods and human beings. This lexical change, which suggests that the origins of human beings and gods may be known whereas the beginning of the physical world cannot be known, implies a fundamental differentiation between the physical universe and the taxonomy of created beings.

The words in this *kpele* text are Ga.

[15]   *Version 1*
         Awi, lo, ngkẹ dzeng ba;
         Awi Tẹte ngkẹ dzeng ba.

         Awi, lo, ngkẹ loo ba;
         Awi Tẹte ngkẹ loo ba.

         Awi, lo, ngkẹ ngmaa ba;
         Awi Tẹte ngkẹ ngmaa ba.

         Awi, lo, ngkẹ nu ba;
         Awi Tẹte ngkẹ nu ba.

         Awi, lo, shwẹmi ye;
         Adeatsẹ mididi mida;
         Awi, lo, shwẹmi ye.

         Awi, lo, I brought the world;
         Awi Tẹte I brought the world.

         Awi, lo, I brought fish;
         Awi Tẹte I brought fish.

Awi, lo, I brought millet;
Awi Tẹte I brought millet.

Awi, lo, I brought water;
Awi Tẹte I brought water.

Awi, lo, look at me well;
At dawn I do not eat, I do not sleep;
Awi, lo, look at me well.

Singer: Akumadze Afieye wọngtsẹ.
Occasion: Recording songs, 1968.

Version 2
Awi, lo, ngkẹ dzeng ba,
Ngkẹ dzeng ba.

Awi Tẹte ngkẹ dzeng ba;
Awi, lo, ngkẹ dzeng ba,
Ngkẹ dzeng ba.

Awi Tẹte ngkẹ nu ba;
Awi, lo, ngkẹ dzeng ba,
Ngkẹ dzeng ba.

Awi Tẹte ngkẹ ngmaa ba;
Awi, lo, ngkẹ dzeng ba,
Ngkẹ dzeng ba.

Awi Tẹte ngkẹ la ba;
Awi, lo, ngkẹ dzeng ba,
Ngkẹ dzeng ba.

Awi Tẹte ngkẹ loo ba;
Awi, lo, ngkẹ dzeng ba,
Ngkẹ dzeng ba.

Awi Tẹte ngkẹ daa ba;
Awi, lo, ngkẹ dzeng ba,
Ngkẹ dzeng ba.

Awi Tetẹ ngkẹ dzoo ba;
Awi, lo, ngkẹ dzeng ba,
Ngkẹ dzeng ba.

Awi, lo, I brought the world,
I brought the world.

Awi Tẹte I brought the world;
Awi, lo, I brought the world,
I brought the world.

Awi Tẹte I brought water;
Awi, lo, I brought the world,
I brought the world.

Awi Tẹte I brought millet;
Awi, lo, I brought the world,
I brought the world.

Awi Tẹte I brought light (fire);
Awi, lo, I brought the world,
I brought the world.

Awi Tẹte I brought fish;
Awi, lo, I brought the world,
I brought the world.

Awi Tẹte I brought drink;
Awi, lo, I brought the world,
I brought the world.

Awi Tẹte I brought dancing;
Awi, lo, I brought the world,
I brought the world.

Singer: Olila wọngtsẹ.
Occasion: Recording songs, 1965.
Commentary: The meaning of this song is disputed. Some informants say that it means that *Awi* created the world, which is suggested by the *Akumadze Afieye* medium's comment, "*Awi Tẹte* is God's first son; he said that he brought the world." The *Olila* medium, however, emphatically maintained that *Awi* is merely the sun (see song 12), which is called to light human activities and is not a creator. She said "Yes, *Awi* brought the world; he holds it, but he did not create it."

Basically, the song enumerates subsistence items and some activities in Ga culture: water, plants, animals, and dancing. If *Awi* is merely the sun, the song pertains to the activities which occur during the day, the time of human activity, as opposed to those activities which take place during the night, the time of divine activity. If *Awi* is the creator of these items, then the song refers to the founding of Ga culture and the preconditions for mortal existence on the earth.

A third, shorter, version of the song was sung by *Kle agbaayoo* in 1968.

The words of the *kpele* text are Ga in Version 2 and in Version 1, with the exception of the last three lines.

Cosmos

This group of songs (16-39) deals with various aspects of the physical world. Song 16 mentions the cylindrical shape of the world, and song 17 elucidates its tripartite division into sky, earth, and sea. The asymmetrical relationship between sky and earth is elaborated in several songs (18-23). The remaining songs concern celestial (24-30) and terrestrial (31-39) phenomena.

[16]   Naa, be ko mba,
          Oshwila, be ko miiba;
          Beni abọ ade, dzee nẹkẹ abọ ade.
          Dzeng ko bamba,
          Oshwila, dzeng ko ba;
          Niimẹi bọ ade dzee nẹkẹ abọ ade.
          Dzeng ko bamba,
          Oshwila dzeng ko ba.

          Dzeng yẹ kokrookokroo;
          Dzeng yẹ koklolonto.
          Atsi lẹ kẹ tee, atsi lẹ kẹ ba.
          Dzeng yẹ koklolonto.

          Dedei Oto, ashimashi obenten,
          Awo bo họ;
          Ale mọni wo bo họ.
          Adzimang naa;

Kwakwa ashi Amaga.
Aamaga yatao onǫ ni owo.

Lo, a certain time is coming,
Oshwila, a certain time is coming;
When the world was created, it was not like this
    that the world was created.
A certain civilization is coming,
Oshwila, a certain civilization is coming;
Grandfathers' world, it was not like this that the
    world was created.
A certain civilization is coming,
Oshwila, a certain civilization is coming.

The world is round;
The world is a cylinder.
It is pushed forwards, it is pushed backwards.
The world is a cylinder.

Dedei Oto, foolish woman,
You were impregnated;
They know who impregnated you.
Adzimang did not beget the child;
Intentionally, it was left to Amaga.
Amaga, go find yours and take it.

Singer: Olila wǫngtsẹ.
Occasion: Discussion of *kpele* cosmogony, 1968.
Exegesis: Lines 13-18: Someone impregnated her and she intentionally said that it was another person. *Dedei Oto* is the
one who is there and acts foolishly and will not talk. When
they asked her the story, then she would not talk.
Commentary: Oshwila is a god who is associated with a stream
near Okai Koi hill and who acts as a linguist for other *kpele*
gods. There is a bird, *shwila*, which is known for its eloquence,
but the bird is not associated with the deity. See song 17 for
note on linguists.

  The three parts of the song pertain to rather different
themes. Lines 1-8 lament the transformation of Ga culture

with the passage of generations (see song 150); lines 9-12 describe the round and cylindrical shape of the universe; and lines 13-18 concern a paternity case. Since this is the only song which refers directly to the shape of the physical world, I have included the song among those relating to the cosmos.

The words of the *kpele* text are Ga.

[17]   Mangnaakpa, obidai;
Ngkǫma Nyampong.
Mangnaakpa, obidai;
Ngkǫma mamra.
Mangnaakpa, obidai;
Ngkǫma bosobro.
Mangnaakpa, obidai;
Ngkǫma wǫwǫi.
Mangnaakpa, obidai;
Ngkǫma lomo.
Mangnaakpa, obidai;
Ngkǫma Tẹte.
Mangnaakpa moomo.

Linguist of the country, no one is to sleep;
I give to God.
Linguist of the country, no one is to sleep;
I give to the earth.
Linguist of the country, no one is to sleep;
I give to the sea.
Linguist of the country, no one is to sleep;
I give to the gods.
Linguist of the country, no one is to sleep;
I give to the prophet.
Linguist of the country, no one is to sleep;
I give to Tẹte.
Linguist of the country of long ago.

Singer: Olila wǫngtsẹ.
Occasion: Recording songs, 1965.

Exegesis: The linguist of the time says that no one is to sleep; everyone should be attentive. He appeals to God, the earth, the sea, the gods, and the prophets.

Commentary: The song elucidates aspects of *kpele* taxonomy, especially the tripartite classification of the physical world into sky, earth, and sea. The ranking of these natural features in *kpele* thought corresponds to their enumerative order in the song.

A linguist is a person who speaks for another person. The mediating role of linguist is variously institutionalized in Ga society. In everyday life, individuals may be asked to act as linguists for individuals or groups for limited and specific occasions, such as the presentation or the acceptance of gifts. In the Ga political system, the linguist is a hereditary status associated with chiefly stools. The preceding song (song 16) suggests that the formal status of linguist exists among divine beings as it does in human society.

See song 55 for note on prophets.

The *kpele* text is non-Ga, with the exception of *mangnaak-pa, wọwọi, lomo,* and *Tẹte.*

[18]   Shikpọng eei,
          Nyọngmọ ni.
          Shikpọng tẹtrẹ, nyọngmọ tẹtrẹ.

          The earth is,
          The sky is.
          The earth is flat, the sky is flat.

Singer: Olila wọngtsẹ.
Occasion: Discussion of *kpele* cosmogony, 1968.
Commentary: This song differentiates the cosmic categories of sky and earth and suggests that they are analogous in physical form. The differentiation between sky and earth is central to *kpele* conceptions concerning the locations of classes of being, for immortal gods dwell in the sky and mortal men on the earth. The differentiation between sky and earth is one

mode of representing the differentiation and complementarity between gods and men (see Chapters 4 and 5).

The words in the *kpele* text are Ga.

[19]   Nyampong dzi onukpa;
        Nyampong, lo, asase Nyampong,
        Lẹ ekwraa wọ.

        God is senior;
        God, lo, it is God's earth,
        He looks after us.

Singer: Olila wọngtsẹ.
Occasion: Discussion of *kpele* ritual, 1968.
Exegesis: The sky is senior; the earth is associated with God, because we walk on the earth. We wish the land to hold us gently, so that we may walk on it. *Asase afia* is the earth; it is not a god.
Commentary: This song conveys notions of differentiation between sky and earth and between gods and men similar to those in song 18.

The words of the *kpele* text are Ga, with the exception of *nyampong* and *asase.*

[20]   Nyampong, lo, asase Nyampong.
        Kẹ ngọngọ bẹ mọhe, maba.
        Ekẹ miti adabra, Okomfo Awu basha lẹ.
        Dzeng teng kwraa wọ.

        God, lo, it is God's earth.
        If no one has a gong, I will come.
        If no one has a gong, Okomfo Awu will catch him.
        The middle of the world guides us.

Singer: Akumadze Afieye wọngtsẹ.
Occasion: Recording songs, 1968.
Exegesis: The gods were created by God. Before we invoke

them, we pour a libation to earth and to sky to ask their permission to perform ritual. Some gods are in the middle of the earth.

Commentary: Adabra is the term for gong (see song 62) in the Adangme *me* cult.

This song text contains two conceptual themes. Lines 1 and 4 pertain to the physical world, and lines 2 and 3 to ritual performance. With respect to the physical world, the differentiation between sky and earth is expressed again, and the concept of the middle of the earth is introduced. As mentioned in Chapter 4, the middle of the earth refers to the air in which gods exist who mediate between the supreme being and mortal men. With respect to ritual performance, in these lines the availability of a gong for beating *kpele* rhythms is assured; consequently, the dance will take place.

Lines 2 and 4 of the *kpele* text are in Ga.

[21]   *Version 1*
        Nyọngmọ kplẹ huu;
        Asase ni ano,
        Asase kantobi;
        Asase ni ano,
        Kasa ni anu.

        The sky roars;
        The earth does not have a mouth,
        The earth cannot speak;
        The earth does not have a mouth,
        It cannot speak but it hears.

Singer: Olila agbaanuu.
Occasion: Recording songs, 1968.
Commentary: The only Ga words in the *kpele* text are *nyọngmọ* and *anu.*

        Version 2
        Asase nyanii, ngkasabi;
        Nyọngmọ kplẹọ huu.

Shikpɔng bɛ naabu ni ekɛ wieɔ Ga.
Nyɔngmɔ kplɛɔ huu,
Ni ekplɛ huu,
Nyɔngmɔ, Nyampong kplɛɔ huu.

The earth is silent, it cannot speak;
The sky roars.
The earth does not have a mouth with which to
   speak Ga.
The sky roars,
And it roars.
The sky, God roars.

Singer: Olila wɔngtsɛ.
Occasion: Recording songs, 1965.
Exegesis: When it thunders, God is speaking. When God speaks
no one else may speak. God is supreme. The sky is associated
with God; the earth is associated with other things.
Commentary: The differentiation and asymmetry of the sky
and the earth are conveyed by the capacity and incapacity for
speech of these physical phenomena. The articulateness of the
sky and the dumbness of the earth relate not only to differentiations between classes of being but to differentiations
within classes of being (see Chapter 4).

The Ga words in the *kpele* text are *nyɔngmɔ* and the words
of line 3.

[22]   Amra bɛdi ade;
       Wɔkwɔ nsu.

       The earth eats;
       We do not fetch water.

Singer: Olila agbaanuu.
Occasion: Recording songs, 1968.
Exegesis: Although the earth fetches neither water nor fire-

wood, it always eats. Since everything which dies is buried in the ground, the earth always gets food to eat.

Commentary: This song and song 23 refer to the empirical fact that the bodies of mortal creatures rest on or in the earth after death and suggest that the earth derives its sustenance from these organic materials. While this song and its exegesis focus upon the passivity of the earth (see Chapter 4), the following song alludes to the implications of mortality for human existence.

The words of the *kpele* text are non-Ga.

[23]   Amama ase gbędzęke;
        Su mingye nǫ tsǫ,

        Death the way is long;
        The earth eats excessively.

Singer: Kle agbaayoo.
Occasion: Recording songs, 1968.
Commentary: E. A. Ammah's statement concerning a similar song is pertinent. He writes:

Earth devours things in excess/We come that we may go,/ Navel cord was cut and left behind./Su miiye no tso,/ Woba ni woya,/Afo lanmo asi. This optimistic hymn was recalled to remind the teachers that the aged or teachers who were passing away, were being buried in the bosom of mother earth with all their knowledge, and that man was a pilgrim, and that they, the teachers, were left behind to continue to impart the acquired knowledge to the people; that the individual dies but the race or mankind abides, *afo lanmo asi*, therefore, whether or not the ethical or moral standard had determined, it was their duty and responsibility as teachers to teach or instruct the people [Ammah, "Ghanaian Philosophy," March 1962, p. 18].

The words in this *kpele* text are non-Ga.

[24]   Awi, lo, mundumu,
        Awi Tẹte mundumu;
        Awi maba onua,
        Awi maba mishia.

        May the sun recede,
        May the sun recede;
        Awi I have come into my house,
        Awi I have come into my house.

Singers: Sakumọ agbaa.
Occasion: Sakumọ ngmaadumọ after return from the sacred
field, 1965.
Exegesis: The sun is implored to recede so that the rain may
fall. The last two lines mean "I have returned safely."
Commentary: The ideas conveyed by this song are analogous
to those expressed in song 12. The *agbaa* entreats God to permit rain to fall so that the seed which has just been sown may
grow. The song, therefore, implies not only a recognition of
natural processes but the belief that these processes are controlled by the supreme being.

    The words of the *kpele* text are Ga, with the exception of
mundumu and *onua.*

[25]   Bonaa lẹ omọ wie able;
        Bonaa lo eha hulu ngtso,
        Amẹletsẹ Ama.

        Gold is like sunshine;
        Gold is like sunshine,
        Amẹle's father Ama.

Singer: Kle agbaayoo.
Occasion: Recording songs, 1968.
Commentary: The song describes the analogous color attributes of gold and sunshine. Ga believe that the first smiths
were members of *Amatsẹ we:* consequently, the song is an al-

lusion and a tribute to the people of this family and their craft.

The last line illustrates the use of teknonymy in Ga culture. The words of the *kpele* text are Ga, with the exception of the first line.

[26]   Nyǫng edze;
       Nyǫngtsere lę edze.

       The night is up;
       The moon has risen.

Singer: Olila wǫngtsę.
Occasion: Discussion of *kpele* ritual, 1968.
Exegesis: Grandfathers [i.e., ancestors] said that the moon rose and went. Thus, the moon is grandfathers' light; it is God's light. The moon will shine during the night, and so all night it stands, but when the sun begins to dance, the moon will set; when the sun sets, the moon stands. At evening the gods will hear God's voice. Then the moon also comes out; the singer says, "Hey, the moon has come out, night has gotten up."
Commentary: As the *Olila* medium explains, the night is the time of divine activity in contrast to the association of the day with human activity. The song illustrates the way in which physical phenomena are utilized to convey differentiations between taxonomic classes in *kpele* thought.

The words in the *kpele* text are Ga.

[27]   Pęhere adi ba;
       Lę ekplęǫ kangkang;
       Ewoso abribri,
       Ekę nyǫngtsere shi akang.

       Pęnyade likes rain;
       It shines brightly;

It shakes violently,
It competes with the moon.

Singer: Olila wǫngtsę.
Occasion: Discussion of *kpele* ritual, 1968.
Exegesis: Pęnyade is a star; they call it "town mother's star" [*mangnyę awale*]. When the moon is out, *pęnyade* is behind it. *Pęnyade* shines brightly, it shakes violently, it competes with the moon. It shines for a long time, then it shakes, then the moon leaves it. *Pęnyade* always follows the moon trying to reach it, but it cannot reach the moon.
Commentary: Pęnyade, the star, is associated with the god *Baawale* (see song 14, note on *Olila*), whose terrestrial location is a river.
The words of the *kpele* text are Ga, with the exception of the first line.

[28]   Owaako, amę nę Gbo nyǫngmǫ.
        Gbo nyǫngmǫ ebawo dudǫkoi amli.

        Owaako, they give Gbo's rain.
        Gbo's rain will fall into empty pots.

Singer: Olila wǫngtsę.
Occasion: Discussion of *kpele* ritual, September 1968.
Exegesis: Owaako [which is a star] cuts off rain and gives rain also. It brings *Gbo*'s rain, which falls into empty wells; wherever there are many water pots, it will not fall. Wherever food is planted, rain will not fall; it will only thunder there. It is now the season of *Gbo*'s rain. And so *owaako* is a cruel star, it is a sinner, so it was created.
Commentary: The Ga year is divided into two major seasons: *Gbo* (September-February) and *Gbienaa* (March-August). *Gbo* is the dry season, which is initiated by the capricious September rains described by the *Olila* medium in her exegetical comments; *Gbienaa* is the rainy season, during which the heavy rains fall. Every *kpele* prayer includes the phrase: "May we eat the produce of *Gbo;* may we eat the produce of *Gbienna*" (*Wǫye Gbo; wǫye Gbienaa*).
The words of the *kpele* text are Ga.

[29]   Obletu wǫ bǫba, kamale.
        Mabǫ otsǫrǫma,
        Mashi tente.

        A dark cloud presages rain, it does not lie.
        I will create a drummer,
        I will beat kpele music.

Singer: *Ashadu wǫngtsǫ.*
Occasion: Recording songs, 1968.
Commentary: Another version of the song was sung by *Kǫǫle agbaayoo* in 1968; the difference between the two versions appears to be based upon multilingual confusion in the second text. The words in this version are Ga.

[30]   *Version 1*
        Nyankutǫng mǫ de?
        Mifo wia,
        Amane.
        Mitǫ nsu,
        Amane.
        Mawie Atsǫfo, Gomua.

        Rainbow, what am I to do?
        When I give sunshine,
        I am blamed.
        When I give rain,
        I am blamed.
        I will talk to Akan people, Gomua people.

Singer: *Akumadze Afieye wǫngtsǫ.*
Occasion: Recording songs, 1968.
Exegesis: Rainbow says, "When I give water, you say that I give too much water; now, when the sun is shining brightly, you say 'Why is the sun shining like this?' " It says that it is finished with them. So this is the song.
Commentary: The words of the *kpele* text are non-Ga, with the exception of the last line.

Version 2
Nyankutǫng, ngtǫ ntswi, amane;
Ngfri wia, amane.
Ablao?

Nyankutǫng, ngtǫ ntswi, amane;
Ngfri wia, amane.
Tsę Nyǫngmǫ Mawu!

Rainbow, when I give water, I am blamed;
When I give sunshine, I am blamed.
What should I do?

Rainbow, when I give water, I am blamed;
When I give sunshine, I am blamed.
God!

Singer: Olila wǫngtsę.
Occasion: Recording songs, 1965.
Exegesis: The rainbow complains to God about human behavior. Human beings are never satisfied; whether there is rain
or sunshine, human beings complain.
Commentary: The only Ga words in the *kpele* text are *tsę* and
nyǫngmǫ.

[31]   Gbǫtsui ashi gbęntę;
       Ngyę dani kanya ba.

       Anthills left the crossroads;
       I existed before kanya came.

Singer: Kle agbaayoo.
Occasion: Recording songs, 1968.
Exegesis: Yes, anthills were before *kanya* came, but we do not
know what *kanya* is.
Commentary: This song asserts the precedence of the earth
over plants which grow on it, for *kanya (Griffonia simplici-
folia)* grows on termite hills on the Ghanaian coastal plains. It

is "a shrub or climber with short strong weedy tendrils. . . .
The hard wood is used, after bending, as walking sticks. . . .
The bursting of the ripe pods is the signal to the farmers on
the Accra Plains that the time has come to plant their crops"
(Irvine, *Woody Plants of Ghana*, p. 309).

Ga believe that anthills are the entrance to the subterranean homes of earth goddesses, *Afieye* (see song 88). Since
kanya is associated with Ga horticulture, the song may connote the earlier origin of divine beings and their superiority
over human beings.

Crossroads are regarded as gathering places for spiritual beings. Since both beneficent and malevolent spirits may con-
gregate at crossroads, they have ambiguous associations. Crossroads are associated positively with *Afieye*, who are believed
to sit near them, and with benevolent ancestral shades. If a
food offering is presented to shades or divine beings, it often
is placed at a crossroad. Nevertheless, witches and malevolent
shades also gather at crossroads. In order to separate human
beings from these malevolent beings, sacrificial offerings to
them also may be placed at a crossroad. Further, mystically
contaminated objects also are disposed of at crossroads. Thus,
whether the connotation of crossroad is negative or positive
depends on the situation. In the text of this song a negative
association seems to apply to the crossroad which the anthills,
symbols of earth goddesses, have left.

The words of the *kpele* text are Ga.

[32]   Kutushi,
        Kẹ ona ba ko,
        Tsẹ obo ha mi.

        A meeting place,
        If you see a leaf,
        Call and give it to me.

Singer: Olila wọngtsẹ.
Occasion: Discussion of trip to Ayawaso, 1968.

Exegesis: I am immobile, therefore, I call others to do things for me.

Commentary: This song was sung in reference to a site on the outskirts of Great Accra which the *Olila* medium said had been a meeting place in former times. Explicitly, the words describe a natural fact that things must be brought to immobile entities. Implicitly, the situation pertains to relations between superordinates and subordinates in Ga society. It is appropriate for a subordinate to visit a superior. Like the preceding song, this song implicitly affirms the precedence of the earth over plants which grow on it.

The words of the *kpele* text are Ga.

[33]   Shadzoo,
         Wulọmọbi eyee;
         Mangtsẹbi eyee.

         Baobab,[1]
         A priest's child does not eat it;
         A chief's child does not eat it.

1. *Shadzoo*, baobab (*Adansonia digitata*).

Singer: Olila wọngtsẹ.
Occasion: Discussion of trip to Ayawaso, 1968.
Exegesis: Shadzoo, this tree does not grow just anywhere. The only place that it grows is where gods are. *Shadzoo* is power; it is good power, Ga's power, and God's own power. It is God's very powerful tree. And so they say that a priest's child cannot eat it; it is chief among chiefs, because God's oath is beside it. It does not just grow, it is God's own power.
Commentary: Another shorter version of the song was sung by *Kle agbaayoo* in 1968.

The text and the *Olila* medium's exegetical comments suggest that the prescription against eating baobab fruits symbolizes the status of the children of the highest-ranking hereditary officials in the Ga secular and religious communities.

Dietary prescriptions are utilized in Ga society to convey status differentiations. The members of some kin groups are forbidden to eat certain animals, and the holders of ritual office are enjoined to refrain from certain foods during ritual periods. Since the baobab tree is associated with divine presence, the interdiction on the consumption of its fruit for people of high status is both an expression of their differentiation from divinity and their special relationship to divine power.

The words in this *kpele* text are Ga.

[34] Mabọ pangtsi,
       Yimi abubu.
       Abọ nase kube ewu,
       Abẹ ewuu.

       I knock on your door,
       Open it for me.
       Since creation the fan palm[1] stands,
       The oil palm[2] dies.

1. *Kube*, fan palm (*Elaeis guineensis*).
2. *Abẹ*, oil palm (*Borassus aethiopium*).

Singer: Olila wọngtsẹ.
Occasion: Checking *kpele* songs, 1968.
Commentary: A shorter version of this song, which *Kle agbaayoo* sang, was distorted by multilingual confusion. The words in this *kpele* text are non-Ga.

Although I do not know the Ga reasons underlying the differentiation in longevity between the fan palm (*Elaeis guineensis*) and the oil palm (*Borassus aethiopium*) in this song, I suggest that it relates to the greater height of the former. Ga often use the expression "since creation" to refer to phenomena that have existed as long as any person can remember or that are believed to antedate other phenomena within the same class. For example, Ga speak of *kpele* gods as having existed from creation (*ade bọ*) in contrast to *akọng* or *otu* gods.

[35]   Odupong bayǫǫ omang;
Wǫngfa suala
Kpletekpetsi tungtungni.
Okron yę dru.

Cedar[1] come watch your town;
Sorcerer cannot challenge
The kpletekpetsi tree.
It is difficult to be a medium.

1. *Odupong*, cedar (*Entangdrophragma*).

Singer: Akumadze Afieye wǫngtsę.
Occasion: Recording songs, 1968.
Exegesis: It is hard to be a medium, because people always
want a little drink. I cannot carry things on my head, because
the god would trouble me if I did. My god is a big woman [see
song 88 for note on *Afieye*]; she wears a lot of beads; she carries a tray; she puts on cloth [*mama*]; she wears a big *atofo*
[a pad for carrying babies]; she does not wear a covershirt or
sandals.
Commentary: I have been unable to identify the tree *kpletekpetsi*. Since the only Ga word in the *kpele* text is *omang*, it is
possible that the singer has distorted the Twi word. She said
that the tree controls thunder and the text implies that this
capacity gives it greater power than a sorcerer. At any rate,
the genus *Entangdrophragma* is found within the forest areas
of Akan peoples and not within the Ga territory.

[36]   Nǫkǫtshǫshishi,
Yoo efǫǫ dzęi shwęmǫ.

Under swamp ebony,[1]
A woman remains in a rich place.

1. *Nǫkǫtshǫ*, swamp ebony (*Diospyros mespiliformis*).
Singer: Olila wǫngtsę.

Occasion: Discussion of trip to Ayawaso, 1968.
Exegesis: Nǫkǫtshǫ is a symbol of joy and plenty. Women
like rich places; no one likes bitter experiences.
Commentary: The words of the *kpele* text are Ga.

[37]   Nẹi dzǫ, nẹi dzǫ;
        Yaakwẹ nǫkǫtshǫ
        Ni abu lẹ mama.

        It is soft grass, soft grass;
        Go to see swamp ebony
        Which is wrapped in cloth.

Singer: Kle agbaayoo.
Occasion: Recording songs, 1968.
Exegesis: Nǫkǫtshǫ is a big tree with fruits that people eat.
One god insults another by saying that she is a tree. Some
gods insult each other, because they are co-wives.
Commentary: The words of the *kpele* text are Ga.

[38]   Shwilale munka;
        Ayao munka.

        Volta come together;
        Let us go together.

Singer: Kǫǫle agbaayoo.
Occasion: Recording songs, 1968.
Exegesis: Its meaning is the noise of the Volta River which
sounds in the grass. When it sounds, one hears its name, so
that is why it is called *shwila.*
Commentary: In *kpele* thought, the Volta River marks the
eastern boundary of the Ga territory. Often the invocation of
deities in *kpele* prayer concludes by calling all the gods from
the Volta River in the east to Langma in the west.
    The words of the *kpele* text are non-Ga.

[39]   Mpo nwea
        Yẹ amu asẹ.
        Tsẹrẹ mi asebi.

        Sea sand
        Has removed her underwear,
        Explain what happened to me.

Singer: Ashiaklẹ wulọmọ.
Occasion: Recording songs, 1968.
Exegesis: Ashiaklẹ wulọmọ: When *Nai* [see song 96] enters
the sea, he walks on the sea sand.
    Olila medium: A person is asking for her underwear [Ga,
mọmọshi], which the sea has removed. What happened was
that she threw her underwear on the sand while she went to
bathe in the sea. While she was bathing, the sea covered her
underwear and removed it. It is a song for the sea sand.
Commentary: Another conceptually similar version of the
song was sung by *Kle agbaayoo* in 1968. She did not know
the Ga meaning of the words of the *kpele* text, which are non-
Ga.

Divine Beings

This group of songs is subdivided into three sections: relations between divine beings and human beings (songs 40-69), relations between divine beings and natural phenomena (songs 70-80), and the attributes and relations of various gods (songs 81-107). The first group of songs elaborates some contractual implications of human dependence upon divine beings. The first songs (songs 40-48) affirm man's reliance for protective assistance upon gods. Several songs specify various forms of economic, political, military, and ritual assistance which human beings desire from gods. (songs 49-52, 54-56, 62-69). Others, however, emphasize the negative consequences of human negligence of divine beings (songs 53, 57-61). As a unit, therefore, the songs in the first section delineate expectations concerning the mutual obligations inherent in relations between gods and men. The songs in the second section describe the association of gods with natural phenomena, such as stars, bodies of water, and rocks (songs 70-80). The songs in the third section pertain to specific deities. Although many songs merely describe the conventional role, attributes, or experience of a god in relation to human society (songs 81, 88-107), several concern the relations between deities as spouses, co-wives, and parents and children (songs 82-87).

[40]   Wọwọi, lo, wọhię amę;
       Wọngshe amę.

Kome, wongshe ame,
Yibume.

The gods, lo, we hold them;
We fear them.
Sakumo, we fear them,
Protect us.

Singer: Kle agbaayoo.
Occasion: Recording songs, 1968.
Commentary: This song articulates the respect which *kpele*
believers have for the powers of divine beings and *Sakumo's*
role as guardian of the interests of Ga people (see song 14 for
note on *Sakumo*).
  The *kpele* text is in Ga, with the exception of *yibume*.

[41]   Madang Ope nima;
        Banu ye banu ye.

        I lean on God and the gods;
        It is good for two to walk together.

Singer: Olila wongtse.
Occasion: Recording songs, 1965.
Exegesis: Man depends on God and the gods. Through the
gods we reach God; man should walk with the gods.
Commentary: The words of the *kpele* text are non-Ga.

[42]   Gbe le dzi wono,
        Shi wowoi ananedzi gbe.

        The way is for us,
        But our gods' steps are the way.

Singer: Kle agbaayoo.
Occasion: Recording songs, 1968.

Commentary: This song and the preceding one emphasize the dependence of human beings upon divine beings and the necessity for human beings to adhere to divine instruction if they are to prosper.

The *kpele* text is in Ga.

[43]   Bisa, bisa.
        Ngto dzwẹng;
        Wọ lee gbẹ;
        Wọbi gbẹ.

        Ask, ask.
        We do not know the way;
        We do not know the way;
        We are asking the way.

Singer: Olila wọngtsẹ.
Occasion: Recording songs, 1965.
Commentary: This song conveys the dependence of human beings on divine beings for guidance in the conduct of their lives.

The third and fourth lines of the *kpele* text are in Ga.

[44]   Omanye oyei;
        Omanye otsẹi.
        Omanye ni ebọlọ wọ;
        Otsẹi wula Omanye miiba.

        Omanye you are for women;
        Omanye you are for men.
        Omanye surrounds us;
        Omanye is coming.

Singer: Olila wọngtsẹ.
Occasion: Discussion of trip to Ayawaso, 1968.

Commentary: The groves of *Omanye* and two of his wives are near the village of Ayawaso, which is said to have been founded before the flight from Great Accra to the coast. *Omanye* means goodness or peace. The customary *kpele* ritual greeting is *"Eei manye,"* to which the addressee responds, *"Omanye aba"* ("May goodness come"). According to the *Olila* medium, all *kpele* usages of *omanye* refer to the god; for most Ga, however, the term *omanye* pertains to the abstract notions of peace and prosperity rather than to the deity per se.

The words in the *kpele* text are Ga.

[45] Bo tee lo?
Dede bo tee?
Omanye fǫ Dede;
Omanye fǫ Kǫkǫ;
Omanye fǫ wǫ.
Kǫkǫ dzi bo ba;
Dede bo tee?

Did you go?
Dede did you go?
Omanye begat Dede;
Omanye begat Kǫkǫ;
Omanye begat us.
Kǫkǫ you came;
Dede did you go?

Singer: Olila wǫngtsę.
Occasion: Discussion of trip to Ayawaso, 1968.
Commentary: This text exemplifies the utilization of anthropomorphic models to characterize relations among divine beings. In this song, the god *Omanye* is said to have begotten two daughters. *Dede* and *Kǫkǫ* are birth-order names for first-born and second-born daughters in Ga society.

The words of the *kpele* text are Ga.

[46]   Otse ba ni ba nam;
        Ohi ba ni ba nam.
        Mi dǫ otse; otse ba dǫ.
        Mi dǫ ohi; ohi ba dǫ.

        A woman came to see me;
        A man came to see me.
        I like a woman; a woman likes me.
        I like a man; a man likes me.

Singer: O*lila wǫngtsę.*
Occasion: Singing for the *Ga mangtsę*, 1965.
Exegesis: The god likes people and goodness. If a person is good, he will achieve good results.
Commentary: The words in the *kpele* text are non-Ga.

[47]   Naa webii nę;
        Wǫhe yę fęęǫ tsǫ,
        Moko na wǫfee.
        Oshi Akwan webii nę;
        Naa Ede webii nę;
        Dedei Adu webii nęę.
        Shi eshwę daa.

        This is grandmother's family;
        We are very beautiful,
        Someone wishes to be like us.
        This is the road blocker's family;[1]
        This is Naa Ede's family;
        This is Dedei Adu's family.
        But the drink remains.

1. *Oshi Akwan,* road blocker; i.e., goddess for women who die in child-birth.

Singers: N*aa Ede agbaa.*
Occasion: N*aa Ede ngmaafaa,* 1965.

Exegesis: You have said that we are beautiful, but you have not given a drink [money or libation] to ratify what you have said.

Commentary: The cult of *Naa Ede Oyeadu*, the goddess of childbirth, is the responsibility of *Abeitsa we* in Accra. Although today her agricultural rites are performed and some pregnant women come to her priest to pray for safe delivery, her cult is not as important as it was in the past. In former times, women who died in childbirth were not buried but taken beyond the limits of the town and "left on the ground exposed to the elements" (Quartey-Papafio, "The Ga Homowo Festival," pp. 231-232). Further, "If anyone dies in childbirth, the Oyeadu Fetish Priest and his people take all the goods of the deceased, and no one goes to the bush towns or farms or the water places for water on the Sunday [*Naa Ede's* day] following the day on which that person so died, till that person's place or house is purified" (Ibid, p. 131). The decline of *Naa Ede's* cult is probably due not only to the government's interdiction on the right of *Abeitse we* to confiscate property about sixty years ago, but to the reduction of maternal mortality rates in recent years through improved medical facilities in Accra and to the secularization of Ga society.

The words in this *kpele* text are Ga, with the exception of *Oshi Akwan.*

[48]   Gua asi moomo;
        Ayelemei awong,
        Ayokomei awong,
        Kwakomei awong.

        Gua lived long ago;
        He is Ayeles' god,
        He is Ayokos' god,
        He is Kwakos' god.[1]

1. These are *Kpakpatse we* names.

Singers: Gua agbaa.
Occasions: Gua ngmaadumǫ and *ngmaafaa,* 1965.
Commentary: Gua, the blacksmith god, is believed to have
created some stars (see song 70). His appellations include:
Gua, lo *Gua,* you have no *Gua,* you call *Gua (Nii Gua, naa
Gua, obǫ Gua, otsę Gua); Gua* is from long ago, *Gua* is unity
(Ayę moomo, Ayę srǫǫ); When you flash lightning, then we
all fall down *(bo mǫni kę okpę flam ekę wǫfęę wǫngbumǫshi).*
Gua's cult is the responsibility of *Kpakpatsę we,* which has
branches in Teshi and Osu; the association between the family
and *Gua* is expressed in the utilization of *Kpakpatsę we* names
in this song. When the Methodist church built a chapel on the
site of *Gua's* shrine in Accra, the shrine was moved to a village, Gbawe, where his agricultural rites are performed cur-
rently. Field says that *"Gua's* real headquarters are in a large
grove in the thick forest near Pokuase. A pot and blacksmith's
tools stand under an *Onyai* [silk cotton] tree, and there annually repair united worshippers from Teshi, Osu, and Accra
and dance every day for two or three weeks" (Field, *Religion
and Medicine,* p. 74).
The words of the *kpele* text are Ga.

[49]   Gua asi moomo.
         Otoi okę nuǫ mang,
         Ohiingmęi kękę okę na nii,
         Okę kwęǫ dzeng.
         Ayękoo, Ayę Kakadono.

         Gua lived long ago.
         You hear the affairs of the town with your ears,
         You see them with your eyes,
         You watch over the world.
         Congratulations, Gua.

Singer: Abudu wulǫmǫ.
Occasion: Recording songs, 1965.

Exegesis: During a war in Okai Koi's time, *Gua* manufactured guns for Okai Koi for which he is congratulated in this song. *Gua* says that he heard and saw what was happening, so he came to aid us; we congratulate him.

Commentary: This song describes explicitly the anthropomorphic physiological attributes of the god *Gua* (see song 48) and his role as guardian of Ga interests.

The words in this *kpele* text are Ga.

[50]   Oshwila Adu Kọme,
        Kọme aduatsọ:
        Afọ awo Kọme, ahe awo Kọme.

        Oshwila Adu Kọme,
        Kọme aduatsọ;
        Beshi tente ni mayọọ kẹtẹkẹtẹ.
        Okẹẹ milaiọ;
        Ngna Nyampong, ngna mamla.

        Sakumọ,
        Sakumọ avers:
        They are born for Sakumọ, they are bought for
          Sakumọ.

        Sakumọ,
        Sakumọ avers:
        Come to beat kpele music so that I may dance.
        I swear to do it:
        I swear to God, I swear to earth.

Singer: Olila wọngtsẹ.

Occasion: Recording songs, 1965.

Exegesis: Sakumọ avers that he is for the free and the slave. When *Sakumọ we* bought a slave, he was named *Kọme;* when a child was born to the family, he was named *Kọme.*

Commentary: The first verse conveys the notion that *Sakumọ* (see song 14) is the guardian of all members of Ga society whether they be slaves or freemen. Ga not only participated actively in the transatlantic slave trade but practiced domestic slavery. Ga say that slaves were obtained primarily through intertribal warfare. With the abolition of domestic slavery by the British colonial government, many former slaves were assimilated into the families of their former owners. The memory of slave status, however, persists and it is thought to be impolite to delve too deeply into genealogies lest this former status be revealed.

The second verse articulates the belief that when possessed mediums dance, gods are dancing.

The words of the *kpele* text are Ga, with the exception of *Nyampong* and *mamla*.

[51]   Kọme, midzara omani;
         Miti ade mproobi.
         Kọme, midzara omani;
         Mihu ade mproobi.

         Sakumọ, I represent the nation;
         When I hear something, I do not reject it.
         Sakumọ, I represent the nation;
         When I see something, I do not reject it.

Singer: Olila wọngtsẹ.
Occasion: Recording songs, 1965.
Exegesis: Sakumọ sings that he is for everyone without distinction; he does not hate anyone.
Commentary: In this song *Sakumọ* (see song 14) is described as watching over human affairs just as *Gua* does in song 49.

The words of the *kpele* text are non-Ga.

[52]   Mprobiale, omangta.
         Nkran Ashi Edu Kẹtẹkrẹ
         Obumi ashi kpoto.
         Mprobiale, omangta.
         Mprobiale, omangtiti, omangta.

Kọme, omangtiti, omangta.
Mprobiale, omangta.

Little children, it is ended.
Ga people
Reckon me as a fool.
Little children, it is ended.
Little children, it is ended, it is ended.
Sakumọ, it is ended, it is ended.
Little children, it is ended.

Singer: Abudu wulọmọ.
Occasion: Recording songs, 1965.
Exegesis: Sakumọ sings that he may be reckoned as a fool,
for he has taken the sins of the people on himself. The sacred
year [agricultural rites] has ended. This song is sung at *Saku-*
mọ's gate at the conclusion of the sacred year.
Commentary: See songs 14 and 61 for notes on *Sakumọ* and
Abudu, respectively.
   The words in the *kpele* text are non-Ga.

[53]   Klọwe Ashi Ẹtẹ,
       Bakpleke ase.

       Komẹ, te ofee tẹ omọ Gblenyo Oko,
       Daa mlamla?
       Mini sao, abrekuma?

       Klọwe,
       Descend to earth.

       Sakumọ, how did you catch a Gbele person, Oko,
       Who has grown quickly?
       What befits you, a foreigner?

Singer: Ashadu wọngtsẹ.
Occasion: Recording songs, 1968.
Exegesis: The people of Gbele [an Akwapim village] and we

do not agree. Someone is asking *Sakumǫ* why he caught a
Gbele person named *Oko* to be his medium.
Commentary: Klǫwe's cult is observed at Nungua. According
to Field, "*Klǫwe* is said to be a blacksmith and thunder-god,
but [it] is also the name of a small lagoon several miles to the
east" (Field, *Religion and Medicine*, p. 27). *Klǫwe* is the son
of *Gbǫbu*, the senior god at Nungua, and his wife *Ohimiya*
(ibid, p. 28).

The basic theme of this song is the possession of mediums.
In the first verse, the Ga belief in the ability of the gods to
come to earth from their home in the sky is expressed clearly.
The second verse relates to the Ga belief that a god selects his
medium.

The words in the *kpele* text are Ga, with the exception of
ase and *abrekuma*.

[54] Wǫye ngtabrako.
      Kǫme Adute, mẹni loo wǫye?

      We eat snails.
      Sakumǫ, what can we eat?

Singer: Kle agbaayoo.
Occasion: Recording songs, 1968.
Exegesis: The season is as it is now [late July]: the fish are
scarce and the people are forced to eat snails.
Commentary: The words in the *kpele* text are Ga.

[55] Kǫme yawa enanẹimẹi;
      Gbamẹi kutǫkutǫkutǫ gbamẹi.

      Oshi Adu Kǫme yawa enanẹimẹi;
      Gbamẹi kutǫkutǫkutǫ gbamẹi.

      Odai yawa enanẹimẹi;
      Gbamẹi kutǫkutǫkutǫ gbamẹi.

Gbamei yawa enaneimei;
Gbamei kutokutokuto gbamei.

Sakumo goes to help his friends;
It is the home of the prophets.

Sakumo goes to help his friends;
It is the home of the prophets.

Sakumo goes to help his friends;
It is the home of the prophets.

The prophet goes to help his friends;
It is the home of the prophets.

Singer: A *budu wulomo.*
Occasion: Recording songs, 1965.
Commentary: In the *kpele* religion, a prophet is believed to
be inspired by *Sakumo.* The *Olila* medium said that *Sakumo*
does not descend upon a prophet to dance, as a medium does,
"but he can give him his spirit so that he will be able to speak"
(*shi ebaanye emumo ke baaha le ni ebaanye ewie*). A prophetic career begins with the person's disappearance into the bush;
on his return several days, weeks or months later, he claims
to have visited the gods and establishes himself as a prophet.
(See Douglas on power and marginality in *Purity and Danger*,
pp. 94-113.) The frankness and unpredictability of prophetic
utterances may provoke hostility from their hearers; angry
townsmen are said to have drowned one *kpele* prophet and to
have destroyed the shrine (*gbatsu*) of another. Among the remembered prophets are Lomo Ayi, Lomo Ama, Lomo Okai,
Lomo Afla, and Lomoko (Lomo Oko). The last recognized
prophet in Accra was Lomoko, a son of *Ga mangtse* Taki
Kome I, who died in 1866. Ga say that before Lomoko's
death, *Sakumo* had never had a medium (see exegesis of song
120).
The *kpele* text is in Ga.

[56]   Osheke ngmaadu ngma krǫmante adzidza.
       Oshwila Adu Kǫme,
       Baangǫ omang ni ohi,
       Koni mang adzǫǫ.

       A stubborn person has disrupted the town.
       Sakumǫ,
       Come and take your town and live,
       So that the town may be peaceful.

Singer: Olila wǫngtsę.
Occasion: Recording songs, 1965.
Exegesis: The townspeople are perishing, because *Sakumǫ* has left. He is urged to return so that the town may be administered properly.
Commentary: This song articulates the Ga belief in the disruptive consequences for human society of the withdrawal of divine support. The text and its exegesis imply that human actions ruptured the harmonious relations between *Sakumǫ* and human beings.

    The words of the *kpele* text are Ga, with the exception of the first line.

[57]   Akansu kplǫsu ope;
       Akankan mǫ le.
       Owie aahu enuu;
       Sane mashi mǫ.

       You speak many times, he does not hear;
       Then I must stop.
       You speak many times, he does not hear;
       Then I must leave.

Singer: Olila wǫngtsę.
Occasion: Recording songs, 1965.
Exegesis: The messenger of the gods speaks to man, "I tell you this, I tell you that; you do not listen to me. Since you do not listen to me, I must leave you."
Commentary: The last two lines of the *kpele* text are in Ga.

[58]   Ngkẹ bo wie Ga;
         Ni oto mi abla,
         Shi abla bọọ mang.

         I spoke Ga to you;
         And you lied to me,
         But falsehood destroys a town.

Singer: Olila wọngtsẹ.
Occasion: Recording songs, 1965.
Exegesis: A god spoke the truth to human beings, but they
lied to the god. A god possessed a person and showed the people what to do to ward off calamity, but they neglected to
follow his instructions and, therefore, destroyed things. What
the god told the people was, "If you do not do this or that,
you will be punished." When the god came and saw that he
had been disobeyed, he killed the person to whom he had
given the instructions.
Commentary: The words of the *kpele* text are Ga.

[59]   Mikpa aahu;
         Mikpa tutulutuu, nulọ enuu, nulọ enuu ngnọ.
         Mikpa hẹẹ nakai ngkẹẹ;
         Mikpa tutulutuu, nulọ enuu, nulọ enuu ngnọ.
         Mikpa aahu;
         Mikpa kẹte;
         Mikpa mlẹshọng.

         I spoke for a long time;
         I spoke with a horn, the hearer does not hear,
             the hearer does not hear me.
         I spoke, so I spoke;
         I spoke with a horn, the hearer does not hear,
             the hearer does not hear me.
         I spoke with a kẹte horn;
         I spoke with a collection of horns.

Singer: *Olila wọngtsẹ.*
Occasion: Recording songs, 1965.
Exegesis: The god told the people what to do to cure the dis-
obedient priest, but they did not do as he said and the priest
died. The priest was defiled by sexual intercourse and did not
purify himself before performing ritual; the god warned him
and in the end killed him. In the same way, the first village
built at Ofankor was destroyed by plague, because the people
disobeyed *Olila.*
Commentary: See song 14 for note on *Olila.*
  The words of the *kpele* text are Ga.

[60] Mangọ tsẹrẹpọng ngkẹẹ bu nyẹ Ga abẹ;
      Shi miwie Ga, onuu.
      Mangọ tsẹrẹpọng ngkẹẹ bu nyẹ Ga abẹ;
      Mabu nyẹ abẹ wudzii.

      I speak tsẹrẹpọng to tell you Ga proverbs;
      But when I speak Ga, you do not hear.
      I speak tsẹrẹpọng to tell you Ga proverbs;
      I shall tell you greater proverbs.

Singer: *Olila wọngtsẹ.*
Occasion: Recording songs, 1965.
Exegesis: The god complains that human beings still do not
listen to him. The plague has come or the priest has died; the
agbaa should have warded off the calamity.
Commentary: Tsẹrẹpọng, which is a Guang language, is said
to be the language of *kpele* ritual. Ga tradition maintains an
intimate connection between Guang-speakers, especially the
Awutu, and the Ga people. In pre-European times, the Awutu
and the Ga are said to have fought and to have intermarried.
The contemporary Ga polity includes the town of Obutu
within its territorial limits. While tsẹrẹpọng is said to be the
language of *kpele* ritual, I do not know the extent to which
contemporary Awutu and Ga cultural traditions are similar.
  The words in the *kpele* text are Ga.

[61]   *Version 1*
       Atsẹ mi kooloobi kooloo;
       Mingtao mangtsẹbii
       Ni mamọmọ amẹ ni mafimọ amẹ.

       I am called animal's child animal;
       I want a chief's children
       In order to catch them and to tie them.

Singer: *Kle agbaayoo.*
Occasion: Recording songs, 1968.

       Version 2
       Atsẹ mi kooloobi kooloo;
       Mitao mangtsẹmẹi mafimọ amẹ.
       Atsẹ mi kooloobi kooloo;
       Mitao mangtsẹmẹi magbe amẹ.
       Nyanyara ehii;
       Okẹẹ mihii, bo hu ohii.

       I am called animal's child animal;
       I want chiefs in order to tie them.
       I am called animal's child animal;
       I want chiefs in order to kill them.
       Nyanyara is not good;
       You said that I am not good; you also are not good.

Singer: *Abudu wulọmọ.*
Occasion: Recording songs, 1965.
Exegesis: Abudu was a captain for *Sakumọ* during a war between Ga and Ashanti. In this song *Abudu* tells the enemy
that he is incarnated in an animal. They are bad, so he wants
chiefs to bind them. The people said that *Abudu* was not
good, therefore, he said that they are not good.
Commentary: Abudu is the senior son of *Sakumọ* at Accra.
His shrine is at Oblogo, a village on the Densu River. According to Field, there is another *Abudu* cult at Tema in which
Abudu is associated with "the horned, black, spitting snake
called *blika*" (Field, *Religion and Medicine*, p. 11).

See song 89 for a note on the *nyanyara* plant.
The words of both *kpele* texts are Ga.

[62]   *Version 1*
      Ashiaklẹ dzẹ wuoyi ta lẹlẹ mli;
      Bosobrobi dzẹ wuoyi ta lẹlẹ mli;
      Akrẹ Kripo dzẹ wuoyi ta lẹlẹ mli.
      Akrẹ, bo mpabi.
      Aklẹ, akẹẹ ehii;
      Ekẹẹ ehi.
      "Mi amralobi, mi kingbi, mi Bosobi, mi mangshọbi;
      Mina ngọngọ enyọ kẹ ha bo."

      Ashiaklẹ came from the south sitting in a canoe;
      Nai's child came from the south sitting in a canoe;
      Ashiaklẹ came from the south sitting in a canoe.
      Ashiaklẹ, you are a quarrelsome person.
      Ashiaklẹ, they said that she is not good;
      She said that she is good.
      "I am the lord's child, I am the king's child, I am
         Nai's child, I am the sea's child;
      I have two gongs to give you."

Singer: Ashiaklẹ wulọmọ.
Occasion: Recording songs, 1968.

      Version 2
      Ataa Naa Nyọngmọ,
      Naibi Aklẹ ha wọ ngọngọi enyọ.
      Akẹẹ ehii kwraa.
      Naibi Aklẹ ha wọ ngọngọi enyọ.
      Akẹẹ ehii, shi ehi nọngng;
      Kingbi Aklẹ ehi nọngng;
      Aklẹ ehi nọngng.
      Gomua ngshra wọ, wọyẹ okuntshẹrẹfo bọ ntsirima;
      Aklẹ Dede, Gomua ngshra wọ, ekuntebi anọ;
      Gomua tsẹrẹa, okuntebi anọ.

God,
Nai's child Ashiaklẹ gave us two gongs.
They said that she is not good at all.
Nai's child Ashiaklẹ gave us two gongs.
They said that she is not good, but she is good;
The king's child Ashiaklẹ is good;
Ashiaklẹ is good.
The Gomua surround us, beat the military drums;
Ashiaklẹ, the Gomua surround us, turn into little
    stones;
The Gomua surround us, turn into little stones.

Singer: Olila wọngtsẹ.
Occasion: Singing for the *Ga mangtsẹ*, 1965.
Exegesis: Nai's people had no gong until *Ashiaklẹ* went to the
kpele people and borrowed a gong. Until this day *Nai's* worshippers do not use drums. The Gomua war was during the
reign of Amugi I [1811]. The Gomua, Akwapim, and Afutu
fought the Ga. When the Ga arrived for battle, they were surrounded by the Gomua forces. The Ga were saved, because
stones turned into human beings and fought with the Ga
against the Gomua.
Commentary: Ashiaklẹ is the eldest daughter of *Nai,* the god
of the sea. Her priest said that she is the goddess of wealth
(*shika,* "money") and that she is a mulatto (*yoo tsuru,* "red
woman"). When her priestess becomes possessed, she may
wear a white veil to symbolize her skin color.

Iron gongs are used to accompany *kpele* songs and dances
and to dispel supernatural beings. In *kpele* musical performances, "One or two gongs may be used, each one playing a
different rhythm pattern . . . in much the same way as drums
may be used, while maintaining a steady tempo" (Nketia,
"Traditional Music of the Ga People," p. 76). When *kpele* mediums travel, they use gongs to clear the road of spiritual beings. Thus, the *Olila* medium explained her use of the gong
while walking to the site of a ritual performance: "You saw
that when I struck, all the grass became cool, because something which was on the road went off it."

A third shorter version of the song was sung by *Kle agbaa-yoo* in 1968.

The words in these *kpele* texts are Ga, with the exception of the last three lines in Version 2.

[63]   Krempe, lo,
        Ayite Krempe ni okwẹẹmọ ni ohaa mọ.
        Angula shi Lome tsọtsọ;
        Klese tsọ Lome, nyangtsọ.

        Krempe, lo,
        Ayite Krempe you do not watch something for him.
        The Ewe have reached Lome little by little.
        Krempe called Lome, they are not there.

Singer: Olila wọngtsẹ.
Occasion: Checking *kpele* songs, 1968.
Exegesis: Ayite Krempe is a god. The gods call him *Klese;* people call him *Krempe.* Yes, little by little he killed everyone as he walked through the Ewe towns; the Ewe moved to the other side [of the Volta River]. Just as *Sakumọ* will speak, so this god, *Ayite Krempe*, speaks.
Commentary: Lome is the capital of modern Togo.

Another shorter version of the song, which *Kle agbaayoo* sang, was distorted through multilingual confusion (see Chapter 3).

The first two lines of the *kpele* text are in Ga.

[64]   Lomo,
        Obene Suẹ
        Lẹ emọ Osei
        Ni ehe egbadza.

        Prophet,
        Obene Suẹ
        He caught Osei
        And disarmed him.

Singer: Olila wǫngtsẹ.
Occasion: Singing for the *Ga mangtsẹ,* 1965.
Exegesis: This song refers to a war with Ashanti [1826]. A Ga caught the Ashanti chief Osei with the help of the warrior god, *Obene Suẹ.* Although human beings fight, the gods may change into human beings to assist them; victory, therefore, is attributed to the gods.
Commentary: The words of the *kpele* text are Ga.

[65] Tǫtroe, Akwamu adze mang.
      Ope Tǫtroe, bahe minanǫ;
      Ope Tǫtroe, batsi minanǫ.

      Tǫtroe, may the Akwamu leave the town.
      Tǫtroe, come and hear my prayer;[1]
      Tǫtroe, come and stop my mouth.

1. Lit., come and take it from my mouth.

Singer: Ashiaklẹ wulǫmǫ.
Occasion: Recording songs, 1968.
Commentary: Tǫtroe, *Nai's* son, associated with a rock on the Abola beach at Accra, is the "key of the sea" (*ngshǫ samfle*) or the bringer of fish. On Tuesday preceding *Lante Dzan we homǫwǫ, Nai wulǫmǫ* performs a rite (*ngshǫ bulemǫ*) to open the bream (*tsile*) fishing season. Bream is used in making *kpekpei,* the traditional *homǫwǫ* food which is shared with ancestral shades.

The first line of the song refers to the Akwamu domination of Accra 1681-1730.

The words in the *kpele* text are Ga.

[66] Tǫtroe,
      Kẹ loo aba wǫye.

      Tǫtroe,
      Bring fish that we may eat.

Singer: Ashiaklẹ wulọmọ.
Occasion: Recording songs, 1968.
Commentary: See song 65 for note on Tọtroẹ.
The words of the *kpele* text are Ga.

[67]   Oshi Koolo,
       Brẹ mi ade.

       Oshi Koolo,
       Bring me food.

Singer: Ashadu wọngtsẹ.
Occasion: Recording songs, 1968.
Commentary: Oshi Koolo is said to be a god.
The words of the *kpele* text are non-Ga.

[68]   Akẹ lẹ dido, akẹ lẹ mba.
       Ataamẹi awọng mba;
       Awomẹi awọng mba.

       She is heavy, they bring her.
       Fathers' god is coming;
       Mothers' god is coming.

Singer: Kle agbaayoo.
Occasion: Recording songs, 1968.
Exegesis: The god is *Naa Ede* [see song 47]. The woman who
is being carried died in childbirth; all dead people are heavy.
When a woman dies during pregnancy, after her burial the
family comes to *Naa Ede we* for ritual, so that such a calamity
may not recur in the family.
Commentary: The words in the *kpele* text are Ga.

[69]   Okrẹ Nyampong dzi onukpa.
       Awi, lo, mẹlomẹ;

Awi, lo, Awi atsẹ ni adzoo,
Awi, lo, mẹlomẹ;
Sakumọ, ngtsẹ wọ.
Awi, lo,
Naa Yoo, ngtsẹ wọ.
Awi, lo,
Tsade, ngtsẹ wọ.
Awi, lo,
Afutuokọ, ngtsẹ wọ.
Awi, lo,
Tsẹkẹtẹ, ngtsẹ wọ.

Great God is senior.
Awi, lo, a person knows a person;
Awi, lo, Awi is called before dancing.
Awi, lo, a person knows a person;
Sakumọ, I call you for us.
Awi, lo,
Naa Yoo, I call you for us.
Awi, lo,
Tsade, I call you for us.
Awi, lo,
Afutuokọ, I call you for us.
Awi, lo,
Tsẹkẹtẹ, I call you for us.

Singer: Ashadu wọngtsẹ.
Occasion: Recording songs, 1968.
Exegesis: When *Awi* calls us then we dance. *Awi* means the drummers who call us to dance [see note on *Awi*, song 15]. *Tsade* is a goddess; she is a river. All of them are gods.
Commentary: With the exception of *Awi*, all the gods mentioned in this song are worshipped by Tema cult groups. The singer who lives in Accra is the medium for another Tema god and was trained in Tema, as her songs reflect.

With respect to the second and third lines, E. A. Ammah writes:

Me lo me is an old expression, meaning in modern Ga, *mo le mo*, 'person knows person.' The hymn gives meaning to worship or religion in its social depth or inmost or intrinsic value: meeting between man and God. In the contact, man knows his fellow man, *mo le mo*, and both of them call or contact God through . . . His Son, *Awi* in dance or prayer [Ammah, "Ghanaian Philosophy," January 1962, p. 17].

The words of the *kpele* text are Ga.

[70]   Ayetei Aye eda moomo eda;
       Esho ngulami kpatsaa;
       Aye moomo Aye.
       Ayelemei miifo ngtse Gua;
       Gua moomo Gua.
       Ayekomei miifo ngtse Gua;
       Gua moomo Gua.
       Aye moomo Aye;
       Gua moomo Gua.

       Gua grew old long ago he grew;
       He created a cluster of stars;
       It is Gua of long ago Gua.
       Ayeles are weeping for Gua;
       It is Gua of long ago Gua.
       Ayekos are weeping for Gua;
       It is Gua of long ago Gua.
       It is Gua of long ago Gua.
       It is Gua of long ago Gua.

Singer: Olila wongtse.
Occasion: Recording songs, 1965.
Exegesis: Kpakpatse we people and other families with names like *Ayetei, Ayele,* and *Ayeko* are weeping for *Gua,* the god of smiths [see song 48]. *Gua* like other gods can change into a human being. When he changes into a person, he appears as a European at night in his shrine or under a tree.
Commentary: The words of the *kpele* text are Ga.

[71] Miba obǫ, Tsiribii Kolo,
Mi Nyǫngmǫ Tsalǫbii.

I came in full, Tsiribii Kolo,
With my children.

Singer: Olila wǫngtsę.
Occasion: Recording songs, 1965.
Exegesis: Tsiribi Kolo is one of the gods of smiths; it is lightning. *Nyǫngmǫ Tsalǫ* is the god of thunder; *Nyǫngmǫ Tsalǫbii* are his children, the elements which fall when thunder
sounds.
Commentary: In Accra, the cult of *Nyǫngmǫ Tsa*, a child of
Nai (see song 96), is the responsibility of *Krokoto we*, which
also provides a drummer for *Sakumǫ* rites. One informant said
that *Nyǫngmǫ Tsa* is one of the blacksmiths, a god of thunder
and lightning; another said that he is the figure which is seen
drumming in the moon. Field suggests that a *Nyǫngmǫ Tsa*
cult exists in every Ga town except Osu. She writes:

In Temma we met a goddess *Tshade* [see song 69]. The
suffix *de* to a Ga name denotes the eldest girl. The male
form of the name, *Tshawe*, recurs in Nungua ... in Labadi
and Teshi we find it as *Nyǫngmǫ Tshawe* and in Accra as
Nyongmǫ Tsha [Field, *Religion and Medicine*, p. 61].

The words of the *kpele* text are Ga.

[72] Awi hii ni.
Wanu anu, opele;
Wanu anu, opele ni opele;
Opele Awi hii ni.

The sun should not shine.
He wants rain, he pleads for it;
He wants rain, he pleads and pleads for it;
He pleads that the sun may not shine.

Singers: Dantu agbaa.

Occasion: Dantu ngmaadumọ, 1965.

Exegesis: Dantu begs God for rain. *Dantu* wants rain to fall, for the seed will not germinate without rain.

Commentary: This song, which is sung by the *Dantu agbaa* outside the shrine after they have returned from sowing the seed in the field, articulates the Ga belief that the gods intercede with God on behalf of human beings.

See songs 15 and 83 for notes on *Awi* and *Dantu,* respectively, and song 24 for an analogous *Sakumọ ngmaadumọ* song.

The words of the *kpele* text are said to be Ga.

[73]   Ashadu nuu tsuru,
         Ogbetserẹ kwọ ngwẹi,
         Etere ongwe.
         Obile nu ba.
         Obile Tẹtẹ Mampong miba.

         Ashadu is a red man,
         Ogbetserẹ climbs to the sky,
         He carries the Pleiades.
         Obile rain is coming.
         Obile Tẹtẹ Mampong is coming.

Singer: Ashadu wọngtsẹ.

Occasion: Recording songs, 1968.

Commentary: Ashadu is a *kpele* god who is worshipped at Tema and whose skin is said to be red or light in color.

The Pleiades (*ongwe*) are said to be seven shrines (*gbatsui*), the seven corners of the world (see Chapter 4). The month *ongwe,* April, in which the constellation appears, marks the commencement of the *kpele* agricultural rites and of the rainy season (*gbienaa*). See song 28 for an analogous song concerning the association between stars and seasonal rain.

The words of the *kpele* text are Ga.

[74] Klǫwe Ashi Ẹtẹ, ba wǫshwẹ dzoo;
   Klǫwe Ashi Ẹtẹ, bawo nyẹ wonu.
   Klǫwe Ashi Ẹtẹ dzẹ wuoyi.

   Klǫwe, come let us play the dance;
   Klǫwe, come and take your song.
   Klǫwe comes from the south.

Singer: Ashadu wǫngtsẹ.
Occasion: Recording songs, 1968.
Commentary: See song 53 for note on *Klǫwe.*
 The words of the *kpele* text are Ga, with the exception of *wonu.*

[75] Afumpe ngdang mpo daa;
   Miyẹ ohene daa.

   Afumpe I lean on the sea always;
   I am always a chief.

Singer: Kle agbaayoo.
Occasion: Recording songs, 1968.
Commentary: The words of the *kpele* text are Ga, with the
exception of *mpo* and *ohene.*

[76] Akẹẹ midzi Tẹnaa.
   Ataamẹi tee wuǫ, amẹ naa loo.
   Kẹ amẹ ba nunaa,
   Amẹ baana loo.

   They said I am Tẹnaa.
   The fathers went fishing, they did not catch any fish.
   When they come to the mouth of the river,
   They will get fish.

Singer: Kle agbaayoo.
Occasion: Recording songs, 1968.

Exegesis: This song is about *Kle*. *Kle* is a god at the village of Faanaa; he is associated with the river, *Tẹnaa* [lit., the mouth of a rock].
Commentary: The god *Kle* is a child of *Sakumọ* (see song 14). The words of the *kpele* text are Ga.

[77]   Nsu tọ mi hi da,
       Kane Abuakwa.

       Full of water always,
       Kane Abuakwa.

Singer: Olila wọngtsẹ.
Occasion: Checking *kpele* songs, 1968.
Exegesis: Kane, the god *Kaneshi*, is associated with a well which gives light. In this song, *Kane* says that whether it rains or not, I am always full of water.
Commentary: Kaneshi is *Naa Kọọle*'s child (song 14). Kaneshi, the site of the god's terrestrial location, was formerly a Ga village; it is now a suburb on the west of Central Accra.
   The words of the *kpele* text are non-Ga. Although *Kle agbaayoo* provided an identical text, she was unable to translate the words into Ga.

[78]   Odai dzatakpọ
       Mi ngto lẹ dzatakpọ.

       Sakumọ's well
       I dug the well.

Singer: Kle agbaayoo.
Occasion: Recording songs, 1968.
Commentary: The words of the *kpele* text are Ga.

[79]   Lemabu;
       Odai, mi ngto lẹ.

It is Lema's well;
Sakumǫ, I dug it.

Singer: Kle agbaayoo.
Occasion: Recording songs, 1968.
Commentary: The words of the *kpele* text are Ga.

[80]   Gbegbe, yaa oyaa lo?
Ba oba lo?
Gigǫng, gigǫng.

Gbegbe, are you going?
Are you coming?
You are limping, limping.

Singer: Kle agbaayoo.
Occasion: Recording songs, 1968.
Exegesis: Gbegbe is a god which is a spring used for drinking
water. The song says that the spring is not bubbling well.
Commentary: The words of the *kpele* text are Ga.

[81]   Ofosu eye edzwa wu mli.
Abaha aye.
Ngpa loo ko ni ye,
Tętę Ogriwu,
Kǫmi Tętę mba, tsina bu "Ooo."

Klang[1] eats broken bones.
They fight to eat.
I despise no meat that I eat.
Klang,
Klang is coming, cows cry "Ooo."

1. *Klang,* spotted hyena (*Crocuta crocuta*).

Singer: Asadu wǫngtsę.
Occasion: Recording songs, 1968.

Commentary: The cult of *Klang*, who is associated with the
spotted hyena, is the responsibility of the *Dzoshi* family,
which has branches in Accra, Labadi, and Teshi. *Klang*, a warrior god who walks before *Sakumo*, is one of the two *kpele*
gods whose mediums carry swords connoting the martial roles
of their gods.

A shorter version of the song, which varied in its expression
of similar ideas, was sung by *Kle agbaayoo* in 1968.

The words of the *kpele* text are Ga.

[82]   Okle dzengke, maba?
        Awo ahoo, maba?
        Dadefo.

        You vie with the world, why?
        They shout at you, why?
        It is the orchestra.

Singer: Olila agbaanuu.
Occasion: Recording songs, 1968.
Exegesis: Klang [song 81] asks her children why they always
fight against the world. Whenever they start to do something,
she shouts, "Do not do that, why do you behave so?"
Commentary: Dadefo and *fifianku* are synonyms for the collectivity of *kpele* musicians: three drummers (*miyiloi*), gong
players (*ngongotswabii*), *olai*, and other singers.

Kle agbaayoo provided a shorter text of the same song.
The words of this *kpele* text are Ga.

[83]   Oshaka, oshaka Dade Aku.
        Le ewoko le.

        Fondle, fondle Dade Aku.
        He fondles her.

Singer: Dantu agbaa.
Occasion: Dantu ngmaadumo, 1965.

Commentary: Dantu, the time keeper, is worshipped by *Lante Dzan we.* His agricultural rites initiate the cycle in Accra. His appellations are: God of long ago, you eat first (*Able Dada, oye ni ko*); God of the container [in which seed is stored] (*Kafu wong*); Herald, first god (*Oka, klengkleng budu*). *Dade Aku* is one of his wives.

At *ngmaadumo,* after the *agbaa* returns from the field where they have planted seed, they dance in a circle outside the shrine. As they dance, they alternately sing this song and song 134.

This song expresses the analogy between divine sexuality and agricultural fertility more explicitly than any other in the collection.

The words of the *kpele* text are Ga.

[84]   Ahu dzengamo oba Dzaadzaabi too,
         Dzaadzaabi doo.
         Dzaadzaabi le solopango.

         Ahu at night you come to sleep with Dzaadzaabi,
         To sleep with Dzaadzaabi.
         Dzaadzaabi is not a horse.

Singer: Koole agbaayoo.
Occasion: Recording songs, 1968.
Exegesis: Ahu's wife is *Dzaadzaabi,* and so he loves her. She told him that she is not a horse; she insults him. She says that all his wives are being dragged by a rope, but she is not a horse. They are quarreling, because she is jealous of her co-wife.
Commentary: Ahu is *Ahulu,* a divine messenger, who is associated with the tortoise (*Kinixyo erosa*).
    The words of the *kpele* text are Ga.

[85]   Ekue tangtang ake ashataa;
         Koole Abooyoo aboomle.

Her neck is as ugly as the fan palm;[1]
Lady Koọle you are called to come.

1. Ga, *weidzo*, fan palm (*Borassus aethiopium*).

Singer: Olila wọngtsẹ.
Occasion: Recording songs, 1968.
Exegesis: This song is sung to insult *Naa Koọle* by her co-wife
Ogbede, who is at Labadi. *Ogbede* says that *Koọle's* neck is
ugly; this is beating-war-talk (*shitawie*).
Commentary: This song and the two following are sung as a
set of hostile exchanges between *Sakumọ's* wives, *Koọle* (song
14) and *Ogbede*, who is associated with the Kpeshi Lagoon.
Another shorter version of the song was sung by *Kle agbaa-
yoo* in 1968.
The words in the *kpele* text are Ga, with the exception of
ashataa and *aboomle*.

[86]   Yakẹẹ Ogbede, mi nọ onaafẹ,
        Toimulọ.

        Go tell Ogbede, I put excrement in your mouth,
        Deaf one.

Singer: Olila wọngtsẹ.
Occasion: Recording songs, 1968.
Commentary: Koọle responds to the taunts of her co-wife
Ogbede (see song 85).
The words of the *kpele* text are Ga.

[87]   Minyọọ La ngoo;
        Akẹ mi tshake sẹbẹ kẹ engmọmi;
        Midzee La ngoo.

        I am not Labadi salt;
        They do not exchange me for garden-eggs and okra;
        I am not Labadi salt.

Singer: Olila wǫngtsẹ.
Occasion: Recording songs, 1968.
Exegesis: So Kǫǫle insults Ogbede again. "As for me, I am not Labadi salt; they do not exchange me for garden-eggs and okra." Formerly, people got salt there [at Kpeshi Lagoon] and exchanged it for okra and garden-eggs [a small variety of eggplant].
Commentary: The words of the *kpele* text are Ga.

[88]   Afieye he yẹ fẹẹǫ tsǫ.

Afieye is exceptionally beautiful.

Singer: Possessed medium.
Occasion: Nai ngmaafaa, 1968.
Commentary: For every male god in the sky, there is a corresponding earth goddess, *Afieye*, who is his wife (see Chapter 4). *Afieye* are associated with termite mounds (*gbǫtsuii*), which are thought to be the entrances to their subterranean homes, and with crossroads (*gbeteng*), because beautiful women do not hide themselves from public view (see song 31 for a note on crossroads).

The words of the *kpele* text are Ga.

[89]   *Version 1*
       Afieye Odame ni,
       Afieye Odame fa;
       Afieye Odame efee nine.

       Afieye Odame,
       Ngshwa akukui;
       Akukui sa mi.

       Afieye Odame,
       Ngwo akǫndǫ;
       Akǫndǫ sa mi.

Afieye Odame,
Ngwo afli;
Afli sa mi.

Afieye Odame,
Ngwo nyanyara;
Nyanyara sa mi.

Afieye Odame,
Ngwo awoyoo;
Awoyo sa mi.

Afieye Odame,
Ngbu bo he.
Bo he egblashi.

It is Afieye Odame.
Afieye Odame are many;
Afieye Odame are more than enough.

Afieye Odame,
I braid the kpele hairstyle;
The kpele hairstyle befits me.

Afieye Odame,
I put on a necklace;
The necklace befits me.

Afieye Odame,
I put on a bracelet;
The bracelet befits me.

Afieye Odame,
I put on a garland of nyanyara leaves;
The nyanyara leaves befit me.

Afieye Odame,
I put on an anklet;
The anklet befits me.

Afieye Odame,
I put on a new cloth;
The new cloth touches the ground.

Singer: Akumadze Afieye wǫngtsę.
Occasion: Recording songs, 1968.
Commentary: Afieye Odame is the son of an *Afieye* (song 88). In this version the accoutrements which he enumerates are those of a *kpele* medium. *Akukui (akukuru)* refers to a medium's hairstyle; the hair is braided in five cones to represent the five corners of the world, which the *kpele* gods support (see Chapter 4). Atop the center cone is placed a parrot feather entwined with the tip of an elephant's tail. This ornament is intended to facilitate possession. A parrot feather is utilized because the parrot is a talking bird and the feather is said to connote peace; the elephant tail is used because the big, strong elephant represents the Ga people.

Akǫndǫ refers to the short necklace of multicolored beads which mediums may wear.

Afli includes the long necklace, bracelets, and anklets which consist either of white beads or of alternating black and white beads. At the bottom of the necklace are two tiny metal horns (*kablę*) which are blown to ward off mystical danger or to summon a deity (see song 62).

Nyanyara is the plant which is used not only in *kpele* rites but in Ga political ceremonies. Unfortunately, I have been unable to classify this plant. The leaf, which may be worn as a garland by ritual performers and always constitutes one of the components of ritual bath water (*bawo*), is a symbol of Ga identity. The *Olila* medium described the significance of the plant in the following words: "The leaf has existed from creation; it is for all Ga gods; it is the jewelry of a chief. And so when a rite is performed, the *Ga mangtsę* does not put on gold, [for] our gods and the sea are gold. And so we do not use red gold. *Nyanyara* is a blessing. And so it is used in all our rites; it is worth more than gold, it comes from the sky itself. *Nyanyara* is a blessing. *Nyanyara* is peace. Its blessing is greater than that of any other leaf; it is the senior one among all the leaves." Another informant said that *nyanyara*'s power is greater than that of a tree, because it is a vine which not only gets nourishment from the sun and the earth but hangs as a tree cannot.

Awoyoo pertains to the metal anklets which mediums wear at ritual dances. When mediums dance, the anklets rattle. As discussed in Chapter 5, Ga believe that contact with immortal beings can be achieved through percussive sounds. Consequently, when mediums wear these anklets at ritual dances, they aspire to induce possession by their gods.

Bo refers to the white waist-cloth worn by a medium. When a medium becomes possessed, her cloth is changed and some of these items are removed lest she be injured by them or they be lost. The objects which are removed include the parrot's-feather ornament and the metal anklets.

A possessed medium at *Nai ngmaafaa* in 1968 sang a shorter version of this song.

The words of the *kpele* text are Ga.

> *Version 2*
> Abia Taki—
> Afieye Odame
> Bu koto;
> Koto sa lẹ.
>
> Afieye Odame
> Wo nyanyara;
> Nyanyara sa lẹ.
>
> Afieye Odame
> Wo kọmi;
> Kọmi sa lẹ.
>
> Afieye Odame
> Wo afli;
> Afli sa lẹ.
>
> Afieye Odame
> Wo ngmọkọ;
> Ngmọkọ sa lẹ.
>
> Ga mangtsẹ—
> Afieye Odame
> Puts on a priest's hat;
> The priest's hat befits him.

Afieye Odame
Puts on a nyanyara garland;
The nyanyara garland befits him.

Afieye Odame
Puts on a fiber necklace;
The fiber necklace befits him.

Afieye Odame
Puts on a bracelet;
The bracelet befits him.

Afieye Odame
Puts on a beaded belt;
The belt befits him.

Singer: Olila wǫngtsę.
Occasion: Recording songs, 1965.
Commentary: In this song *Afieye Odame*, the god of hunting, describes his dress, which is that of a *kpele* priest.

Koto is the term for the hats worn by chiefs and priests; these hats are made of rush (*woma*) or raffia (*so*).

Kǫmi is a long necklace of raffia worn at *kpele* agricultural rites by priests and sometimes by *agbaa* members and mediums.

Ngmǫkǫ is a "sash of precious beads" worn by *Otu* cult members.

See version 1 for notes on *nyanyara* and *afli.*

The words of the *kpele* text are Ga.

[90]   Afieye yoo kpakpa;
        Efa mǫ nibii,
        Etutua sabi.

        Afieye is a good woman;
        She uprooted things;
        She uprooted things.

Singer: Olila wǫngtsę.
Occasion: Discussion of trip to Ayawaso, 1968.
Exegesis: Afieye (song 88) shows how beautiful she is by revealing herself naked. When an *Afieye* medium is possessed, she usually sings this song.
Commentary: The words of the *kpele* text are Ga, with the exception of the third line.

[91]　　*Version 1*
　　　　Oma ni mo, gbętsę;
　　　　Ni oma ni mo, gbętsę.
　　　　Oma ni mo, gbętsę;
　　　　Niimęi anane kę wǫ tsęmęi anane dzio.

　　　　Congratulate, father of the road,
　　　　And congratulate, father of the road.
　　　　Congratulate, father of the road,
　　　　Grandfathers' messenger and our fathers'
　　　　　　messenger he is.

Singer: Olila wǫngtsę.
Occasion: Recording songs, 1965.
Commentary: In the *kpele* text, the fourth line and *gbętsę* are Ga.

　　　　Version 2
　　　　Ma ni moę, gbętsę,
　　　　Wǫwǫi adzangmęi baamale.

　　　　Congratulate, father of the road,
　　　　Gods' followers will tell lies.

Singer: Kǫǫle agbaayoo.
Occasion: Recording songs, 1968.
Commentary: The second line of the *kpele* text is in Ga.

[92]   Ahulu dzẹ ngwẹng,
       Bata wọ sane;
       Nyọngma shishiishi.

       Ahulu came from the sky,
       And told us a story;
       It was the truth.[1]

1. Lit., it is precisely ten.

Singer: Olila wọngtsẹ.
Occasion: Recording songs, 1965.
Exegesis: Ahulu [see song 84] is a messenger of the gods.
Whatever he says from the sky is true.
Commentary: The words of the *kpele* text are Ga.

[93]   Susu mufahada?
       Bọni odzeng ebaa nakai?

       How do you think that it does not happen so?
       How do you think that it does not happen so?

Singer: Olila wọngtsẹ.
Occasion: Recording songs, 1965.
Commentary: This song, which was sung after song 92, continues the theme of the truthfulness of *Ahulu*, the divine messenger.
    The second line of the *kpele* text is in Ga.

[94]   Ahulu Bẹsẹ Ahulu,
       Mbọ lale mbọ tsẹdi atọọ;
       Mifa shika to Ama Oplabi.
       Dzee Dede dzi mi;
       Debi yẹ amane ni dzi minaa kọsha.
       Mito ankwa; mikẹẹ
       Na shikpọng, na ngwẹi.

Ahulu Bẹsẹ Ahulu,
I come to speak, I do not come to deceive;
I lent money to Ama Oplabi.
I am not Dede;
Debi has trouble which is my evil mouth.
I hold the truth; I said
Lo earth, lo sky.

Singer: Akumadze Afieye wọngtsẹ.
Occasion: Recording songs, 1968.
Exegesis: Ahulu says, "I come to speak, but I do not come to gossip." He says that he went somewhere and saw something with his eyes.
Commentary: This song continues the theme of *Ahulu*, the truthful messenger, who reports the events he has witnessed.

Another shorter version of this song was sung by *Kọọle agbaayoo* in 1968, which differs slightly in the ideas which it expresses.

With the exception of the second line, the words of the *kpele* text are Ga.

[95]   Shwila, Oshwila, Oshwila,
Oshwila, gbo ogbo lo loo wọ owọ lo?

Afutu kẹẹ enyangta;
Ayigbe kẹẹ egblẹ;
Gamẹi kẹẹ ehii.

Shwila, Oshwila, Oshwila,
Oshwila, gbo ogbo lo loo wọ owọ lo?

Oshwila mingkpa ade mangka.
Oshwila gbo ogbo lo loo wọ owọ lo?
Oshwila wọ owọọ lo?

Oshwila nte mingka.
Ayoo mungka?
Misẹrẹ alọbi.

Oshwila mingkpa ade mangka.
Oshwila gbo ogbo lo loo wọ owọọ lo?
Oshwila wọ owọọ lo;

Miti mibua;
Okomfo Aku Lomo, miti mibua.

Oshwila mingkpa ade mangka.
Oshwila gbo ogbo lo loo wọ owọọ lo?
Oshwila wọ owọọ lo?

Afutu kẹẹ enyangta;
Ayigbe kẹẹ egblẹ;
Gamẹi kẹẹ ehii.

Shwila, Oshwila, Oshwila,
Oshwila, are you dead or are you sleeping?

Afutu say it is destroyed;
Ewe say it is destroyed;
Ga say it is destroyed.

Shwila, Oshwila, Oshwila,
Oshwila, are you dead or are you sleeping?

Oshwila sings at dawn.
Oshwila, are you dead or are you sleeping?
Oshwila are you sleeping?

Oshwila sings at dawn.
Do you hear him?
I will soar to the stars.

Oshwila sings at dawn.
Oshwila, are you dead or are you sleeping?
Oshwila are you sleeping?

When I hear, I do not decide immediately.
Okomfo Aku Lomo, when I hear, I do not decide
    immediately.

Oshwila sings at dawn.
Oshwila, are you dead or are you sleeping?
Oshwila are you sleeping?

Afutu say it is destroyed;
Ewe say it is destroyed;
Ga say it is destroyed.

Singer: Olila wǫngtsę.
Occasion: Recording songs, 1965.
Exegesis (*Olila olai*): *Oshwila* speaks. After a war, when one looks at the dead, one says that it is bad. *Oshwila* is calling the gods, have they been sleeping during the war? *Oshwila* does not talk until he hears both sides of a dispute. *Oshwila* tells *Lomo* that he must not say what he has not heard. *Oshwila* is a true prophet, for he only says what he hears.
Commentary: See songs 16 and 55 for notes on *Oshwila* and prophets, respectively.

This *kpele* text combines Ga and non-Ga words, not only in different lines, but sometimes in the same line. The lines with Ga lexemes are 1, 2, 5, 6, 7, 9, 10,. 15, 16, 20, 21, 24; the non-Ga lines are 12, 13, 17, 18; the lines which combine Ga and non-Ga words are 3, 4, 8, 11, 14, 19, 22, 23.

Two shorter versions of the song were sung by *Olila agbaa-nuu* and *Akumadze Afieye wǫngtsę* in 1968. The *Olila agbaa-nuu*'s version contains two lines, which are lines 8 and 10 in the version presented here. Thus, the *kpele* text of his version is: "Oshwila mingkpa ade mangka./ Oshwila wǫ owǫǫ lo?" When asked for an interpretation of the song, the *Olila agbaa-nuu* said, "*Oshwila* is at Dzongkobli at Okai Koi [hill]'. And so if something happens, he will tell us. If anything happens, the story will be told to *Oshwila* and he will come to see Okai Koi or our ancestors [*wǫ blema sisai*, "our ancient ghosts"]. You see, they are two: Okai Koi and *Oshwila*. *Oshwila* is a god, but Okai Koi is a person. There is also Opoku Adzimang; his god is *Oshwila*. If anything harms him, he will inform *Oshwila*. Something has hurt Opoku Adzimang and so he sang this song; he said '*Oshwila*, are you sleeping;'"

The *Akumadze Afieye wǫngtsę*'s version was based on four substantive lines, lines 1, 8, and 9 of the above text and a fourth line, "Oshwila I know, I do not know" (*Shwila le ni nglee*). Thus, the *kpele* text of her version is: "Shwila, Oshwila, Oshwila,/ Oshwila mingkpa ade mangka./ Oshwila gbo ogbo lo loo wǫ owǫǫ lo?/ Shwila le ni nglee." The medium explained the first three lines, "So *Oshwila* cries, 'Are you dead or are you sleeping?' *Oshwila* cries so, because he is calling the people behind." She said that the fourth line meant, "He heard a sound, but he did not know whether or not it was the people behind him."

The text and the exegetical statements express clearly the Ga belief that the *kpele* gods protect Ga people.

[96]   Bosobro mi kafo mi yę dę;
        Bosobro amralobi;
        Bosobro wǫyę sęęteng.
        Bosobro amralobi;
        Bonso wǫdiri mang.
        Bosobro amralobi;
        Amralobi wǫdiri mang.
        Bosobro amralobi;
        Kingbi wǫdiri mang.
        Bosobro amralobi;
        Shitsę wodiri mang.

        Nai I do not praise my sweetness;
        Nai is the ruler;
        Nai we have many children.
        Nai is the ruler;
        The whale rules the town.
        Nai is the ruler;
        The ruler rules the town.
        Nai is the ruler;
        The king rules the town.
        Nai is the ruler;
        The land owner rules the town.

Singer: Ashiaklę wulǫmǫ.
Occasion: Recording songs, 1968.
Exegesis: When they sow millet, what do they sing that shows a certain chief at the riverside?

Commentary: After *ngmaadumǫ, Nai agbaa* sings this song at various houses in Accra to announce the beginning of the three-week ban on noise (see song 133).

Nai, the highest ranking god at Accra, is the god of the sea. His cult group, *Nai we,* is said to have lived at coastal Accra before other Ga fled from Okai Koi Hill. These conceptions are expressed in his appellations: Owner of the land (*shitsę; mę wura odoma*); King of kings (*kingbi king*); Lord of lords (*amralobi amralo*); *Nai* you cut your tree on the ground (i.e., first settler, *Nai bo ofo tso ongmaashii*); You kill always (*ogbe dada*); He cleanses and dirties the shore (*afunya*). *Nai*'s children are said to include the creatures of the sea and divine beings associated with rocks on the shore or in the sea: *Amugi, Oyeni, Ashiaklę, Abledede, Ablekǫkǫ, Tǫtroe, Osekan, Mamang, Obutu,* and *Nyǫngmǫ Tsa.*

In this song, *Nai*'s superiority over other gods is conveyed through metaphors of seniority which are based on physical phenomena (*bosobro,* "sea"), animals (*bonso,* "whale"), and social categories (*shitsę,* "land owner"; *kingbi king,* "king of kings"; *wǫyę sęę teng,* "we have many offspring"). Each of which represents seniority within its category: the whale is the largest sea creature, the sea is the most extensive topographical feature, and the land owner has precedence over other members of the community. Through these metaphors of physical and social magnitude, *Nai*'s high status among other gods is expressed.

This multilingual *kpele* text includes some Ga words, such as *mi, kafo, wǫyę sęę teng, mang,* and *shitsę;* some European loan words, such as *amralo-bi* and *king-bi;* and some words from other African languages, such as *yę dę* and *wǫdiri.*

[97]   Nai kǫte ni ba mi.
       Nai, Ogbe Dada, efǫ mi.
       Nai, Ogbe Dada, womi.

       Nai's penis brought [begat] me.
       Nai, you kill always, begat me.
       Nai, you kill always, begat me.

Singer: *Ashiakle wulomo.*
Occasion: Recording songs, 1968.
Exegesis: This is the boast of one of *Nai's* children [see song 96].
Commentary: This song illustrates the use of anthropomorphic imagery to characterize the physiological attributes and relations of divine beings, discussed in Chapter 4.

The words of the *kpele* text are Ga.

[98]   Nai, Ogbe Dada, mutoi;
        Afowo mutoi ni ahe wo.

        Nai, you kill always, is deaf;
        While he was deaf, he begat us and he bought us.

Singer: *Ashiakle wulomo.*
Occasion: Recording songs, 1968.
Exegesis: The sea is deaf; he eats, he kills; he begets a person; he goes with us and he comes with us. He does not hear a person speak. Look, as we are talking now, if we were nearer the sea, the words that we speak could not be heard. The sound of the sea blocks our ears; it shows his greatness; it shows how he is.
Commentary: See song 96 for note on *Nai.*

The notion of *Nai* as a god for free man and slave is also expressed for *Sakumo* in song 50.

The words of the *kpele* text are Ga.

[99]   Opete Kwatse Kotsiakong,
        Miwo ade;
        Miwo abosua.
        Onipa ni hu;
        Midi fifiankuhene.
        Omang beshwe.
        Ayoko Adu Dunkai,
        Nkra beshwe.

Opete Kwatse Kotsiakong,
I have possessions;
I have family.
Anyone who has not seen me, come and see;
I rule over the orchestra.
May the people come and see.
Ayoko Adu Dunkai,
May Accra come and see.

Singer: Abudu wulomo.
Occasion: Recording songs, 1965.
Exegesis: Kotsiakong is a goddess under *Abudu* [see songs 14
and 61]. She has things and people; she asserts her royal sta-
tus; she invites people to come to see her.
Commentary: See song 82 for note on *fifianku.*
The words of the *kpele* text are non-Ga, with the exception
of *omang.*

[100] Olila moomo Olila;
       Olila, ngye ni aba;
       Olila moomo Olila.

       Olila of old Olila;
       Olila, I was before they came;
       Olila of old Olila;

Singer: Olila wongtse.
Occasion: Recording songs, 1965.
Exegesis: Olila [song 14] existed before all the other gods.
Commentary: The words of the *kpele* text are Ga.

[101] Opobi, Opobi, Opobi, Opobi,
       Miye bokaibi.
       Opobi, Opobi, Opobi, Opobi,
       Miye tsafalobi.
       Agbe wuo hu, miyee;

Ni agbe shwǫ hu, miyee;
Akrama gbe wuo hu, miyee;
Ogbe loo fęę, miyee.
Miye bǫkaibi.

Opobi, Opobi, Opobi, Opobi,
I eat the blue shark.[1]
Opobi, Opobi, Opobi, Opobi,
I eat the blue shark.
When they kill a fowl, I do not eat it;
And when they kill an elephant[2] also, I do not eat it;
When Opobi kills a bushcow[3] also, I do not eat it;
If you kill any animal, I do not eat it.
I eat the blue shark.

1. *Tsaflǫbi/bǫkaibi,* blue shark (*Scoliodon terrae novae*).
2. *Shwǫ,* elephant (*Loxodonta africana*).
3. *Wuo,* bushcow (*Syncerus caffer beddingtoni*).

Singer: Olila wǫngtsę.
Occasion: Discussion of *kpele* gods, 1968.
Exegesis: Tsaflǫbi, the gods call it *bǫngkalebi. Opobi* is *Akrama.* The meaning of the song is that *Opobi* is a hunter who kills animals. And so he does not like any of the animals that he kills; if he eats them, it is not good for him. He eats only the blue shark.
Commentary: Opobi or *Akrama* is a hunter and a warrior whose grove is near the foot of Okai Koi Hill. In his martial role, he carries a sword like *Klang;* in his hunting role, he carries a bow and arrow.

In this song, *Opobi* asserts that he prefers to eat blue shark, a large species which subsists primarily on other fish (Irvine, *The Fishes and Fisheries of the Gold Coast,* p. 88). Although I could not get a satisfactory explanation of this food preference from Ga informants, a number of points are relevant. First, the food preference per se represents a form of anthropomorphism. In human society, individuals avoid certain foods either as a requirement of their social statuses or as a means of avoiding physical illness. The *Olila* medium's exegetical comments suggest that the latter interpretation pertains to *Opobi's* food preference. Secondly, since *Opobi* is a forest hunter, he does not kill blue shark himself. This fact has a number of implications. It means that he does not kill animals to satisfy his own subsistence requirements, but the needs of others who may be gods or men. Further, in order for him to obtain blue shark, someone must bring it to him. A person who wishes to achieve propitious contact with *Opobi*, therefore, would be well advised to sacrifice a blue shark to him. Catching the fish would be a difficult and possibly dangerous task, for the mature shark may be eight feet in length. The person who wishes to please *Opobi* by presenting blue shark to him involves himself in a hazardous situation. I observed one sacrifice at *Opobi's* shrine which utilized a white fowl rather than a blue shark.

The words of the *kpele* text are Ga.

[102]   Ode Akrama Ode
        Na mi shi enyọ.

        Opobi
        Give it to me twice.

Singer: Olila wọngtsẹ.
Occasion: Recording songs, 1968.
Exegesis: Opobi said to give him just two fowls. He has already said that he eats nothing [song 101], but when someone said that they wanted to give him something, he said to give him just two fowls.
Commentary: In *kpele* worship, the sincerity of the officiant who performs a sacrificial act is conveyed through double prestations (see Chapter 5).

The words of the *kpele* text are Ga.

[103]   Dantu Able Dade,
        Bo ole dzuuhe,
        Ni ole faahe.

        Dantu,
        You know the stealing place,
        And you know the borrowing place.

Singer: Kle agbaayoo.
Occasion: Recording songs, 1968.
Exegesis: It means that this senior god knows the place where
he will go to get things to eat. You see that he knows the bor-
rowing place and the stealing place so that they will have
things to eat.
Commentary: This song refers to *Dantu* (see song 83) as the
initiator of agricultural tasks. Since *Dantu* begins to work his
field first, he must know where the seed can be obtained.
Moreover, since Ga believe that the gods in the sky perform
the same tasks as men on the earth, the song refers not only to
Dantu's activities but to those of his cult group, which ini-
tiates the annual set of agricultural rites in Accra.
    The words of the *kpele* text are Ga.

[104]   Kǫǫle minam abente;
        Okle dzengke;
        Nami atia, ye.
        Dede odiko,
        Kǫǫle nami atia, ye;
        Minam abente.

        Kǫǫle is a warrior;
        She is omnipresent;
        She is carried by dwarfs, it is good.
        Dede she cooks for you.
        Kǫǫle is carried by dwarfs, it is good;
        She is a warrior.

Singer: Kɔɔle agbaa.
Occasion: Kɔɔle ngmaadumo, 1965.
Exegesis: Gods may appear as dwarfs. *Kɔɔle* [see song 14] cooks for people to enjoy the food. Although there may not be much food, many people will eat it; the food will never be finished.
Commentary: This song is sung by *Kɔɔle agbaa* as they return from the field where they have planted the millet seed.

Although Ga do not attribute special powers to human dwarfs, they believe that there is a class of immortal beings *(adope)* who resemble tiny human beings. These dwarfs, who live in the bush and often in termite mounds, know about the medicinal properties of plants. When a human being approaches, the dwarfs vanish. Sometimes, however, a person can observe their activities without seeing them. One informant claimed that he had seen the game *wari* being played by invisible dwarfs and that he had seen fire being carried by them into the bush. Ga say that frequently gods manifest themselves as dwarfs, though they may assume any form.

The words of the *kpele* text are non-Ga, with the exception of *Kɔɔle* and *Dede.*

[105]   Dudɔ, lo,
        Kɔɔle edudɔ;
        Afɔ awo lɛ ni ahe awo lɛ.

        The lagoon, lo,
        It is Kɔɔle's lagoon;
        They are born for her and they are bought for her.

Singer: Kɔɔle agbaayoo.
Occasion: Recording songs, 1968.
Commentary: The notion of a deity being for all people, which pertains to all gods, is expressed also for *Sakumɔ* and *Nai* in songs 50 and 98, respectively.

The *kpele* text of the song is in Ga.

[106] *Version 1*
Miwoa ḳotuẹ ni ngkẹ fo shwila;
Shwila nyẹẹ mi.

I wore afli to cross the Volta River;
The Volta River cannot defeat me.

Singer: Ḳoọle agbaayoo.
Occasion: Recording songs, 1968.
Exegesis: She said that she wore ḳotuẹ to cross the Volta River. We Ga call ḳotuẹ, afli.
Commentary: See song 89 for a discussion of afli and koto. The words of the kpele text are Ga.

Version 2
Ngọngọi enyọ amẹ fo
Shwila Aku;
Wọngya wọyakwe.

With two gongs they are crossing
The Volta River;[1]
We are going to see.

1. *Aku* is a name for a person who is born on Wednesday.

Singer: Kle agbaayoo.
Occasion: Recording songs, 1968.
Commentary: See song 62 for note on the utilization of gongs by kpele musicians and mediums.
The words of this kpele text are Ga.

[107] Nsu su mi, Ogbame,
Midamọ Olẹwu nọ;
Nsu su mi.

Water drowns me, Ogbame,
I stand on Olẹwu;
Water drowns me.

Singer: Kle agbaayoo.

Occasion: Recording songs, 1968.

Exegesis: Ogbame is standing on a hill, the water is rising, and he is drowning.

Commentary: According to the *Olila* medium, the god *Ogbame* is *Sakumo*'s slave, "but truly we do not know where he bought him. It is a creation story." By which she means that it is a *kpele* belief that *Ogbame* is *Sakumo*'s slave. Ga differentiate *kpele* gods from those of other cults by saying that the former have existed from the time of creation (*adebo*) and that the latter have been bought (*he*) from other cultures. The usual way to identify the cult of an unfamiliar god, however, is to inquire "what food it eats" (*meni eye*). If the god eats millet (*ngmaa*), it is a *kpele* god; if it eats yam (*yele*), it is not a *kpele* god.

The second line of the *kpele* text is in Ga.

Ritual Performance

This group of songs concerns various aspects of ritual performance through which human beings attempt to achieve contact with divine beings. The songs in this section are grouped together because they express ideas about ritual performance; their performance, however, is not restricted to ritual events. While most of the songs relate to ritual actions, some concern specific agricultural rites and ritual objects. The songs pertaining to ritual action are ordered to express the sequence of events at a *kpele* dance: the appropriate time for ritual has come and gods and men gather (songs 108-114), the drummers are called (songs 115-119), the gods possess their mediums (songs 120-127), the gods depart, and the performers go home (songs 128-131). These songs are followed by several songs which refer to particular annual rites, such as *ngmaa-dumo̧*, *ho̧mo̧wo̧*, *mangnaamo̧*, and *ngmaatoo* (songs 132-140). The remaining songs concern various ritual structures and objects: the fence and entrance of a shrine, incense, drums, stools, and the accoutrements of a medium (songs 141-147).

[108]   Obene Asere obene; Asere obene anyado.
       Asere Kotopong, ba kami mia.
       Obene Asere obene; Asere obene anyado.
       Ganyo Ayite, ba kami mia.
       Obene Asere obene; Asere obene anyado.
       Kotokpe, anyado.

Obene Asere obene; Asere obene anyado.
Ope Nyampong, ba kami mia.
Obene Asere obene; Asere obene anyado.
Boi Tono, ba kami mia.
Obene Asere obene; Asere obene anyado.
Kuọkọ Adzimang, ba kami mia.
Obene Asere obene; Asere obene anyado.
Ayi Kushi, ba kami mia.
Obene Asere obene; Asere obene anyado.
Mamate, ba kami mia.
Obene Asere obene; Asere obene anyado.

The new year is due, Asere, the new year is due;
  Asere, the new year is due, come and count
  your children.
Asere Kotopong, come and count your children.
The new year is due, Asere, the new year is due;
  Asere, the new year is due, come and count
  your children.
Ga person Ayite, come and count your children.
The new year is due, Asere, the new year is due;
  Asere, the new year is due, come and count
  your children.
Kotokpe, come and count your children.
The new year is due, Asere, the new year is due;
  Asere, the new year is due, come and count
  your children.
God, come and count your children.
The new year is due, Asere, the new year is due;
  Asere, the new year is due, come and count
  your children.
Boi Tono, come and count your children.
The new year is due, Asere, the new year is due;
  Asere, the new year is due, come and count
  your children.
Kuọkọ Adzimang, come and count your children.
The new year is due, Asere, the new year is due;
  Asere, the new year is due, come and count
  your children.

Ayi Kushi, come and count your children.
The new year is due, Asere, the new year is due;
　Asere, the new year is due, come and count
　your children.
Earth, come and count your children.
The new year is due, Asere, the new year is due;
　Asere, the new year is due, come and count
　your children.

Singer: Olila wǫngtsẹ.
Occasion: Recording songs, 1965.
Exegesis: The song shows that the sacred year is about to begin.
Commentary: In this song various natural features, deities,
and historical personalities are called to assist human beings
in the performance of agricultural rites. Asere, one of the sev-
en quarters of Accra, was founded by the Ga who fled from
Great Accra to the coast in 1677. *Kotokpe* is the god of the
Clottey family of Asere. According to tradition, Ayi Kushi
and Ayite were the first and second *Ga mangtsẹmẹi* at Great
Accra, Kuǫkǫ Adzimang was the wife of Nikoi Olai, the
brother of Dǫde Akabi, and Boi Tono of *Nai we* was the chief
of coastal Accra in 1734 to whom the Dutch gave authority
to collect duty from European trading vessels.
　Apart from the names, the words of the *kpele* text are non-
Ga.

[109]　Oshwila Adu Kǫme,
　　　　Kǫme olai,
　　　　Ngtsẹ awonyo.
　　　　Ganyo Ayi,
　　　　Ngtsẹ awonyo.
　　　　Lomo,
　　　　Ngtsẹ awonyo.
　　　　Lomo Ama,
　　　　Ngtsẹ awonyo.
　　　　Okai,

Ngtsẹ awonyo.
Lumo Okai,
Ngtsẹ awonyo.
Afi eshẹ, agbaamẹi,
Ngtsẹ awonyo.
Anan Lomo Anan,
Ngtsẹ awonyo.
Aklẹ,
Ngtsẹ awonyo.
Aflan,
Ngtsẹ awonyo.

Sakumọ,
Sakumọ's singer,
I call for the sacred dance.
Ga person Ayi,
I call for the sacred dance.
Prophet,
I call for the sacred dance.
Prophet Ama,
I call for the sacred dance.
Okai,
I call for the sacred dance.
Prince Okai,
I call for the sacred dance.
The year has come, agbaa,
I call for the sacred dance.
Prophet Anan,
I call for the sacred dance.
Ashiaklẹ,
I call for the sacred dance.
Aflan,
I call for the sacred dance.

Singer: Olila wọngtsẹ.
Occasion: Recording songs, 1965.
Commentary: The time for the performance of agricultural
rites has arrived and various transcendental beings are called

to participate in the rites: *Sakumo* (see song 14), *Ashiakle* (see song 62), prophets (see song 55), former chiefs and elders who include Ayi, Okai, and Aflan, the son of Ayite (see song 108).

In this song, *awonyo* (see song 89) refers not simply to the anklet which mediums wear at *kpele* dances but to the dance performance itself.

The words in this *kpele* text are Ga.

[110]   Mi kong ma Nyampong,
         Nami ayeledi.
         Mi kong ma mama,
         Nami ayeledi.
         Mi kong ma wowoi,
         Nami ayeledi.

         I play a sacred dance to God,
         So that I may be congratulated.
         I play a sacred dance to the earth,
         So that I may be congratulated.
         I play a sacred dance to the gods,
         So that I may be congratulated.

Singer: Olila wongtse.
Occasion: Recording songs, 1968.
Commentary: This song recapitulates the cosmogonic ordering of the *kpele* world: God and the sky, the earth, and the gods, and articulates the intentions which motivate the performance of ritual.

The words of the *kpele* text are non-Ga, with the exception of *wowoi*.

[111]   Agbaa ngmiingmii
         Wo song.

         The pure agbaa
         We are.

Singer: *Kle agbaayoo.*
Occasion: Recording songs, 1968.
Exegesis: We gather ourselves to make a dance.
Commentary: Another version of this song was sung by *Olila agbaanuu* in 1968. The two versions differ only in the mode of expressing similar ideas; both *kpele* texts are in Ga.

[112] Wǫdze ngkwa maba;
       Gbę he wǫwǫ.

       We prepared the road and came;
       We slept by the roadside.

Singer: Possessed medium.
Occasion: *Nai ngmaafaa,* 1968.
Commentary: The first line means that the people have prepared the road to the farm and returned. E. A. Ammah suggested that an alternative translation for the first line was,"We received life and came." He further hypothesized that the second line referred to the wanderings of the Ga before they arrived at Great Accra.
   The words in the *kpele* text are Ga, with the exception of *ngkwa.*

[113] Ananse ase
       Fa oti bra,
       Tsęrę mi ade.
       Ananse lo,
       Tsęrę mi akǫng.
       Ananse lo,
       Tsęrę mi sa.
       Ngǫngǫi nǫngng wǫti ngde;
       Miti adabra maba oba,
       Wǫwǫi, atele shamo,
       Kę wǫtee ni kę wǫba.
       Atsę wǫ, wǫmba, wǫmba.

Atsẹ wọ kẹdzẹ kooyi kẹ atsẹ wọ ngshọnaa.
Awo blẹtsẹ, nyẹ ba,
Blẹ yẹ niimẹi ayinọ naamẹi ayinọ.
Wọwọi blẹtsẹ.

Spider's story
Bring me your knowledge,[1]
Show me something.
Spider lo,
Show me akọng dancing.
Spider lo,
Show me dancing,
We do not understand the same gongs.
When I hear a gong, I come.
Gods, who dance shamo,
Go with us and come with us.
They call us, we are coming, we are coming.
They call us from the north and they call us
    to the south.
Hornplayer, you come.
The horn has existed from grandfathers' time
    and from grandmothers' time.
It is the gods' horn player.

1. Lit., bring me your head.

Singer: Ashadu wọngtsẹ.
Occasion: Recording songs, 1968.
Commentary: In Ga thought, the spider symbolizes knowledge. It is called in this song to show human beings how to
perform various dances. One Ga informant said that "spider
thinks that it is wise, others think that spider is greedy." He
continued: "Ga people rarely kill spiders, but they destroy
their webs, because it is believed that if a person does not destroy them, he will not get money." This statement suggests
that spider's web catches not only insects but information.
By destroying the spider web, ideas are released for use by
human beings.

Although all chiefs have horns, the only *kpele* cult in Accra
that utilizes a horn is the *Sakumo* cult. This horn is supposed
to arouse the people to participate in ritual and in warfare.

The last six lines of the *kpele* text are in Ga; the words of
the first ten lines are non-Ga, with the exception of a few
words, such as *ngongoi, wowoi, wo*, and *mi*.

[114] Nyẹ dzoo nẹ?
Tsiaaa!

Is this your dance?
Hsss!

Singer: Olila agbaanuu.
Occasion: Recording songs, 1968.
Exegesis: It is as though someone asked you to come to a certain place to see what he is doing. When you arrive, you see
that the drummers are beating incorrectly. The music that
they are playing is done badly.
Commentary: The words in this *kpele* text are Ga.

[115] Okọni bo ba,
Ayi Anafo baaherẹ mi okọni,
Okọni bo ba,
Ayi Anafo baala mi.
Okọni bo ba,
Okọni okọni fritete.
Okọni bo ba,
Ayi Anafo baaherẹ mi okọni.

Drum you come,
Ayi Anafo will receive the drum.
Drum you come,
Ayi Anafo will beat the drum.
Drum you come,
It is the drum, the drum of long ago.

Drum you come,
Ayi Anafo will receive the drum.

Singer: Olila woŋgtsẹ.
Occasion: Recording songs, 1965.
Exegesis: A god is calling Ayi Anafo to come.
Commentary: Ayi Anafo of *Krokoto we* (see song 71) is said
to have been the first *kpele* drummer. According to the *Olila*
medium, at Great Accra the *kpele* drums were stored at *Krokoto we*, and *kpele* dances were performed there. Today
kpele drums are stored at *Sakumo we* theoretically, but usually cult groups have their own sets of drums. Each of the three
drums utilized in performing *kpele* music is named. The
largest, which is medially placed (see Chapter 5), is called
okoni or *dzengtenghi le* ("the middle of the world"); the latter is a title for the Asere chief whom the *Olila* medium claims
was responsible for the initiation of *kpele* ritual at Great Accra. The medium-sized drum, which is placed to the right of
the big drum, is named *mikumalewa* ("I play for old woman"), *afuakpe* ("thousand hunchbacks"), and *ablaba* ("*Abla*
come"). The smallest drum, which is placed on the left of the
big drum, is called *dzengtengdzii* ("little middle of the world").
The drums, the music performed on them, and the dances
they accompany may be termed either *tente* or *kpele*.
 The words of the *kpele* text are Ga.

[116] Ayi Anafo bashi tente;
    Anaa mo ayi.

    Ayi Anafo come and beat the kpele drum;
    They do not have anyone to beat it.

Singer: Kle agbaayoo.
Occasion: Recording songs, 1968.
Exegesis: Sometimes when a god descends, there is no one to
beat the drum.
Commentary: See song 115 for notes on Ayi Anafo and *tente*.
 The words of the *kpele* text are Ga.

[117]   *Version 1*
  Anaa oyabala ni ala;
  Ayi Anafo, baala.
  Anaa mọ ayi mi lẹ.
  Ayi Anafo, baayi.

  They do not have anyone to sing;
  Ayi Anafo, come to sing.
  They do not have anyone to beat the drum;
  Ayi Anafo, come to beat.

Singer: *Olila wọngtsẹ.*
Occasion: Discussion of trip to Okai Koi Hill, 1968.

  Version 2
  Anaa mọ ayi;
  Odai, anaa mọ ayi;
  Ayatsẹ Ayi, mi lẹ tsẹ,
  Ni ebayi.

  They do not have anyone to beat;
  Sakumọ, they do not have anyone to beat;
  Call Ayi, the drummer,
  To come and beat.

Singer: *Olila wọngtsẹ.*
Occasion: Recording songs, 1965.
Commentary: See song 115 for note on Ayi Anafo.
 The words of both versions of the *kpele* text are Ga.

[118]   *Version 1*
  Ayi eka koong.
  Naa, kpele efo,
  Kpeletsẹ bẹ.

  Ayi remained in the forest.
  Lo, kpele is weeping,
  There is not a kpele drummer.

Singer: Olila wǫngtsẹ.
Occasion: Discussion of trip to Okai Koi Hill, 1968.
Exegesis: Ayi remained in the forest, because he was angry.
He would not come and so the people were unable to perform the dance. Now, the drummer should be treated well,
so that he will teach you what he knows; that is correct, and
the gods will like it too. And so when you go to a god, you
should treat the drummer and the singer well.

> *Version 2*
> Ayi eka koong;
> Tene mingfo.
> Ayi eka koong;
> Tenetsẹ bẹ lo?
> Tene mingfo.
>
> Ayi remained in the forest;
> Kpele is weeping.
> Ayi remained in the forest;
> Is there not a kpele drummer?
> Kpele is weeping.

Singer: Olila wǫngtsẹ.
Occasion: Recording songs, 1965.
Commentary: See song 115 for notes on Ayi Anafo and *tente*
(*tene*).

The words of both versions of the *kpele* text are Ga.

[119] Ayi Anafo bawo ni akǫmi.
       Kilikitiko.

       Ayi Anafo come to put kǫmi on me.
       Kilikitiko.[1]

1. The sound of the drum.

Singer: Kle agbaayoo.

Occasion: Recording songs, 1968.
Commentary: See songs 89-2 and 115 for notes on *kǫmi* and Ayi Anafo, respectively. When *kǫmi* is put around a person's neck, it shows that he has been acknowledged as a ritual performer.

The first line of the *kpele* text is in Ga.

[120] Ekęę, beka na mingka;
       Okomfo, beka na mingka;
       Obloo, beka na mingka.
       Ekęę, gbalǫ dzi wǫnǫ;
       Okomfo Lomoko, bagba wǫ;
       Gbalǫ dzi wǫnǫ.

       He said, come speak that I may speak;
       Medium, come speak that I may speak;
       Medium, come speak that I may speak.
       He said it is our prophet;
       Okomfo Lomoko, come speak for us;
       It is our prophet.

Singer: Akumadze Afieye wǫngtsę.
Occasion: Recording songs, 1968.
Exegesis: First three lines: Come speak so that I may speak; *Obloo* is a medium. This song is sung when a god comes.

Last three lines: The person whom a god first caught in Accra was named Okomfo Lomoko. It is said that he did not die; it is said that he sat down for a long time, he rotted, and he turned into a fan palm tree. What that person spoke was true, and so it is said that he should come to prophesy so that we too may prophesy.

Commentary: This song and the six succeeding songs refer to the possession of a medium by her god. When a god wishes to communicate with human beings, he descends from the sky to speak through his medium (songs 120-122). *Kpele* gods are believed to select their mediums (songs 123-126). After a god has chosen a person to be his medium, the price for refusing to become his medium is insanity and/or death. Mediums undergo a lengthy period of training during which they live with and learn from an established medium. During their vocational training, novices learn how to sing *kpele* songs, to dance, to pray, to divine, and to control trance states. The termination of a novice's education is determined partly by her instructor's decision that she has acquired the requisite skills to be a medium and partly by her relative's ability to pay the fees of her training and initiation, which amount to at least $1,000.

See song 55 for additional information on prophets and Lomoko.

The first three lines of the *kpele* text are not in Ga, with the exception of *ekee;* the last three lines are in Ga.

[121]   Ahu Gbomo,
        Miko ngteng maba ngteng.

        Ahulu,
        I come quickly so that I may return quickly.

Singer: Akumadze Afieye wongtse.
Occasion: Recording songs, 1968.
Exegesis: When a god is coming to possess you, he says that he is coming. This song is what he will say so that he may leave quickly.
Commentary: See song 84 for note on *Ahulu.*

The words of the second line of the *kpele* text are non-Ga, with the exception of *maba.*

[122]   Ayemfu ahia mi, otsirima ahia mi.
        Beka namenti.
        Oshwila Adu Kome,
        Beka namenti.

        I need a man, I need a drummer.
        Come speak that I may hear.

Sakumǫ,
Come speak that I may hear.

Singer: Olila wǫngtsę.
Occasion: Recording songs, 1965.
Commentary: See song 14 for note on *Sakumǫ.*
The words of the *kpele* text are non-Ga.

[123] Obsum ma yę dzoo;
       Mingtao obsum ma manyra ade.

       A god's child has danced;
       I sought a god's child, by luck I got someone.

Singer: Kle agbaayoo.
Occasion: Recording songs, 1968.
Commentary: The words of the *kpele* text are non-Ga, with
the exception of *dzoo* and *mingtao.*

[124] Tęte, mǫbi mashi nyę.

       Sakumǫ, someone's child I will have you.

Singer: Kle agbaayoo.
Occasion: Recording songs, 1968.
Commentary: See the exegesis of song 125.
The words of the *kpele* text are Ga.

[125] Awi lo, ngtra mǫ, ngtra Saku;
       Ngtra mǫ ngtra Saku;
       Ngfa oba.

       Awi lo, I swear by Sakumǫ;
       I swear, I swear by Sakumǫ;
       I will take your child.

Singer: Olila woŋgtsẹ.
Occasion: Recording songs, 1965.
Exegesis: When a god vows to possess a person, that person must become a medium for the god.
Commentary: The words of the *kpele* text are non-Ga.

[126] Lomo,
       Wusi bẹ nam;
       Teteete wọkọng.
       Odzwani bẹ nam;
       Teteete wọkọng.
       Okomfo Aku Lomo wọkọng,
       Teteete wọkọng.

       Prophet,
       You cry to meet me;
       It is our ancient dance.
       You ran to meet me;
       It is our ancient dance.
       Prophet Aku it is our dance,
       It is our ancient dance.

Singer: Olila wọŋgtsẹ.
Occasion: Singing for the *Ga mangtsẹ*, 1965.
Exegesis: Our religion has been handed down from unknown times. The song describes a person whom a god wishes to possess; the person ran to a prophet and said, "Look, what is happening to me?" The prophet allays her fears, nothing unusual has happened; it has happened for a long time.
Commentary: See song 55 for note on prophets.
      The words of the *kpele* text are non-Ga, with the exception of *Aku* and *lomo*.

[127] Mihu onipa onimisẹ,
       Matsi mawie,
       Makọng mawie,
       Obolo.

Mihu onipa onimisę,
Matsi mawie,
Makǫng mawie,
Dantsęrę.

Kǫtię ni pa nǫng,
Lę ewo mi nyanyara.
Dantsęrę,
Lę ewo mi nyanyara.

I have not seen my equal,
I have finished my training,
My name encompasses the world,
Obolo.

I have not seen my equal,
I have finished my training,
My name encompasses the world,
Dantsęrę.

A good person has trained me,
She puts nyanyara on me.
Dantsęrę,
She puts nyanyara on me.

Singer: Olila wǫngtsę.
Occasion: Recording songs, 1965.
Commentary: This song is for a medium who has completed her training. It was sung for me, named Obolo in the song, at my last recording session with the *Olila* medium, Dantsęrę, in 1965. When a medium has completed her training, she is permitted to wear *nyanyara* (see song 89), which is forbidden during her years of apprenticeship.

The words of the *kpele* text are non-Ga, with the exception of Obolo, Dantsęrę, and the line *"Lę ewo mi nyanyara."*

[128] Ngbasra nyę, maya;
       Akǫntswi nana bę hę.
       Ngbasra nyę, maya;

Sane ko bę ehę.
Ngbasra nyę, maya;
Ngbasra lomo momo;
Ngbasra Buadza momo;
Ngbasra Kǫme momo;
Ngbasra Dǫde momo;
Ngbasra Nkranpong momo.

I have visited you, I will go;
If one prolongs a visit, one sees another's secret.
I have visited you, I will go;
Nothing is against him.
I have visited you, I will go;
I have visited the prophet already;
I have visited Olila already;
I have visited Sakumǫ already;
I have visited Dǫde already;
I have visited Great Accra already.

Singer: Olila wǫngtsę.
Occasion: Singing for the *Ga mangtsę,* 1965.
Exegesis: This song should be followed by song 131 to close a
kpele dance.
Commentary: This song and the three following songs refer to
the conclusion of a ritual performance. This song enumerates
some transcendental beings who have appeared at a *kpele*
dance: a prophet (song 55), *Olila* (song 14), *Sakumǫ* (song
14), and Dǫde Akabi (song 178).

The words of the *kpele* text are Ga, with the exception of
the second line and *Nkranpong.*

[129]   Ataa lami,
        Mangǫ ta ngna.

        Father's shell,
        I shall put it to my lips.

Singer: Olila wǫngtsẹ.
Occasion: Singing for the *Ga mangtsẹ*, 1965.
Exegesis: Lami is a shell. When a chief puts it to his mouth, no one may speak again. Everything has been completed [see commentary, song 128].
Commentary: Another identical version of the song was sung by the *Olila wǫngtsẹ* on another occasion in 1965.

The words of the *kpele* text are Ga.

[130] Ayi tse awoyoo;
       Lumǫ Ayi tse awoyoo.
       Ayi tse awoyoo;
       Nuumo tse awoyoo.
       Ayi tse awoyoo;
       Nii tse awoyoo.
       Ayi tse awoyoo;
       Etse awoyoo.

       Ayi tore off the anklet;
       Prince Ayi tore off the anklet.
       Ayi tore off the anklet;
       The old man tore off the anklet.
       Ayi tore off the anklet;
       Grandfather tore off the anklet.
       Ayi tore off the anklet;
       He tore off the anklet.

Singer: Olila wǫngtsẹ.
Occasion: Singing for the *Ga mangtsẹ*, 1965.
Exegesis: This song, which is sung to conclude a sacred dance, means that the music has stopped.
Commentary: See song 89 for note on *awoyoo*.

The words of the *kpele* text are Ga.

[131] Agbaa yawǫ,
       Kukui kẹ kakai.

The congregation will go to sleep,
Everyone.

Singer: Olila wǫngtsę.
Occasion: Singing for the *Ga mangtsę,* 1965.
Commentary: A concluding song for a *kpele* dance (see song 128).
The words of the *kpele* text are Ga.

[132] Ngmaa hewǫ,
Atokong dzwa Kakenyę hiingmęi tsoo.
Ngmaa hewǫ,
Enama akǫng sǫng.
Kakenyę, Kakenyę,
Ayidǫng.
Agbaamęi, angmee, angmee.

It was because of millet,
A tree hurt Kakenyę's eye badly.
It was because of millet,
She did not work carefully.
It was Kakenyę, Kakenyę,
She is a one-eyed person.
Congregation, it was a thorn, it was a thorn.

Singers: Sakumǫ agbaa.
Occasion: Sakumǫ ngmaadumǫ, 1965.
Exegesis: This song is about a one-eyed person, *Kakenyę.*
Once when she went to the field during *ngmaadumǫ,* she was careless and pricked her foot on a thorn which made her stumble. She fell on a tree and put out one eye.
Commentary: The words of this *kpele* text are said to be Ga, by which I mean that although my informants said that the words of the *kpele* text are Ga, I cannot identify certain lexemes as Ga, such as *ayidǫng* and *akǫng sǫng.*

[133] Adu ngmaa fẹẹ;
Akpaa blẹ, akpaa blẹ.

Ofori edu ngmaa fẹẹ;
Adu ngmaa fẹẹ;
Akpaa blẹ, akpaa blẹ.

Odai edu ngmaa fẹẹ;
Adu ngmaa fẹẹ;
Akpaa blẹ, akpaa blẹ.

Lomo edu ngmaa fẹẹ;
Adu ngmaa fẹẹ;
Akpaa blẹ, akpaa blẹ.

Lomo edu ngmaa fẹẹ;
Adu ngmaa fẹẹ;
Akpaa blẹ, akpaa blẹ;
Alaa, alaa;
Afoo, afoo;
Atswaa ntsoa, atswaa ntsoa;
Ayii mi, ayii mi;
Adzoo, adzoo;
Atuu ampe, atuu ampe;
Ashwee adawe, ashwee adawe;
Ashii dzama, ashii dzama;
Atswaa ngọngọ, atswaa ngọngọ.

Adu ngmaa fẹẹ;
Akpaa blẹ, akpaa blẹ.

They have planted all the millet;
Do not blow a horn; do not blow a horn.

Ofori has planted all the millet;
They have planted all the millet;
Do not blow a horn, do not blow a horn.

Sakumọ has planted all the millet;
They have planted all the millet;
Do not blow a horn, do not blow a horn.

A prophet has planted all the millet;
They have planted all the millet;
Do not blow a horn, do not blow a horn;
Do not sing, do not sing;
Do not weep, do not weep;
Do not clap ntsoa, do not clap ntsoa;
Do not beat a drum, do not beat a drum;
Do not dance, do not dance;
Do not play ampe, do not play ampe;
Do not play adawe, do not play adawe;
Do not push, do not push;
Do not beat a gong, do not beat a gong.

They have planted all the millet;
Do not blow a horn, do not blow a horn.

Singer: Olila woŋgtsẹ.
Occasion: Recording songs, 1965.
Exegesis: Dantu agbaa sing this song as they walk around the town after *ngmaadumọ* to inform the townspeople that the three-week period of silence has begun. During the last Akwamu war in 1730, Akim were hired by Ga to rout Akwamu. Ofori, the Akim chief, came to Accra during the period of silence and blew his horn [see commentary below].
Commentary: This song enumerates various kinds of noise which are prohibited during the period of silence. Among the activities which are prohibited are clapping games for men (*ntsoa*), women (*adawe*), and children (*ampe*). In Chapter 5, I have argued that these restrictions on noise aim to avoid disrupting the attention of the gods from their more important activity of ensuring the successful growth of the millet seed.

Although the *Olila* medium said that Ofori is the name of an Akim chief, it is also the name of the Ga chief, Okai Koi's son and successor, who twice eluded the invading Akwamu. In 1677 he fled to coastal Accra from Great Accra and from thence to Little Popo in 1681 (Wilks, "The Rise of the Akwamu Empire," pp. 107-111).

The words of the *kpele* text are Ga.

[134] Okplẹ kẹ sẹsẹ,
       Adzabento.

No one high or low is to make noise,[1]
They have sown the seed.

1. Lit., no one high or low.

Singers: Dantu agbaa.
Occasion: Dantu ngmaadumọ, 1965.
Exegesis: This song announces the period of silence.
Commentary: When *Dantu agbaa* return from the field, they
form a circle outside the shrine and dance. As they dance,
they alternately sing this song and song 83.
    The words of the *kpele* text are non-Ga.

[135] Gbi ko mana minọ;
       Wọwọi Adangọte kẹ tsina mingba.

One day I will get my own;
The gods at Adangọte are bringing cows.

Singer: Kle agbaayoo.
Occasion: Recording songs, 1968.
Exegesis: Adangọte is an inland town near Ayawaso where La
[Labadi] people settled before they migrated to the coast.
When *họmọwọ* [annual feast to celebrate ancestral shades] is
celebrated at Labadi, people bring cows and corn.
Commentary: The words of the *kpele* text are Ga.

[136] Wọyawọ họmọ yi;
       Na ngmaa yi eyẹ.
       Wọyawọ.

We are going to hoot at hunger;
Look, the millet top is white.
We are going to hoot.

Singer: Olila wǫngtsę.
Occasion: Discussion of trip to Ayawaso, 1968.
Exegesis: This is a *kpele homǫwǫ* song.
Commentary: The second line means that the millet is ripe and ready for harvesting. When the harvest is in, the threat of hunger is dispelled and may be ridiculed safely.

The words of the *kpele* text are Ga.

[137]   Mitsiri omang,
        Mitsiri bii yę dang,
        Mitsiri bii yę kǫ.

        I stroll in the town,
        I go round and return,
        I go round and go.

Singer: Olila agbaanuu.
Occasion: Recording songs, 1968.
Exegesis: This song is sung [at *mangnaamǫ*] when *Sakumǫ agbaa* goes about the town to purify and bless the people after the harvest.
Commentary: The words of the *kpele* text are non-Ga.

[138]   Yę atsi mang, agbaamǫbi,
        Ni ena nii ni eye.

        Go round the town, agbaa person's child,
        So that he may get food to eat.

Singer: Kle agbaayoo.
Occasion: Recording songs, 1968.
Commentary: This song may refer either to *Sakumǫ*'s walk around the town at *mangnaamǫ* (see song 137) or to the licensed looting of food by children on the morning of that rite.

The words of the *kpele* text are Ga.

[139] Mprobiale, họmọ teteete họmọ ta;
       Mprobiale, biale;
       Mprobiale, biale.

       Children, hunger of long ago, hunger is ended;
       Little children;
       Little children.

Singer: Olila wọngtsẹ.
Occasion: Recording songs, 1965.
Commentary: The words of the *kpele* text are Ga, with the exception of *mprobiale.*

[140] Okolomo, ngmaatoilọi;
       Kaaya dzẹi.
       Awo yẹ dzẹi;
       Kaaya dzẹi.
       Nii yẹ dzẹi;
       Kaaya dzẹi.
       Ataa yẹ dzẹi;
       Kaaya dzẹi.

       Okolomo, it is the millet storers;
       Do not go there.
       Mother is there;
       Do not go there.
       Grandfather is there;
       Do not go there.
       Father is there;
       Do not go there.

Singer: Kle agbaayoo.
Occasion: Recording songs, 1968.
Exegesis: This *Okolomo,* I do not know who he is. The year has come, they have eaten, the year is finished; the priests are going to perform a rite. Yes, they are going to store the millet seeds.

Commentary: This song is sung at *ngmaato*. As the text suggests, this is a private rite in which only the men of *Sakumǫ agbaa* may participate. The men are joined in the performance of the rite by ancestral shades.

According to E. A. Ammah, in leeward towns they sing *Afromo* rather than *Okolomo*, who, he suggested, is a trespasser.

The *kpele* text is in Ga.

[141]   Akrabatsa wǫnǫ;
        Ngdamǫ pampi sęę,
        Mayę biibri matsęrę mang.

        The fence is ours;
        I stand behind the pampi,
        I will do something to show the people.

Singer: Ashiaklę wulǫmǫ.
Occasion: Recording songs, 1968.
Exegesis: The fence is there [around the shrine], we paddle to its mouth, then we enter the center, then we cover the fence. That is how we enter the house.
Commentary: The *akrabatsa* is the fence which surrounds a *gbatsu* (lit., "telling room") or shrine of a god. In former times, all *gbatsui* were circular with grass roofs, but today only *Sakumǫ* has such a *gbatsu* in Accra (see Danniell, "On the Ethnography of Akkrah and Adampe," p. 27). The thresholds (*pampi*) to the entrances of both a *gbatsu* and the courtyard of the shrine where ritual is performed consist of a number of small sticks (I have seen them with four, seven, and nine sticks). The *pampi* constitute a mystical hindrance to impure or ill-intentioned persons, who will be unable to cross the *pampi*, as they will fall or will be unable to put their feet down on the opposite side of the threshold.

According to E. A. Ammah, at naming rites in leeward towns, the baby is placed inside a circle which is drawn on the ground. This circle symbolizes Ga society.

The words of the *kpele* text are Ga, with the exception of the third line.

[142]   Fanti meni oye
Ni oteke pampi, pampi aduase?

Fanti person, what did you eat
That you crossed the pampi, the thirty pampi?

Singer: Kle agbaayoo.
Occasion: Recording songs, 1968.
Exegesis: The Fanti person is uncircumcised; therefore, he should not enter a *kpele* shrine.
Commentary: This song expresses amazement that a Fanti person has succeeded in entering a *kpele* shrine from which non-Ga are excluded. The practice of circumcision differentiates Ga from their Akan neighbors (Kaye, *Bringing Up Children in Ghana*, pp. 122-123; Christensen, *Double Descent among the Fanti*, p. 85). Ga males are circumcised usually in infancy and certainly before puberty. An uncircumcised male is regarded as ritually unclean and as a jural minor who cannot achieve the status of an ancestral shade.

See song 141 for note on *pampi*.

Another version of the song was sung by *Ashiakle wulomo* in 1968. The two versions are identical except that the priest's version omits the significant word *Fanti*.

The words of the *kpele* text are Ga.

[143]   Akee wongwongtsu yango omanye obahawo.
Afieye Okropong yango wongwongtsu obahawo;
Wongwongtsu ke omanye abahawo.
Afieye ngo manye obahawo;
Wongwongtsu ke omanye abahawo.
Akee wongwongtsu yango omanye obahawo;
Wongwongtsu ke omanye abahawo.
Afieye Okropong lasu ni tsuko mo;
Wongwongtsu ke omanye abahawo.

They said incense procure peace for us.
Afieye Okropong procure incense for us;
May incense and peace be given to us.
Afieye procure peace for us;
May incense and peace be given to us.
They said incense procure peace for us;
May incense and peace be given to us.
Afieye Okropong, smoke cleanses a person;
May incense and peace be given to us.

Singer: Abudu wulǫmǫ.
Occasion: Recording songs, 1965.
Exegesis: Wǫngwǫngtsu is incense made from palm fronds.
When it is lighted, the smoke removes all pollution. When sins
are removed, one has peace. This song refers to purification
before worship.
Commentary: Incense is used to purify places and sometimes
people in *kpele* ritual. At agricultural rites, incense burns in
the courtyard of the shrine, the leader of the procession of
agbaa members is the incense carrier, often the field is fumigated before the ritual performers enter, and the bodies of
participants are fumigated before some rites.

See song 88 for note on *Afieye.*

The words of the *kpele* text are Ga, with the exception of
wǫngwǫngtsu and *okropong.*

[144] Afumpe Okǫni di abaa;
Kokobi te.

The big drum brings all this;
It is the medium-sized drum.

Singer: Olila wǫngtsę.
Occasion: Checking *kpele* songs, 1968.
Exegesis: Abla-ba [the medium-sized drum] says that *Afumpe
Okǫni*, the big drum, brought all their suffering, because the
drummer beats on the big drum to call all the people. *Kokobi,*

the drum on the right, complains that when the drums are played, their ears are slapped.

Commentary: See song 115 for note on drums.

The words of the *kpele* text are non-Ga.

[145]   Manya akongua pa matran ase;
        Akongua pa ne eye.

        I have a good stool to sit on;
        A good stool is good.

Singer: Kle agbaayoo.
Occasion: Recording songs, 1968.
Exegesis: A god or an important person is speaking.
Commentary: A stool (Ga, *sẹi*) is the symbol of political and ritual office. In the god's room (*wọngtsu*) of a medium, where she invokes deities, there are two ritual stools: one for the spirit of the god whom she worships and one for her to sit on during invocations. After her death, her stool, like those of chiefs and family elders, will be kept and used only for propitiating her soul with food on ritual occasions.

The words of the *kpele* text are non-Ga.

[146]   Wiri tsẹrẹ bẹ lo?
        Kaangọ korobata owo kpaa mli?

        Is there not a parrot feather?
        Do not put a parrot feather into twine.

Singer: Olila wọngtsẹ.
Occasion: Recording songs, 1965.
Exegesis: The song means that one should put something in its appropriate place. When you know the way, go that way. Specifically, the song refers to the red feather which is part of a medium's hair style.

Commentary: In *kpele* ritual, red parrot feathers are utilized solely as part of the hair ornament of *kpele* mediums (see song 89). Consequently, it is appropriate to put a parrot feather into the hair of a medium and into nothing else. Since the parrot feather is thought to facilitate possession, the analogy between talking birds and talking mediums is clear. Red, as I have noted in Chapter 5, is the color associated with chieftaincy, particularly in its military aspect. Since *kpele* gods are thought to assist in the military exploits of the Ga, it is probably their martial role that is connoted by the utilization of a red feather.

The words of the *kpele* text are Ga, with the exception of *wiri* and *korobata.*

[147] Atinka ni sa;
       Oshwila Adu Kọme,
       Atinka ni sa;
       Esa mi——e.

       Ahulu dzenamọ,
       Bakwẹ mi atinka.
       Atinka ni sa;
       Esa mi——e.

       Akọndọ ni sa;
       Odai,
       Akọndọ ni sa;
       Esa mi——e.

       Nuumo dzenamọ,
       Bakwẹ mi akọndọ.
       Akọndọ ni sa;
       Esa mi——e.

       Abakle ni sa;
       Oshwila Adu Kọme,
       Abakle ni sa;
       Abakle ni dọme.

Ahulu dzenamǫ
Bakwę mi abakle.
Abakle ni sa;
Esa mi——e.

Afutu, eye bangka oye,
Bakwę nsaado.

Ahulu dzenamǫ;
Bakwę mi bęshwę.

Afutu, eye bangka oye,
Bakwę mi bęshwę.

Tsę Nyǫngmǫ Mawu,
Bakwę mi bęshwę.

The hairstyle befits me;
Sakumǫ,
The hairstyle befits me;
It befits me.

Ahulu of all times,
Come look at my hairstyle..
The hairstyle befits me;
It befits me.

The necklace befits me;
Sakumǫ,
The necklace befits me;
It befits me.

Ahulu of all times,
Come look at my necklace.
The necklace befits me;
It befits me.

The bracelet befits me;
Sakumǫ,
The bracelet befits me;
The bracelet befits me.

Ahulu of all times,
Come look at my bracelet.
The bracelet befits me;
It befits me.

Afutu, the bracelet is good,
Come look at my bracelet.

Ahulu of all times,
Come look at me and see.

Afutu, the bracelet is good,
Come look at me and see.

God,
Come look at me and see.

Singer: Olila wǫngtsę.
Occasion: Recording songs, 1965.
Exegesis: The dress of a medium is described in this song.
Commentary: In this song a medium calls upon God, gods
(*Sakumǫ* and *Ahulu*), and men (Afutu, a neighboring Guang-
speaking people) to see her accoutrements.

Abakle is the term for the bracelet which a novice wears
during her training to become a medium. When a novice's
"mouth is opened" to determine the identity of the god who
wishes to possess her, this bracelet is put on her right wrist
and it is thought that the god alights on the bracelet. The
bracelet consists of a closely fitting cord on which two small
beads are strung; the beads are worn on the back of the right
wrist. The positive associations of right with power, goodness,
and masculinity have been discussed in Chapter 5. When a
medium is initiated at the completion of her training, she is
permitted to wear *afli* on both wrists and is given all the other
accoutrements of a medium specified in song 89. The bracelets of an initiated medium consist of white or alternating
black and white beads which completely encircle her wrists.
Although a medium wears *afli* on both wrists as a symbol of
her initiated status, it is believed that the god continues to
descend on her right wrist. Theoretically, mediums only re-

move their bracelets after the death of a close relative in order to avoid contaminating the god through contact with mortal pollution. In practice, bracelets may be removed if a medium has injured her wrist in some way and wishes to remove all sources of pressure from her arm.

See song 89 for note on *atinka* and song 84 for note on *Ahulu*, the divine messenger.

The words of the *kpele* text are Ga, with the exception of *atinka*, *beshwe*, *nsaado*, and *bangka*.

Human Society

These songs deal with aspects of human society. Some songs concern the temporal continuity of Ga culture and society (songs 148-156), others emphasize reciprocity in social life (songs 157-163).

[148] Abǫ ade naamęi ayinǫ,
       Niimęi ayinǫ.

       Creation was in grandmothers' time,
       In grandfathers' time.

Singer: Ashadu wǫngtsę.
Occasion: Recording songs, 1968.
Commentary: The central theme of this song and the succeeding one is that Ga culture originated during the lifetimes of distant ancestral shades. In Chapter 6, I hypothesized that the internal evidence provided by certain songs in the light of recent archaeological and historical studies suggests that *kpele* time begins in the late sixteenth century. The authoritative precedent which the continuity of Ga culture over the years gives to present activities is implicit in these songs.

The words of the *kpele* text are Ga, with the exception of *ade.*

[149] Ataamẹi shi ha wọ;
       Tsẹmẹi shi ha wọ.

       Fathers left it to us;
       Fathers left it to us.

Singer: E. A. Ammah.
Occasion: Discussion of *kpele* rites, 1968.
Exegesis: This song refers to the performance of agricultural rites. Whatever we do, our ancestors left it to us to continue; they passed it on to us.
Commentary: The *kpele* text is in Ga.

[150] Dzeng bọ ade wọyẹ mli;
       Tsutsu blema bẹ nẹkẹ.

       The created world we are in;
       Former times were not like these.

Singer: *Olila agbaanuu.*
Occasion: Recording songs, 1968.
Exegesis: We are living in a situation created by society; it was not like this in the olden days. Human beings create their social environment. What our forefathers had was better than what we know now. Formerly there was contentment; now things have gone wrong; man changes things.
Commentary: This song introduces the notion of cultural change. The culture of contemporary Ga does not correspond to that of the ancestors, which in retrospect represents a golden age.

    An identical text was sung by *Kle agbaayoo* in 1968.

    The words of the *kpele* text are Ga, with the exception of *ade* and *tsutsu.*

[151] Tsatsa awekumẹi;
       Wọmli egblẹ yaa.
       Shi wọle wọhe.

Tsatsa awekumẹi;
Wọle tso ni wowọ,
Shi wọle wọhe.

The relatives are scattered;
We are scattered,
But we know ourselves.

The relatives are scattered;
We know the tree that bore us,
(But) we know ourselves.

Singer: Olila wọngtsẹ.
Occasion: Discussion of trip to Okai Koi Hill, 1968.
Exegesis: It is God's tree where he commanded and the sea divided. God himself made them settle there. That tree is the place that all Ga come from; there is the road we came on. "The relatives are scattered; we are scattered, but we know ourselves," so we sing it in *kpele.* Some went to Labadi, some to Nungua. "The relatives are scattered; we know the tree that bore us, we know ourselves." We like to add God's name to everything that we do in *Ga Mashi.* "We are scattered but we know ourselves, the relatives are scattered," that is, we know the tree that bore us, we know our mother who bore us, we left our mothers and fathers.
Commentary: Ga Mashi (lit., *Ga mangshishi,* "under Ga town") is a synonym for Accra. According to the *Olila* medium, the specific reference of the term is to a tree on Okai Koi Hill under which the townspeople used to gather in Great Accra. On the day before *Lante Dzan we homọwọ,* the *Olila* medium and representatives of the Asere chief sacrifice a sheep under this tree to the ancestors (*Okai Koi kẹ ewebii,* Okai Koi and his family) of the Ga people, who thereby enjoy *homọwọ* before any living Ga.

The words of the *kpele* text are Ga.

[152] *Version 1*
Wǫdzę Ga mli;
Wǫhi Ga mli;
Wǫdzę wuoyi;
Wǫdzęę kooyi.

We came among Ga people;
We live among Ga people;
We came from the south;
We did not come from the north.

Singer: Possessed medium.
Occasion: Nai ngmaafaa, 1968.
Exegesis: This refers to the people of *Nai we* who lived at
coastal Accra before the migration from Great Accra.

Version 2
Wǫdzę Ga mli;
Wǫya nina Gamęi.

We came among Ga people;
We met Ga people.

Singer: E. A. Ammah.
Occasion: Discussion of *kpele* songs, 1968.
Exegesis: This song refers to the wanderings of the Ga people
before they came to Accra. *Nai* people say that they came
from the seaside; other Ga say that they came from the forest.
Commentary: The ancestors of *Nai we* are believed to have
lived on the coast before other Ga migrated from the inland
town of Great Accra. This song asserts the southern coastal
origins of *Nai we* in contrast to the northern hinterland origins of other Ga. This differentiation between family units is
maintained in the utilization of white clay for ritual body
markings by the *Nai* cult and of red clay by other *kpele* cults
(see Chapter 4).

The *kpele* texts are in Ga.

[153] Wuoyi wǫnǫ.
Atsę wǫ kooyi;
Wǫyaa kooyi.

The south is ours.
They called us to the north;
We did not go to the north.

Singer: Ashiaklę wulǫmǫ.
Occasion: Recording songs, 1968.
Exegesis: Okai Koi's people called us to the forest, and we said that we would not go there.
Commentary: This song refers to the members of *Nai we* (song 152) who state that they refuse to travel to the north. In contemporary *kpele* thought, the south and the north represent a complementary asymmetrical pair in which the south is superior to the north. The south connotes the sea, its god *Nai,* who outranks all other *kpele* gods, and civilized culture, in contrast to the north, which represents the land, lesser deities, and rustic culture (see Chapter 4). Since in Ga society a superior does not visit an inferior, the refusal of the people of *Nai we* to travel to the north is an assertion of their superordinate status.

This song and its exegesis exemplify the way in which historical tradition may be utilized to rationalize contemporary social relations. Wilks' historical studies show that until 1677 the transatlantic trade at coastal Accra was controlled by the chief at Great Accra, who did not leave his town. European factors had to travel to him, and it may be presumed that coastal Ga also had to respond to his summons. Consequently, in fact, during the reign of Okai Koi, members of *Nai we* undoubtedly did go to the north, when they were called. When Great Accra was destroyed and some of its inhabitants escaped to coastal Accra, the structure of relations between seaside Ga and hinterland Ga was reversed and assumed its present form, to which the song alludes.

The *kpele* text is in Ga.

[154] Womang moomo, womang;
Womangtiase wo ye mli.
Dzeng bo ade aye mli;
Womang moomo, womang.

It is our town from long ago, it is our town;
We are in our capital.
The created world they are in;
It is our town from long ago, it is our town.

Singer: Olila wongtse.
Occasion: Singing for the *Ga mangtse*, 1965.
Commentary: See song 150 for a line which is similar to the third line in this text.

The words of the *kpele* text are Ga, with the exception of *ade* and *-tiase*.

[155] Tsemu to langmo;
Aba ni aya.
Afo langmo ashi.
Tsemu to langmo.

Tsemu keeps the navel;
They come and they go.
Navel was cut and left;
Tsemu keeps the navel.

Singer: Kle agbaayoo.
Occasion: Recording songs, 1968.
Exegesis: Tsemu, a god who is associated with the river at Tsoko [which is a village on the west of Accra] and a river at Tema, is the keeper of life, *Tsemu to langmo*. The navel is the center of life, for it ties all things together; through the umbilical cord, which links mother and child, the child is part of the mother. When a person dies, he lives on through his descendants [*afo langmo ashi*]. People are born to die [*aba ni aya*].
Commentary: The words of the *kpele* text are Ga.

[156] Oshiki nto mẹi ale wọ ato;
       Niimẹi le wọ to moomo.
       Oshiki nto mẹi ale wọ ato;
       Tsẹmẹi hu le wọ to moomo.
       Dedebi Bọtre.

       We are well known;
       Grandfathers knew us well already.
       We are well known;
       Fathers knew us well already.
       It is Dede's child Bọtele.

Singer: Olila wọngtsẹ.
Occasion: Recording songs, 1965.
Exegesis: The *Ga Mashi* [see song 151] people sing that Nungua people have said something which was known already. *Bọtele* is a female name at Nungua.
Commentary: The words of the *kpele* song are Ga.

[157] Mọ nitsọmọ—

       Oshwila,
       Ni eshẹ wọnọ
       Mọ nitsọmọ.

       Oshwila Adu Kọme,
       Ni eshẹ wọnọ
       Mọ nitsọmọ.

       Lawate Samua,
       Ni eshẹ wọnọ
       Mọ nitsọmọ.

       Lawate Kọme,
       Ni eshẹ wọnọ
       Mọ nitsọmọ.

       Olete Anyado,
       Ni eshẹ wọnọ
       Mọ nitsọmọ.

Teaching a person—

Oshwila,
And now it is our turn[1]
To teach someone.

Sakumo,
And now it is our turn
To teach someone.

Old person Sakumo,
And now it is our turn
To teach someone.

Old person Sakumo,
And now it is our turn
To teach someone.

Intelligent Venus,
And now it is our turn
To teach someone.

1. Lit., and it reaches us.

Singer: Olila wongtse.
Occasion: Recording songs, 1965.
Exegesis: It is now our turn to transmit what we know. Venus, the planet, is believed to send lightning; in this song she is asked to be gentle.
Commentary: The words of the *kpele* text are Ga.

[158] Mokome fo;
       Mokome elee.
       Afo le aha dzeng fee;
       Aha le aha dzeng blublu.

       One person bears a child;
       One person does not train a child.
       He is born for all the world;
       He is bought for all the world.

Singer: Kle agbaayoo.
Occasion: Recording songs, 1968.
Exegesis: You see, only one person will bear a child, but one person does not bring him up. And so, a child is born for everyone. If a person buys a slave, the slave's services will be used by others as well.
Commentary: See song 50 for note on slavery in Ga society.
The words of the *kpele* text are Ga.

[159]   Ngkome ngka nga teng;
        Mibẹ tsẹbi,
        Mibẹ nyẹbi.

        I lie alone in the field;
        I do not have a father's child,
        I do not have a mother's child.

Singer: Kle agbaayoo.
Occasion: Recording songs, 1968.
Exegesis: A person complains that he is alone without any companions.
Commentary: Since kinship is cognatic in Ga society, a person is affiliated with individuals and groups through both parents and achieves rights and obligations through these affiliations. Ga differentiate between relatives on the mother's side (*nyẹsẹẹ*) and those on the father's side (*tsẹsẹẹ*). Moreover, the frequency of both polygyny and divorce in Ga society means that an individual often has a number of uterine and nonuterine siblings with whom he shares certain rights and duties. This song emphasizes the existence of and differentiation between uterine and nonuterine siblings in Ga society.
The words of the *kpele* text are Ga.

[160]   Ayabi Ayitsẹ Oko,
        Mẹni mibaaye ni mawọ?
        Ka mi diale;
        Ahi bo mia, atse bo mia.

Ask Ayi's father Oko,
What will I eat before I sleep?
You will eat;
Men eat, women eat.

Singer: Olila wǫngtsę.
Occasion: Singing for the *Ga mangtsę,* 1965.
Exegesis: The first two lines mean that unless one cooks on a stove [*oko*], one does not get any food; more generally, the song means that if one needs something, one asks the appropriate person for assistance. The last line means that men and women work together.
Commentary: The first two lines of the *kpele* text are in Ga.

[161] Amęletsę shika ayenǫ:
Kǫble shika ayenǫ;
Ayenǫ, shika ayenǫ.
Duętę shika ayenǫ;
Ayenǫ, shika ayenǫ.
Dade shika ayenǫ;
Ayenǫ, shika ayenǫ.

Amęle's father eats with money:
He eats with copper money;
He eats with it, he eats with money.
He eats with silver money;
He eats with it, he eats with money.
He eats with iron money;
He eats with it, he eats with money.

Singer: Olila wǫngtsę.
Occasion: Checking *kpele* songs, 1968.
Commentary: The *Olila* medium sang this song after correcting song 25. Both songs refer to the traditional occupation of *Amatsę we* as smiths.
The words of the *kpele* text are Ga.

[162] Seę kpe ni Odolo,
Męni Odolo ye,
Ni kpe sęę woba?

It is tardy Odolo,
What does Odolo eat,
Since we were late in coming?

Singer: Ashadu wongtsę.
Occasion: Recording songs, 1968.
Exegesis: This song is sung during the millet feast [*ngmaayeli*];
it expresses gratitude for some gift.
Commentary: The words of the *kpele* text are Ga.

[163] Anya sibisi, anya siaoba.
Anya monka mootsuii;
Anya sibisi, anya siaoba.
Afoo Soobi ni ahe bo Hoobi;
Anya sibisi, anya siaoba.
Angme bo gbęnta;
Anya sibisi, anya siaoba.
Koole Adu, monka mootsuii;
Oshwila Adu, monka mootsuii;
Koote abongka yo ope.

You were bought as a slave, you were sold as a slave.
Give the slave water to drink;
You were bought as a slave, you were sold as a slave.
You were born on Thursday, and you were sold on
    Saturday;
You were bought as a slave, you were sold as a slave.
You were put on a crossroad;
You were bought as a slave, you were sold as a slave.
Koole, give him water to drink;
Oshwila, give him water to drink;
Sakumo surrounds him.

Singer: Olila wǫngtsẹ.

Occasion: Singing for the *Ga mangtsẹ,* 1965.

Exegesis: This song refers to a war between Ga and Akan peoples. *Kǫǫle* cooked *kpekpei* for the Akans [see song 14]. When they ate, they became weak; the gods said that the Ga should give them water to revive them. A slave has no identity; his name may be changed at his master's whim, but a slave should be well treated.

Commentary: As the exegetical statement says, the central theme of this song is the subjugation of a slave to his master's will (see song 50). The despised social status of a slave is conveyed through allusions to crossroads where waste may be dumped (see song 31) and to changes in a slave's day name (line 4).

The Ga words in the *kpele* text are the names of deities and the words of the fourth and sixth lines.

Ga Polity

This group of songs deals with three political themes: the requirements and conduct of political office (songs 164-169), the destructive implications of war (songs 170-176), and some events in Ga traditional history (songs 177-185).

[164] Ngda ni ngda ndoro omang;
      Afutu, madang kwai.

      I grew old before I ruled the country;
      Afutu, I became like a forest.

Singer: Olila wǫngtsẹ.
Occasion: Recording songs, 1965.
Exegesis: Line 1: I was mature in thought if not in years before I ruled. Line 2: I became wise.
Commentary: As the text and exegesis state, the holder of a political office should be an intellectually mature person who will make wise decisions on behalf of his subjects. In this song, the luxuriant growth of the forest is used as a metaphor for wisdom. This association of the forest, wisdom, and social order assumes additional interest when it is appreciated that in other contexts Ga utilize the forest as the habitat of wild animals to represent nonrationality and social disorder. I discuss this second connotation of the forest and its fertility in "Twin Beliefs and Ceremony in Ga Culture."

246

The *kpele* text is in Ga, with the exception of *ndoro* and *kwai*.

[165] Dzebi Akwano,
Ohene sa bo;
Akwe bo ni ato.
Afutu ohene, bo ohene;
Ohene, bo ohene.

Dzebi Akwano,
The chieftaincy befits you;
They watched you before they enstooled you.
Afutu chief, you are a chief;
Chief, you are a chief.

Singer: Olila wongtse.
Occasion: Recording songs, 1965.
Exegesis: Dzebi Akwano is the name of a chief. The song suggests that the chief was not really eligible for office, but that he was such a fine person that he was enstooled.
Commentary: In the Ga polity as in Akan polities, stools symbolize chiefly office and authority. Since the central act in the investiture of a chief involves placing the new chief on his stool, the accession ceremony is referred to as the enstoolment. In Ga society succession to political office depends partly upon hereditary criteria and partly upon personal factors. A chief must be the descendant of a preceding chief through either his father or his mother. Usually the chieftaincy, like the priesthood, rotates among three component houses (*shia*) of a chiefly family. The elders of the appropriate house select their candidate from among eligible kinsmen. The candidate whom the succeeding house selects is confirmed by the council of elders of the entire chiefly family before he is enstooled.

The *kpele* text is in Ga, with the exception of *ohene*.

[166]   *Version 1*
Aku Abia mǫ mang nyo;
Taki mǫ mang nyo—
Mang nyo blẹblẹ.

Ga mangtsẹ hold the town well;
Ga mangtsẹ hold the town well—
The town well and gently.

Singer: Ashiaklẹ wulǫmǫ.
Occasion: Recording songs, 1968.

Version 2 .
Ohi blẹo;
Mǫ mang nyo;
Otsi blẹo.
Abia, mǫ mang nyo;
Taki, mǫ mang nyo;
Mǫ mang nyo.
Abia, mǫ mang nyo;
Taki, mǫ mang nyo;
Ohi blẹo.

Live quietly;
Hold the town well;
Reign quietly.
Ga mangtsẹ, hold the town well;
Ga mangtsẹ, hold the town well;
Hold the town well.
Ga mangtsẹ, hold the town well;
Ga mangtsẹ, hold the town well;
Live quietly.

Singer: Olila wǫngtsẹ.
Occasion: Singing for the *Ga mangtsẹ*, 1965.
Commentary: This song articulates the peaceful prosperity
which Ga expect to enjoy under the leadership of a wise para-
mount chief. Taki and Abia are titles for the *Ga mangtsẹ*.
The words of both versions of the *kpele* text are Ga.

[167] Okaidza Ofroso, ba mang, owelefo;
Eshẹ mang, eshẹ onọ;
Kwẹmọ mang odzogbang;
Mọ mang dzo.

Gbese mangtsẹ, come to the town, avenger;
He arrives in the town, it is your turn;
Look after the town well;
Hold the town well.

Singer: Ashiaklẹ wulọmọ.
Occasion: Recording songs, 1968.
Commentary: When the Ga paramount stool is vacant, the chief of Gbese quarter in Accra acts as chief during the interregnum. The *Gbese* stool, which is said to be the nephew of the *Ga mangtsẹ*'s stool, is the second-ranking Ga stool. The relative status of these stools is reflected in the spatial orientations of their occupants on ceremonial occasions when the *Gbese mangtsẹ* is stationed either before or to the right of the *Ga mangtsẹ* (see Chapter 5). The Gbese quarter of Accra was founded by Okaidza, whom tradition maintains was the first Ga person to be buried in a coffin. He was buried by the Dutch in Ussher Fort, where every *họmọwọ* the *Gbese mangtsẹ* offers *kpekpei* to his soul.

The words of the *kpele* text are Ga.

[168] Ayi Bonte, bubu mang nyo;
Bubu mang nyo.

Gbese mangtsẹ, watch the town well;
Watch the town well.

Singer: Ashiaklẹ wulọmọ.
Occasion: Recording songs, 1968.
Commentary: See song 167 for note on the *Gbese mangtsẹ*'s role during interregna of Ga paramount chiefs. Ayi Bonte is one of the titles of the *Gbese mangtsẹ*.

Kle agbaayoo sang another version of the song that was identical with this one, except for the use of the first person in the second line.

The *kpele* text is in Ga.

[169]   Modzawe
        Teteete;
        Adaimẹi to lẹ.

        It is Modza we
        Of long ago;
        The ancestors instituted it.

Singer: Olila wọngtsẹ.
Occasion: Singing for the *Ga mangtsẹ*, 1965.
Exegesis: In the time of Amugi [early nineteenth century], the people instituted a criminal court of highest appeal. Punishments for the guilty included: shooting oneself with a gun, being thrown into the sea with a rock around the neck, and sitting on a red hot arrow.
Commentary: Until the British colonial government terminated its activities in 1910, *Modza we* was the *Ga mangtsẹ's* court of appeal in Accra (Amartey, *Adzenuloo!*, pp. 48-49).

The words of the *kpele* text are Ga.

[170]   Adai aponsa;
        Oku aba na sisi aba.

        People who know adai come and play;
        When war comes then deceit comes.

Singer: Olila wọngtsẹ.
Occasion: Discussion of *kpele* ritual, 1968.
Exegesis: When the world was created, this was the first song. It is a song of sorrow. As I have said, *kpele* existed from the beginning; this song is *kpele ayida*, which is a warrior's and

hunter's dance. The song says "*Adai* come and play," but the first song says that "when war comes then deceit comes." That is the first song. This person says one thing, that one says another; when war comes, that is how it is. And so when war comes, then deceit comes. Now the warriors call the priest to come to play a war dance.
Commentary: The words of the *kpele* text are non-Ga.

[171] Ngkra bę shwęmi,
      Dzę Ashanti eba;
      Dzę Odǫnkǫ eba,

      He swore to come to see me,
      He came from Ashanti, he comes;
      He came from the northern territories, he comes.

Singer: Olila wǫngtsę.
Occasion: Checking *kpele* songs, 1968.
Commentary: Another version of the song, distorted by multilingual confusion, was sung by *Kle agbaayoo* in 1968.
    The second and third lines of the *kpele* text are in Ga.

[172] Angula ba, eye wo;
      Akwamu ba, eye wo;
      Ashanti ba, eye wo;
      Anyę awo atee ashi lę.

      Ewe came, he was not defeated;
      Akwamu came, he was not defeated;
      Ashanti came, he was not defeated;
      They cannot defeat him, they went and left him.

Singer: Olila wǫngtsę.
Occasion: Discussion of Ayawaso trip, 1968.
Commentary: The *Olila* medium sang this song to explicate

the invincibility of the Ga under *Omanye*'s protection (see song 44 for note on *Omanye*).

The words of the *kpele* text are Ga.

[173] Afutu kęę enyangta;
Ayigbe kęę egblę;
Gamęi kęę ehii.
Atsę mi Ganyo krong,
Atsę mi Ganyo Ayite.

Afutu say it is destroyed;
Ewe say it is destroyed;
Ga say it is destroyed.
I am a pure Ga person,
I am a Ga person, Ayite.

Singer: Olila wǫngtsę.
Occasion: Recording songs, 1965.
Exegesis: Ayite, the second chief of Great Accra, sang this song. When some dissident Ga wished to follow an Obutu chief, Ayite sang, "I am a pure Ga person, follow me."
Commentary: See song 95, which incorporates the first three lines of this song in quite a different context.

Another version of the song, sung by *Olila agbaanuu* in 1968, was distorted by multilingual confusion.

The last three lines of the *kpele* text are in Ga; the first two lines each include one Ga word, *kęę.*

[174] Aye eta, Gamęi aye eta;
Atsu atsu banga;
Kę nyię akutsęi amli.
Kę nyię mangdzi anǫ,
Kę nyię mangdzi asęę,
Kę nyię wǫ mli,
Kę nyię gbomęi wudzii anǫ,
Kę nyię gbomęi lumęi anǫ.

Gamẹi aye eta;
Atsu atsu banga.

They ate everything; Ga people ate everything;
They collected, they collected everything:
When walking through the quarters,
When walking through the town,
When walking through other towns,
When walking among ourselves,
When walking among big men,
When walking among princes.
Ga people ate everything;
They collected, they collected everything.

Singer: Olila wọngtsẹ.
Occasion: Recording songs, 1965.
Commentary: This song differentiates the various units of the Ga polity: the quarter within a town, the town, and the confederation of towns.

With the exception of the second and tenth lines, the words of the *kpele* text are Ga.

[175] Ashi edu kẹtẹkre.
Dantu able dada,
Bo ole toohe, bo ole dzuuhe.
Nkran, Ashi edu kẹtẹkre,
Odom ni amangfọng;
Ana ngmẹẹ, anaa tẹ; ana tẹ, anaa ngmẹẹ.
Afutu kẹẹ enyangta;
Ayigbe kẹẹ egblẹ;
Gamẹi kẹẹ ehii.
Ashi edu kẹtẹkre.
Dantu able dada,
Bo ole toohe, bo ole dzuuhe.

It is Great Accra.
Dantu of old,

You know the storing place, you know the stealing
  place.
It is Great Accra,
Which is not subject to destruction;
When they have a palm nut, they do not have a stone;
  when they have a stone, they do not have a palm nut.
Afutu say it is destroyed;
Ewe say it is destroyed;
Ga say it is destroyed.
It is Great Accra.
Dantu of old,
You know the storing place, you know the stealing
  place.

Singer: *Olila wǫngtsę.*
Occasion: Recording songs, 1965.
Commentary: This song is an amalgam of songs (e.g., songs
95, 103, 173, 176), which through the repetition of thematic
elements achieves an integrated and distinctive unity.
  See the exegesis and commentary of song 176.
  The Ga lines in the *kpele* text are 2, 3, 6, 9, 11, 12.

[176] Nkran, Ashi edu kętękre,
       Odom ni amangǫng,
       Ana ngmęę, anaa tę; ana tę, anaa ngmęę.
       Wuǫwǫlǫ tufui ni awo lę kpaa ni efule.
       Afutu kęę enyangta;
       Ayigbe kęę egblę;
       Gamęi kęę ehii.

       It is Great Accra,
       Which is not subject to destruction.
       When they have a palm nut, they do not have a stone;
         when they have a stone, they do not have a palm nut.
       A rotten egg hangs on a loose thread.
       Afutu say it is destroyed;
       Ewe say it is destroyed;
       Ga say it is destroyed.

Singer: Olila woŋgtsẹ.
Occasion: Singing for the *Ga mangtsẹ,* 1965.
Exegesis: This is one of the great *kpele* songs; it rouses the
martial spirit of the Ga. Line 3 refers to Ga stoicism. Line 4 is
a proverb: what happens when a rotten egg falls? There is a
bad smell, so people leave; the Ga people are stinking, that is,
they are invincible in war.
Commentary: The central theme of this song is the invincibility of the Ga in battle. This idea is expressed clearly in the
first two lines of the song. The third line, which states that
when the Ga have a palm nut, they do not have a stone to
crack it, and conversely, when the Ga have a stone, they do
not have a palm nut to crack, refers to the indomitable forti-
tude of the Ga people in adverse circumstances. The fourth
line asserts the invincibility of the Ga in the form of a proverb: the enemies of the Ga flee from them, just as people run
to avoid the stench of a rotten egg. The last three lines concern the destruction that befalls all protagonists in war.

Like song 175, this song utilizes a number of thematic elements which may appear as separate units or as parts of a
variety of complex units.

The Ga lines of the *kpele* text are 3, 4, and 7.

[177]   Feemọ blẹọ, blẹọ afeeọ;
        Ngfee blẹọ dani ngmọ Nyanao;
        Feemọ blẹọ ni omọ Nyanao.
        Mibuushi ni mimọ Nyanao,
        Shi mi dzran tengteng ni ngmọ Nyanao.
        Blẹọ afeọ ni agbla alọ.
        Yaakwẹ adẹtẹtemẹi agbẹdzianọto.

        Go quietly, one goes quietly;
        I go quietly before I catch Nyanao;
        Go quietly so that you may catch Nyanao.
        I do not lay an ambush to catch Nyanao,
        But I stand straight to catch Nyanao.
        One goes quietly before one draws something.
        Go to see how the ancient people order things.

Singer: Olila wọngtsẹ.

Occasion: Recording songs, 1965.

Exegesis: If one wants something, one should be patient and brave. This song was sung when the Akwamu were conquered. Nyanao is a hill near Nsawam, a *Sakumọ* carrier [i.e., a god who is subordinate to *Sakumọ* and whose terrestrial location is the hill Nyanao], where the Akwamu resided. The general meaning of the song is that one should deal honestly and patiently with people.

Commentary: In general this song asserts the values of patient integrity in pursuing goals in human society. Specifically, the song refers to the conduct of a military foray against the Akwamu capital of Nyanao (see Chapter 6). Not withstanding the exegetical statement above, the Akwamu conclusively defeated the Ga in 1681.

An identical version of the song was sung by the *Olila* medium for the *Ga mangtsẹ* in 1965.

The words of the *kpele* text are Ga.

[178] Legọng, Tẹte Legọng;
    Adzẹ ni aba.
    Legọng, Tẹte Legọng;
    Adzẹ mangdzii ni aba.
    Legọng, Tẹte Legọng;
    Adzẹ boka.
    Legọng, Tẹte Legọng;
    Adzẹ anai.
    Legọng, Tẹte Legọng;
    Adzẹ dzeng fẹẹ.
    Legọng, Tẹte Legọng;
    Adzẹ dzeng teng.
    Legọng, Tẹte Legọng;
    Adzẹ dzeng kodzii kpawo.
    Legọng, Tẹte Legọng.

    It is Legọng, Tẹte Legọng;
    They arrived.

It is Legong, Tẹte Legong;
They arrived from other towns.
It is Legong, Tẹte Legong;
They came from the east.
It is Legong, Tẹte Legong;
They came from the west.
It is Legong, Tẹte Legong;
They came from all the world.
It is Legong, Tẹte Legong;
They came from the seven corners of the world.
It is Legong, Tẹte Legong.

Singer: Olila wọngtsẹ.
Occasion: Recording songs, 1965.
Exegesis: The song refers to the death of Dọde Akabi. She
told the Ga to dig a well with their hands. After they had dug
for some time, they told her that they could not dig any
further, because someone in the well told them that they
should not dig anymore. She became angry and went into
the well; people took stones and threw them in on her and
made a hill. When people were coming from north, south,
east, and west, they were told that the work was finished already. A god called *Tẹte Legong* told them that Dọde Akabi
was dead.
Commentary: According to Ga tradition, Dọde Akabi was the
wife of the *Ga mangtsẹ* Mampong Okai who died in 1642 and
the mother of Okai Koi who died in 1677. She is remembered
as a tyrannical regent during the latter's youth. In this song
people and gods come from all directions to witness her welcome death. The middle of the world and the seven corners
of the world refer to the location and supportive role of the
gods who mediate between the supreme being and mortal men
(see Chapter 4).
  The words of the *kpele* text are Ga.

[179]   *Version 1*
    Dọde Akabi,

Miba oye;
Oma ntẹm anto.

Dọde Akabi,
It is good that I came;
You are late and missed the burial.

Singer: Olila wọngtsẹ.
Occasion: Recording songs, 1965.
Exegesis: I came promptly so I saw Dọde Akabi's burial.
Those who came late did not see her burial.

> *Version 2*
> Adọde Aka, miba oye;
> Adọde Aka, mba ni ehi.
> Ba makwẹ minaa.
>
> Adọde Aka, it is good that I came;
> Adọde Aka, it is good that I came.
> If I do not come promptly, I do not see it.

Singer: Olila wọngtsẹ.
Occasion: Checking *kpele* songs, 1968.
Commentary: This song continues the theme of song 178 concerning the death of wicked Dọde Akabi.

A shorter rendition of the second version was sung by *Ashiaklẹ wulọmọ*, who inserted a different name and, therefore, provided a very different exegesis of the song.

The words of the first version of the *kpele* text are non-Ga; those of the second version are Ga, with the exception of the first line.

[180] Ani lomo bẹ mọ kwraa?
Aha lomobii fẹẹ;
Nyẹha lomobii fẹẹ;
Nyẹha lomobii blublu.
Oshi Adu Kọme, lomo bẹ moko kwraa.
Aha Buadzabii fẹẹ;

Naa, Buadza bę mǫ.
Aha Kǫmebii blublu;
Aha Kǫmebii fęę;
Kǫme bę mǫ kwraa.
Nyęha Dǫdebii fęę;
Naa Dǫde bę mǫ;
Aha Dǫdebii fęę.
Naa nyę ha Nkranpong fęę.
Nyę ha foloi eha Nkranpong fęę;
Wǫ Atsimbii amęha Nkranpong fęę.
Eta.
Amęha Nkranpongbii blublu;
Mua Nkranpong bę mǫ.

Does man have anyone at all?
They snatched all man's children;
You snatched all man's children;
You snatched all man's children.
Sakumǫ, man has no one at all.
They snatched all Olila's children;
Lo, Olila has no one.
They snatched all Sakumǫ's children;
They snatched all Sakumǫ's children;
Sakumǫ has no one at all.
You snatched all Dǫde's children;
Lo, Dǫde has no one;
They snatched all Dǫde's children.
Lo, you snatched all Great Accra.
You let uncircumcised people snatch all Great Accra;
Our Akims have snatched all Great Accra.
It is finished.
They have snatched all the people of Accra;
So Accra has no one.

Singers: Olila wǫngtsę and old woman.
Occasion: Greeting, 1968.
Commentary: The song refers to the Akwamu destruction of
Great Accra in 1677. Since the Ga have been routed, the gods

and ancestors have no one to honor them (see song 14 for notes on *Sakumo* and *Olila* and song 178 for note on Dǫde Akabi).

In the text circumcision is mentioned as a means of differentiating Ga from non-Ga (see song 142).

Stylistically, the song, which is presented as it was sung, illustrates how singers may vary the pattern of a song by altering words and the order of lines slightly.

The words of the *kpele* text are Ga, with the exception of *Nkranpong*.

[181]   Lakote Adu Awushi ku Anglo;
        Lakote ku˙Ashanti;
        Yęsoo mbęyę bi.

        Lakote Adu Awushi conquered Ewe;
        Lakote conquered Ashanti;
        I will do it again.

Singer: Ashiaklę wulǫmǫ.
Occasion: Recording songs, 1968.
Commentary: According to tradition, Lakote Adu Awushi was an elder of *Nai we.*

The words of the *kpele* text are non-Ga.

[182]   Ashi mlętęhu;
        Nyę kuadzing nęę ahię!

        Look at the faces of these people;
        You have monkey[1] faces!

1. *Kwakuo*, mona monkey (*Cercopithecus mona*).

Singer: Ashiaklę wulǫmǫ.
Occasion: Recording songs, 1968.
Exegesis: Lakote is angry with the people of Osu. When the

Osu people came from Fantiland to fish at Accra, Lakote gave
them a place to live. Sometimes the Okai Koi people [the
people of Great Accra] go after the Osu people's fish and so
the Osu people complained to Lakote. Lakote became angry,
because the Osu people did not send their elders to talk to
him. Lakote said that the Osu people did not respect him, but
that he respects himself.

Commentary: In this song Lakote of *Nai we* (song 181) insults the people of Osu by calling them monkeys. This form
of insult, whereby members of one class of being are identified as members of a lower class, also characterized the hostile exchanges between divine co-wives in songs 85 and 87.

The second line of the *kpele* text is in Ga.

[183]   Naa, mǫ yę;
     Mǫ yę;
     Mǫ yę.
     Akǫ Plaaku;
     Akǫ Plaaku, atsinete.
     Abola pong,
     Amǫ Ashantitsęmęi ayi bǫ.
     Ongwe Tęte,
     Ade, ngtsę mǫ bloa.

     Lo, there is someone;
     There is someone;
     There is someone.
     They took Plaaku;
     They took Plaaku, doubter.
     Great Abola,
     They caught many Ashanti elders.
     Pleiades Tęte,
     Ade, I call someone.

Singers: Olila wǫngtsę and old woman.
Occasion: Greeting, 1968.
Commentary: This song, which was sung in response to song
180, asserts that the Ga still exist.

The words of the *kpele* text are Ga, with the exception of *plaaku, atsinete,* and *pong.*

[184]   Abola pong,
        Mọyẹ, mọbẹ;
        Obi ni Abola.

        Great Abola,
        Someone is there; no one is there;
        No one is in Abola.

Singer: Kle agbaayoo.
Occasion: Recording songs, 1968.
Exegesis: The superior people have gone to Little Popo; those who remain are inferior.
Commentary: Abola is the quarter of Accra in which the Ga paramount chief resides. This song refers to the paramount chief Ofori's flight from coastal Accra to Little Popo in 1681 (see song 133).

The second line of the *kpele* text is in Ga.

[185]   Ashi edu kẹtẹkre,
        Tseremi ase obọmẹi aso kọngkọng;
        Omoẹ lẹ.

        Great Accra,
        Tell me what I did before you struck my ears;
        You are not good.

Singer: Olila wọngtse.
Occasion: Singing for the *Ga mangtsẹ*, 1965.
Exegesis: The prophet Lomoko [see song 55] speaks to the Asere people who burned his *gbatsu*. This *gbatsu* was *Olila*'s *gbatsu*, but Lomoko used it to prophesy. Originally, *Olila*'s *gbatsu* was at Ofankor [a village at the foot of Okai Koi Hill]. When the villagers came to coastal Accra, they brought the

gbatsu with them. After the *gbatsu* was destroyed, the water bowl [*tsẹsẹ*] was taken to *Sakumọ*'s *gbatsu* [see song 14], where it is today.

Commentary: The words of the *kpele* text are non-Ga.

Ga Culture

This group of songs concerns various premises and values of Ga culture. Several songs illuminate the stoical orientation of Ga culture toward social and biological experience (songs 186-189, 196). The impossibility of mutuality between persons of variant statuses or cultures and, conversely, the necessity of reciprocity between persons of similar status constitute the themes of a number of songs (songs 191-195, 197-199). Finally, several songs of salutation disclose the positive metaphysical connotations of certain physical qualities and properties, such as straightness, the right, white color, and white clay (songs 200-205).

[186] Ehi kɛ ehii,
   Wɔngɔ lɛ nakai.
   Mitsɛ lomo;
   Wɔngɔ lɛ nakai,
   Ehi kɛ ehii.
   Odai mitsɛ;
   Wɔngɔ lɛ nakai,
   Ehi kɛ ehii.

   Whether it is good or bad,
   We shall take it so.
   I call a prophet;
   We shall take it so,

Whether it is good or bad.
I call Sakumǫ;
We shall take it so,
Whether it is good or bad.

Singer: Olila wǫngtsẹ.
Occasion: Recording songs, 1965.
Exegesis: One must stoically accept any situation.
Commentary: The *Olila* medium sang a shorter version of the song on another occasion in 1965.
The words of the *kpele* text are Ga.

[187]   Odzweni akronto;
        Mile akẹ gbomǫ ehii.

        It is a ram's horn;
        I knew that the person was bad.

Singer: Olila wǫngtsẹ.
Occasion: Singing for the *Ga mangtsẹ*, 1965.
Exegesis: We were friends until something happened and you revealed your true bestial character.
Commentary: Ga believe that the spirits of animals may possess human beings. When the spirit of an animal is localized in a person, the person behaves like the animal. Although this notion is particularly relevant to twins who are thought to have bushcow (*Syncerus caffer beddingtoni*) spirits, in this song a person is possessed by the spirit of a ram, which suggests that his aggressive and irrational behavior violates the norms of reciprocal mutuality between friends.
The words of the *kpele* text are Ga, with the exception of *odzweni*.

[188]   Kaamǫ ashaman, kaamǫ,
        Ni ohẹ na koo nẹ;
        Shi gbele fǫ gbẹ loo.

Do not catch a thorn, do not catch it,
And do not cover this forest [with thorns];
For death's fat does not have any flesh.

Singer: Kle agbaayoo.
Occasion: Recording songs, 1968.
Exegesis: If a person covers a forest with thorns, he himself
may be pricked, which could result in his own death.
Commentary: With the exception of *ashaman*, the words of
the *kpele* text are Ga.

[189]   Obla yata moomo;
Mawo madā,
Laye Katamantọ.

Youth ended long ago;
I do not know where I will die,
It is Laye Katamantọ.

Singer: Abudu wulọmọ.
Occasion: Recording songs, 1965.
Exegesis: This is an old song, but I added my name, Laye, to
it. The song is about life—youth, old age, and death. A per-
son can die at any time, so it is essential to lead a good life.
Commentary: The words of the *kpele* text are Ga.

[190]   Kwao nyẹẹ aba;
Eyakwẹ heni ni
Ekẹẹ enaanii.
Oblo Oshi Edu Kọme kẹẹ
Kwao nyẹẹ aba.

Kwao cannot come;
He is looking for a place where
He may give his messages.
Sakumọ said
Kwao cannot come.

Singer: Koọle agbaayoo.
Occasion: Recording songs, 1968.
Exegesis: Kwao [Thursday-born male] wants a place where he can speak; he is beautiful.
Commentary: The text suggests that *Kwao* is a medium whose duties as a spokesman for divine beings take precedence over his obligations to other human beings.

A shorter version, which omits the fourth line, was sung by *Kle agbaayoo* in 1968. The principal difference between the two texts is that while this one is in the third person, that of *Kle agbaayoo* is in the first person. Both *kpele* texts are in Ga.

[191]   Opo lase,
        Ngkọ mia;
        Mishwẹẹ mọ mang;
        Miyee mọ we.

        I am a noble person,
        I do not go to another country;
        I do not drum in someone's town;
        I do not eat at someone's house.

Singer: Ashiaklẹ wulọmọ.
Occasion: Recording songs, 1968.
Exegesis: Nai we people say that they do not visit, play, or eat with others.
Commentary: A person should not endebt himself in any way to a person of lower status. Thus, in this song, the members of *Nai we* assert their superiority over other Ga by refusing to involve themselves in situations which might entail the establishment of reciprocal relations of equality.

The last two lines of the *kpele* text are in Ga.

[192]   Otswi ni krewii
        Afutu ni Gomua asem, ni Gomua asem
        Apam ni mlẹ wa yẹ.

Ngkẹ bo yee ongwẹ;
Ongwẹ ni angwẹtẹle.
Ahu ahuu mplenuu;
Ngmẹnẹ ngna wọhu mana.

A Twi person does not know
Afutu and Gomua customs, and Gomua customs
An Apam person does not know.
I do not share my privileges with you;
I share with my equals.
Today I see, tomorrow I will see;
Today I see, tomorrow also I will see.

Singer: Olila wọngtsẹ.
Occasion: Recording songs, 1965.
Exegesis: We are ignorant of other people's customs; we perform them without understanding. The last two lines mean that you reveal your character to me today, and tomorrow you will do the same.
Commentary: The fourth and seventh lines of the *kpele* text are in Ga.

[193] Akẹẹ wọọya wọyakwẹ;
Ngleshi blọfo engma wolo folo.

They said we are going to look;
The Englishman has written a worthless letter.

Singer: Kle agbaayoo.
Occasion: Recording songs, 1968.
Commentary: When the *Sakumọ agbaa* goes around the town either to announce the imposition of the period of silence after *ngmaadumọ* or to purify the town after the harvest, they sing this song at the *Alata mangtsẹ*'s house. Ga say that the Alata or Ngleshi quarter of Accra was established by non-Ga immigrants who settled in the vicinity of James Fort where

they worked for the British. In the course of time, these people became "Ga."

The words of the *kpele* text are Ga.

[194] Yẹdi na huma mu.
King blọfo
Wọde asem bi aba.
Wọbaaye lẹ wọdzi amli.
Yẹdi na huma mu.
King blọfo
Wọde asem bi aba.
Wọtee, wọnaa; wọba, wọnaa.

We are dealing in books.
The European
Has brought stories.
We are dealing in books.
We are dealing in books.
The European
Has brought stories.
We went, we did not understand; we came, we did not understand.[1]

1. *Wọnaa,* we did not see.

Singer: *Olila wọngtsẹ.*
Occasion: Recording songs, 1965.
Exegesis: The song is about the advent of European languages in Accra. The last line means that we went, we did not understand the European language; we returned, we did not understand the European language.
Commentary: This song, like the preceding one, is sung at the *Alata mangtsẹ*'s house by the *Sakumọ agbaa* during *mangnaamọ.*

The Ga lines in the *kpele* text are 2, 4, 6, and 8.

[195] Oshingkẹ kẹ otsi ofọ wọnọ,
Kẹ wọtsi wọfọ onọ.

Powerful one, when you push us,
Then we push you.

Singer: Kọọle agbaayoo.
Occasion: Recording songs, 1968.
Exegesis: The song means that when someone pushes me, I also push him. *Oshingkẹ* means "you say you are powerful"; so when you fight and hit me, I also will hit you.
Commentary: The basic theme of this song is the norm of reciprocity among equals in human society.

The words of the *kpele* text are Ga, with the exception of *oshingkẹ.*

[196] Asomua nyẹlọi.
Anyẹ aahu ni anyẹ.
Eko awo tọ mli ni atsi naa.
Anyẹ aahu ni anyẹ.

They do not comprehend people who hate.
They hate and they hate.
They put some hatred in a bottle and corked it.
They hate and they hate.

Singer: Olila wọngtsẹ.
Occasion: Singing for the *Ga mangtsẹ,* 1965.
Exegesis: This song describes a venomous individual whose hatred becomes part of his soul.
Commentary: The fact that the *Olila* medium sang this song for the *Ga mangtsẹ* before he assumed the full responsibilities of his office suggests that she intended to warn him of one kind of person who might cause discord during his rule.

The words of the *kpele* text are Ga, with the exception of *asomua.*

[197]   Saki Ayikwe eye edzawu eta;
        Eshwę ekome.

        Saki Ayikwe has eaten all the yams;
        There remains only one.

Singer: Olila agbaanuu.
Occasion: Recording songs, 1968.
Exegesis: You are staying with someone, you do not have any
food, you are hungry for a long time. Both of you feel hungry. You work together for some time. He has one yam which
both of you eat. When you finish eating the yam, you run
away and leave him. When you see that he has more food,
you return, but he says, "I have eaten all the yams."
Commentary: The exegetical statement further illuminates
the principle of reciprocity among peers. Saki Ayikwe's com-
panion violated this norm by greedily eating the yam but refusing to share the task of growing more food; consequently,
he was denied food later.
    The words of the *kpele* text are Ga.

[198]   Ngmada agoo,
        Moko bę dzęi?
        Ngkęę "Kikǫikikǫi,
        Ya oya lo ba oba?"

        I knock at the door.
        Is no one there?
        I said "Silent one,
        Are you going or are you coming?"

Singer: Olila agbaanuu.
Occasion: Recording songs, 1968.
Exegesis: When you enter a house, you should explain why
you have come. The song describes a rude person who does
not speak.
Commentary: The *kpele* text is in Ga.

[199] Ngtsẹ bo aahu;
Kpaako okẹ okantoi hẹlẹọ shi.

I called you many times;
Now your knees are knocking on the ground.

Singer: Olila agbaanuu.
Occasion: Recording songs, 1968.
Exegesis: The singer says that he often has called the person
who now begs for help, but the person never heeded his call.
Now that things have gone badly for the man, he begs on his
knees for help, but it is too late.
Commentary: The words of the *kpele* text are Ga.

[200] Okwandzo loome,
Nọni osumọ afee aha bo.

Okwandzo man,
What you like is done for you.

Singer: Kle agbaayoo.
Occasion: Recording songs, 1968.
Exegesis: Okwandzo is a *gbobalọ*. When he leaves a place, he
sings this song.
Commentary: When a woman successively loses a number of
babies, it is believed that the same spirit is being reborn each
time. The spirit does not remain on earth, because it is too
well liked by other spirits. In order to make the spirit stay, a
baby will be scarified to make it ugly and will be given a name
which implies that its human parents do not value it. If a child
who has been disfigured and named in this way survives, it is
called a *gbobalọ* (die-come-person).
   The *kpele* text is in Ga.

[201] Ndaose akunyanka,
Ani tọọ, ani dọọ.

> You are thanked, benefactor,
> For your gift, for your gift.

Singer: Kle agbaayoo.
Occasion: Recording songs, 1968.
Exegesis: When various *agbaa* go from house to house at
ngmaadumo to announce the period of silence, they may be
given money or drinks. When they are presented with a gift,
they sing this song.
Commentary: The words of the *kpele* text are non-Ga.

[202] Naa Tẹtẹ,
    Mọbi,
    Tẹtẹ baanyẹ masha gbẹ mli;
    Awaa, awaa, atuu, atuu;
    Nghe bo ninẹi dzurọ, nghe bo abeku.

    Behold Tẹtẹ,
    He is someone's child,
    Tẹtẹ will reach into the pot;
    Welcome, welcome, welcome, welcome;
    I receive you with the right hand, I receive you
        with the left hand.

Singer: Olila wọngtsẹ.
Occasion: Singing for the *Ga mangtsẹ*, 1965.
Exegesis: This song may be sung on any occasion to welcome
a person with blessing. On this occasion, the *Ga mangtsẹ* is
being blessed. *Tẹtẹ* refers to the god *Klang* [song 81]. *Masha
gbẹ mli* means "to reach into the pot" which contains *fotoli*
[a ritual food made from millet].
Commentary: In this song the cordial reception of the visitor
is conveyed through the images of sharing food and of a dual
handclasp. Since commensuality connotes amicable mutuality
in Ga society, an invitation to share food cannot be refused
politely. The *Olila* medium states in her exegesis that the visitor will join in eating *fotoli*, which is reserved for *kpele* ritual

meals in which gods and men participate; her statement suggests the unusual intimacy of the visitor's welcome. In Ga culture the greeting of a person with two hands rather than with the right hand alone connotes sincerity and respect (see Chapter 4). Thus, the greeting which is proffered in this song is unmistakably cordial and intimate.

The words of the *kpele* text are Ga.

[203]   Ngkwa,
         Okwa dzo;
         Oye kę awo,
         Oba hu awo.
         Gbę mli yę dung;
         Otsę ninei dzurǫ kę ayilǫ,
         Otsę abeku kę ayilǫ.
         Na, Kǫme gbę miiya,
         Dede gbę miiya.
         Ayatsę Nyampong ni eya dzię bo gbę;
         Ataa Nyǫngmǫ ni eya dzię bo gbę.
         Gbę miiya;
         Na, gbę edzę.

         The road,
         May your road be good;
         May you go with blessing,
         May you come with blessing.
         Darkness is on the road;
         May you turn to the right with white clay,
         May you turn to the left with white clay.
         Lo, on Sakumǫ's road I am going;
         On Dede's road I am going.
         Go call God that he may lead you on the road;
         May God lead you on the road.
         I am going on the road;
         Lo, the road is clear.

Singer: Olila wǫngtsę.

Occasion: Farewell, 1968.
Commentary: This song of farewell utilizes the image of the road as a metaphor for human experience in which darkness (*dung*) symbolizes difficulty, white clay (*ayilọ*) connotes success, and clarity (*gbẹ edzẹ*) signifies prosperity. The song also articulates the belief that success in human life ultimately depends upon the supreme being and harmonious relations with the gods.

The *kpele* text is in Ga, with the exception of *ngkwa* and *okwa.*

[204] Agblama fuu,
  Oba kẹ omanye;
  Oya kẹ omanye.
  Agblama fuu,
  Ayilọ fuu,
  Omanye fuu.
  Oba kẹ omanye;
  Oya kẹ omanye.
  Otee kẹ awo,
  Oba kẹ awo.

  May it be white,
  May you come with peace;
  May you go with peace.
  May it be white,
  White clay,
  White peace.
  May you come with peace;
  May you go with peace.
  May you go with blessing,
  May you come with blessing.

Singer: Olila wọngtsẹ.
Occasion: Farewell, 1965.
Commentary: In this song, as in song 203, whiteness is used as a propitious symbol.

The *kpele* text is in Ga, with the exception of *agblama.*

[205]   Okwa bladza,
         Okwa ayilǫ,
         Omanye ngkwa,
         Okwa dzodzo;
         Baya kwǫ bayaba.

         May your road be straight,
         May your road be white clay,
         May your road be peace,
         May your road be good;
         Go that you may return.

Singer: Olila wǫngtsẹ.
Occasion: Farewell, 1965.
Commentary: This song, which utilizes the metaphor of the road for human experiences (song 203), is a compendium of propitious symbols which are based upon physical qualities (straight, white) and abstract conceptions (peace, good).

The words of the *kpele* text are Ga, with the exception of *okwa* and *ngkwa.*

Animals

This final group of songs pertains to all kinds of animals. In accordance with Ga taxonomic principles (see Chapter 4), the group is subdivided into three categories: domestic animals (songs 206, 207), land animals (songs 208-223), and sea animals (songs 224-243). Within each category, however, the songs relate to one of two conceptual models. Some songs represent animal behavior as analogues of human behavior. Other songs provide existential descriptions of animal life which may or may not include references to the pragmatic utilization of these creatures by human beings.

[206] Akǫkǫ bo kokolikoo,
Ade bęsa, ade bętsę.

The cock crows kokolikoo,
It is morning, it is evening.

Singer: Kle agbaayoo.
Occasion: Recording songs, 1968.
Commentary: The crowing of the cock signals the limits of the day, the period of human activity, and, conversely, those of the night, the period of divine activity.

The words of the first line of the *kpele* text are Ga, with the exception of *akǫkǫ.*

277

[207]   Akǫkǫ ni mto onya dabloye;
        Wuǫ ni mito enaa wǫhe.

        The fowl that I keep cannot find a sleeping place;
        The fowl that I keep cannot find a sleeping place.

Singer: Olila agbaanuu.
Occasion: Recording songs, 1968.
Exegesis: When *Afieye* have children, whatever they say to
them, they will do. When *Afieye* says pass here, the children
will pass here; when *Afieye* says pass there, the children will
pass there. But if you have a child who does not agree to do
what you say, then he is like your fowl which does not like
her nesting place. She lays eggs wherever she likes. Even if you
beat her with a stick, she will lay wherever she wishes. And so
we made the song. If a fowl does not have a customary place
to sleep, it will wander about just as children who do not have
a good place to stay become truants.
Commentary: The second line of the *kpele* text is in Ga.

[208]   Gǫdǫi amɛnyiɛ amɛ momoɛ,
        Amɛtao amɛ kpakpo.

        The cranes walk on their old paths,
        They want their lake.

Singer: Olila agbaanuu.
Occasion: Recording songs, 1968.
Exegesis: The cranes are walking on the walls, they want their
lake so that they may swim. A lake is the source of life for
cranes; they seek a lake in order to swim and wash.
Commentary: The words of the *kpele* text are Ga.

[209]   Kwakwa lobite,
        Obaanyɛ kǫle lo?

Kwakwa lobite,
Ekẹẹ kọle ni mọmọ,
Kọle ni shamọ.
Ah, Lobite baanyẹ kọle lo?
Kọle ni mọmọ.

Crow,[1]
Can you compete with kọle?
Crow,
She said kọle which catches,
Kọle which snatches.
Ah, crow, can you compete with kọle?
Kọle which catches.

1. *Kwakwa lobite*, pied crow (*Corvus albus*).

Singer: Akumadze Afieye wọngtsẹ.
Occasion: Recording songs, 1968.
Exegesis: The crow cannot compete with *kọle*, which is another bird.
Commentary: Although unfortunately I have been unable to identify *kọle*, the text implies that the *kọle* bird is a better insect catcher than the crow. In Ga thought such natural abilities are considered to be immutable and are attributed to the intention of the supreme being. The wording of the text suggests the crow does not appreciate fully this fundamental principle of the Ga universe (cf. songs 9 and 11).

The words of the *kpele* text are Ga.

[210]   Apatuplẹ,
        Yẹ mi na mi yọọ.
        Apatuplẹ, plẹ, plẹ, kọmfoẹ,
        Yẹ mi na mi yọọ.
        Okọdi wusa, wusa kẹ wutum;
        Yẹ mi na mi yọọ.
        Okọdi mako wọshiu onuam;
        Yẹ mi na mi yọọ.

Apatuplẹ, plẹ, plẹ, kọmfoẹ,
Yẹ mi na mi yọọ.

Pepper-eating bird,[1]
It is not my fault.
Pepper-eating bird, pepper, pepper, pepper,
It is not my fault.
You eat a sponge, the sponge gets stuck in your anus;
It is not my fault.
You eat pepper, it hurts your eye;
It is not my fault.
Pepper-eating bird, pepper, pepper, pepper,
It is not my fault.

1. *Apatuplẹ*, garden bulbul (*Pycnonotus barbatus*).

Singer: Akumadze Afieye wọngtsẹ.
Occasion: Recording songs, 1968.
Exegesis: When you eat a sponge and the sponge gets stuck in
your anus, I did not do it; when you eat pepper and pepper
also gets stuck in your anus, I did not do it.
Commentary: This text suggests two social norms. The first is
that persons must assume responsibility for their actions; the
second is that persons should not attempt tasks without
knowing how to perform them. Thus, the pepper-eating bird
asserts that those who imitate him and get pepper in their
eyes should not blame him for their clumsiness. Similarly, if a
person eats a sponge which gets stuck in his gut, this is his
own responsibility. Ga informants often have stated that although human beings depend on divine beings ultimately for
success in their endeavors, people shape their own destinies
through their capacity to reason.

A similar version of the song was sung by *Kọọle agbaayoo.*
The differences between the texts are due to multilingual dis-
tortions in the second text. The words of the *kpele* text are
non-Ga.

[211]   Dodo mi eei,
        Dodo mi Obleku,
        Shwẹmi tiri mi ye;
        Shwẹmi nua mi ye;
        Shwẹmi so mi ye;
        Shwẹmi nuii mi ye;
        Shwẹmi na mi ye;
        Shwẹmi kuma mi ye;
        Shwẹmi siye mi ye;
        Shwẹmi ko mi ye;
        Shwẹmi koko mi ye;
        Shwẹmi basa mi ye;
        Shwẹmi breku mi ye;
        Shwẹmi yẹfu mi ye;
        Shwẹmi nuku mi ye;
        Shwẹmi fifi mi ye;
        Shwẹmi sa mi ye;
        Shwẹmi natu mi ye;
        Shwẹmi namu mi ye;
        Shwẹmi ngwọba mi ye.

        I am Dodo,
        I am Dodo Obleku,[1]
        Look at my head, it is good;
        Look at my eye, it is good;
        Look at my ear, it is good;
        Look at my nose, it is good;
        Look at my mouth, it is good;
        Look at my tongue, it is good;
        Look at my tooth, it is good;
        Look at my neck, it is good;
        Look at my chest, it is good;
        Look at my right arm, it is good;
        Look at my left arm, it is good;
        Look at my torso, it is good;
        Look at my breast, it is good;
        Look at my waist, it is good;
        Look at my thigh, it is good;

> Look at my calf, it is good;
> Look at my leg, it is good;
> Look at my toe, it is good.

1. *Obleku*, Senegal coucal (*Centropus senegalensii*).

Singer: Akumadze Afieye wǫngtsę.
Occasion: Recording songs, 1968.
Exegesis: Obleku counts all his parts, look at his head, look at his eyes; he counts all his body parts down to his toes.
Commentary: The most notable feature of this song is that the body parts which the bird enumerates are human and not avian (see Chapter 4).

A similar version of the song was sung by *Kǫǫle agbaayoo* in 1968. The two versions differ with respect to some of the body parts that are enumerated. Both *kpele* texts are non-Ga.

[212] Anuma lisu;
       Anuma lisu;
       Mikǫ Lampasa;
       Anuma lisu.

       Anuma kasa;
       Anuma kasa;
       Mikǫ Lampasa;
       Anuma kasa.

       A bird cries;
       A bird cries;
       I climbed Lampa hill;
       A bird cries.

       A bird speaks;
       A bird speaks;
       I climbed Lampa hill;
       A bird speaks.

Singer: Akumadze Afieye wǫngtsę.

Occasion: Recording songs, 1968.
Exegesis: When I went, a bird was crying on Lampa hill; he stood on the top of the hill. When I went there again, I met the bird standing there. When I went there again, I met the bird walking on the top of the hill. I do not know the name of the bird, that is how it is sung.
Commentary: The second and seventh lines of the *kpele* text are in Ga.

[213]　Angọbi ba he wọ ade;
　　　　Angọbi, frabra.

　　　　Bird, come take our thing;
　　　　Bird, come take it.

Singer: Ashiaklẹ wulọmọ.
Occasion: Recording songs, 1968.
Exegesis: Angọbi do not eat all our millet. Come and eat some, but do not eat all our millet.
Commentary: This is a *ngmaadumọ* song for *Nai we.*

　　The *Ashiaklẹ wulọmọ* said that *angọbi* was a "fine, small bird," which I have been unable to identify further.

　　The first line of the *kpele* text is in Ga, with the exception of *ade.*

[214]　Wuọ fọọ looflọ.
　　　　Patu li kọng kọ ni dẹle.
　　　　Patu tsẹ komia;
　　　　Patu tsẹ kọngfia.
　　　　Mi dọ otse mi dọ ohi.
　　　　Mitiri kọng,
　　　　Kooloo patu na mi adawute.

　　　　A fowl does not understand a wild bird.
　　　　What the owl knew he has left for you.
　　　　The owl said that what you like [likes you].

The owl said that it likes you.
I like women and I like men.
I carry my head,
The owl's head contains knowledge.

Singer: Olila wo̧ngtsȩ.
Occasion: Singing for the *Ga mangtsȩ*, 1965.
Exegesis: You know only what your master teaches you; the pupil resembles his teacher [line 1]. You have been taught so that you may teach [line 2].
Commentary: In Ga thought the owl is an ambiguous creature, for owls are associated with witches (*ayȩ*). Although Ga believe that witches, who are human beings with unusual psychic powers, may use their powers for benevolent purposes, witches are expected to act malevolently. Witches are believed to transform themselves into animals, that is, into beings of a lower taxonomic class, and most frequently into owls. The cry of the owl, therefore, is interpreted usually as an omen of impending disaster in human society (songs 215, 216). There are a number of reasons why owls and witches should be associated. Both are believed to be primarily nocturnal creatures. Both, therefore, are differentiated from the normal diurnal beings of their respective classes. This habitual differentiation is associated with unusual powers and further with moral inversion, or at least moral ambiguity. Thus, nocturnal witches and nocturnal owls are beings which may utilize their unusual powers either positively or negatively.

The words of the *kpele* text are non-Ga, with the exception of *wuo̧, looflo̧, patu,* and *kooloo.*

[215] *Version 1*
Patu hu ade;
Huhu edzang.
Patu nsu
Edzang;
Daadaa ha edzang, edzang.

The owl sees something;
He saw nothing.
The owl cries
Without cause;
Always he cries without cause.

Singer: Olila agbaanuu.
Occasion: Recording songs, 1968.
Exegesis: When an owl cries, people say that it means something bad will happen; but actually his cry portends good.

> *Version 2*
> Akęę huhu de dzang.
> Patu eye; patu su.

> They said that he sees nothing.
> The owl is good; the owl cries.

Singer: Kle agbaayoo.
Occasion: Recording songs, 1968.
Commentary: The conventional notion that the cry of an owl presages evil is contradicted in this song (see song 214).

The words of the *kpele* text are non-Ga, though *patu* is the term for owl in both Twi and Ga.

[216] Akęę mi hu mihii;
Patu su mihu ade;
Mihu ade.
Shwila tee bahere omang;
Oshwila Adu Kǫme bahere omang.

They said I too I am bad;
The owl cries I have seen something,
I have seen something.
Oshwila, go and save your town;
Sakumǫ, come and save your town.

Singer: Abudu wulǫmǫ.
Occasion: Recording songs, 1965.
Exegesis: The owl's cry shows that something calamitous will happen. Perhaps someone will die. The owl appeals to the gods for salvation.
Commentary: Contradictory ideas about the meaning of an owl's cry are expressed in songs 214 and 215.

The first, fourth, and fifth lines of the *kpele* text are in Ga.

[217] Kǫkǫbi Dene;
Mahi faahe,
Manu wǫlǫmǫ.

Kǫkǫbi Dene;
Mahi dzǫǫhe,
Manu wǫlǫmǫ.

It is the frog;
I will live near rivers,
I will hear coughing.

It is the frog;
I will live near valleys,
I will hear coughing.

Singer: Olila wǫngtsę.
Occasion: Recording songs, 1965.
Exegesis: Kǫkǫbi Dene is a species of frog which says that it will live near rivers to hear people cough. The frog is the father of the river. Whenever you hear a frog croak, you know that there is water for you to drink.
Commentary: The words of the *kpele* text are Ga.

[218] Atswele wǫ nsu;
Kǫkǫbi nggbo faa.

The frog lives in water;
The frog dies in the river.

Singer: Olila wǫngtsẹ.
Occasion: Recording songs, 1965.
Exegesis: The frog lives and dies in the river. But a frog can leap out of the river; sometimes when it jumps out of the river, it dies, because it cannot find its way back to the river.
Commentary: The second line of the *kpele* text is in Ga.

[219] Ahura sasaplẹfo
Lẹ etseǫ amẹ naa ba.

The tortoise[1] is a busy-body
He plucks their leaves.

1. *Ahura*, hinged tortoise (*Kinixys erosa*).

Singer: Kle agbaayoo.
Occasion: Recording songs, 1968.
Exegesis: The tortoise meddles where he is not wanted. Sometimes he picks the leaves which people want for their ritual bath water.
Commentary: The second line of the *kpele* text is in Ga.

[220] Bẹtsẹ minka;
Oshishibrishi nangka gbo.

The puff adder lies;
When you handle it, it will bite.

Singer: Abudu wulǫmǫ.
Occasion: Recording songs, 1965.
Exegesis: Bẹtsẹ is a short but poisonous snake. The meaning of the song is that when you handle something dangerous, you get bad results; one, therefore, should use caution in one's pursuits.
Commentary: See song 61 for a note on the association of the god *Abudu* with *blika* or the puff adder.
The words of the *kpele* text are non-Ga.

[221] Lomo Aku blika,
       Blika ebaaye wuǫ.

       Lord Wednesday-born puff adder,[1]
       Puff adder will eat fowls.

1. *Blika*, puff adder (*Bitis arietans*).

Singer: Kle agbaayoo.
Occasion: Recording songs, 1968.
Commentary: Although this song appears merely to present an existential description of relations between two animal species, it may be considered as an analogue of intersocietal relations. A number of songs (e.g., songs 142, 192, 214) have conveyed the notion of social distance between groups of different cultures. This song suggests not only social distance between societies, but the expectation that intersocietal relations will be hostile. This song further suggests that the wild bush as represented by the puff adder can destroy the civilized village as connoted by the domesticated fowl (see song 164). Ga appreciate the struggle between passion and reason in human life; while they assert the primacy of reason over passion in human society (*dzengmǫ dzi gbomǫ*, "the mind is the person"), they acknowledge the tenuousness of this balance.
       The words of the *kpele* text are Ga.

[222] Tsutsua akpene,
       Ofobii mingtu, hǫǫbii mingtu.

       Moving slowly,
       The monkeys[1] are climbing, the monkeys are
         climbing.

1. *Ofo* (*ofobi*), white-thighed colobus (*C. polykomos vellerosus*).

Singers: Gua agbaa.

Occasion: Gua ngmaadumǫ and *ngmaafaa*, 1965.
Exegesis: When one tries to catch monkeys, they climb to the
tops of trees on tendrils. This is the situation described in this
song. *Gua*'s people [i.e., the members of the *Gua* cult] do not
eat monkeys.
Commentary: The second line of the *kpele* text is in Ga.

[223]   Aduẹlẹ dzio amane;
         Gbomǫ ngǫǫtsǫ,
         Shi akǫǫ gbomǫ ayee.

         The squirrel[1] has done wrong;
         Man is very sweet,
         But one does not bite and eat man.

1. *Aduẹlẹ*, northern ground squirrel (*Euxerus erythropus*).

Singer: Olila agbaanuu.
Occasion: Recording songs, 1968.
Exegesis: A squirrel tells a snake that man is sweet. The snake
assumes that the squirrel means that man's flesh is sweet. The
snake bit a hunter, but he did not taste any sweetness. So the
squirrel told the snake that he did not mean that the flesh of
man is sweet, but he meant that to have a man [as a com-
panion] is sweet.
Commentary: A shorter version of the song was sung by *Kle
agbaayoo* in 1968.
    The second and third lines of the *kpele* text are in Ga.

[224]   Mpo mu mi ni dua
         Ni kita mu.

         The sea does not have a tree
         To hold.

Singer: Olila wǫngtsẹ.

Occasion: Checking *kpele* songs, 1968.
Exegesis: The sea cannot hold a tree.
Commentary: Another version of the song, sung by the *Ashiakle wulomo*, was distorted by multilingual confusion, for the *kpele* texts are non-Ga. Although the *wulomo* garbled the *kpele* text and could not provide a Ga transliteration of it, he knew the general meaning of the song.

[225]   Nti Mpo Dede ti mponaa ase ba;
     Mpo Dede, bo oha sane ba.

     When Sea Dede hears things from the sea, she
       repeats them;
     Sea Dede, you bring trouble.

Singer: Olila agbaanuu.
Occasion: Recording songs, 1968.
Exegesis: Mpo Dede is the name of a bird who brings trouble. She reveals things that are happening. Consequently, she has been exiled to the sea where she must sleep and hatch her eggs.
Commentary: This song may be interpreted as an analogue of human society. Its message is that people who gossip will be socially ostracized. The value which Ga attach to circumspection in social life is expressed clearly in the following lines, which form part of a prayer at the naming rite of an infant:

     The wind blows before a Ga person speaks;
     Gafomobi ke keyoo tswa dani ewie;
     He sees, he has not seen;
     Ena, enako;
     He hears, he has not heard.
     Enu, enuko.

A shorter version of the song was sung by the *Ashiakle wulomo* in 1968, who provided a similar exegesis of the song.

The second line of the *kpele* text is in Ga, with the exception of *mpo.*

[226]   Alangmaibi lẹ shwẹẹ kwea.

The sand crab[1] does not go to the forest.

1. *Alangmai,* sand crab (*Ocypoda africana*).

Singer: Ashiaklẹ wulọmọ.
Occasion: Recording songs, 1968.
Exegesis: The crab does not go to the forest; he lives in the sea. He is one of *Nai*'s children, and all *Nai*'s children are in the sea.
Commentary: Just as the human members of *Nai we* assert their superiority over members of other Ga families by refusing to visit them (songs 152 and 153), so the animal members of *Nai we* assert their superiority over other members of their class in this song.

The words of the *kpele* text are Ga, with the exception of *kwea.*

[227]   Somo eku yaa;
        Agbaamẹibii nyẹ haa somo.

The fiddler crabs[1] are scattered around;
May the agbaa's children collect fiddler crabs.

1. *Somo,* fiddler crab (*Gelasimus tangeri*).

Singer: Kle agbaayoo.
Occasion: Recording songs, 1968.
Exegesis: Lots of fiddler crabs have come, may the *agbaa* collect them.
Commentary: The words of the *kpele* text are Ga.

[228]   Somo Dede,
        Somo Kọkọ,
        Milẹ mibẹẹ mọ.

It is fiddler crab Dede,
It is fiddler crab Kǫkǫ.
As for me, I do not pinch a person.

Singer: Kle agbaayoo.
Occasion: Recording songs, 1968.
Commentary: The names *Dede* and *Kǫkǫ* denote first-born and second-born daughters, respectively.
The words of the *kpele* text are Ga.

[229]   Atshitshi flu ba yęng.
Obise, malate.

The mangrove crab[1] gives fever.
If someone speaks, I reply.

1. *Atshitshi*, mangrove crab (*Goniopsis cruentata*).

Singer: Kǫǫle agbaayoo.
Occasion: Recording songs, 1968.
Exegesis: The mangrove crab is in the sea and people eat it. When some people eat it, they become sick; when others eat it, nothing happens to them. But if sickness catches a person, it is not the mangrove crab's concern at all.
Commentary: The song conveys the notion of personal responsibility for one's actions that was expressed in song 210.
The first line of the *kpele* text is in Ga.

[230]   Bonso Aku efri mpomu;
Eba ebęshwę ade.

The Wednesday-born whale came in the sea;
He came to see what is being done.

Singer: Kle agbaayoo.
Occasion: Recording songs, 1968.

Exegesis: The whale came from the sea; he went to the forest also; he came from the sea to Accra to look at things. The whale guides the sea.

Commentary: The whale, the largest sea creature, is superior to other sea animals, just as *Nai,* the god of the sea, outranks all other *kpele* gods in Accra. Sometimes the term whale is used as a symbol of *Nai* (song 96). The correlation between physical magnitude and social ranking is covered in Chapter 4.

The Ga words in the *kpele* text are *bonso, aku,* and *eba.*

[231]   Bonso mba yẹ shọng;
        Anaa nine amọ Bonso;
        Akpaa nine mli amọ Bonso.

        The whale is coming from afar;
        They do not have a hand to catch the whale;
        They stretch out a hand to catch the whale.

Singer: Kle agbaayoo.
Occasion: Recording songs, 1968.
Commentary: The second and third lines of the *kpele* text are in Ga.

[232]   Atsi wọkẹtee.
        Akẹẹ wọmashi nọọng:
        Atsi wọkẹtee;
        Atsi wọkẹba.

        They push, we go.
        They said that we remain the same:
        They push, we go;
        They push, we come.

Singer: Ashiaklẹ wulọmọ.
Occasion: Recording songs, 1968.

Exegesis: We *Nai* people, when they push us forward and when they push us backward, we remain the same.

Commentary: The *Nai* people, that is, sea creatures always remain in the sea. This song is said to refer specifically to sea algae which moves to and fro in the water with the tides.

The words of the *kpele* text are Ga.

[233] *Version 1*
     Mpo minaa;
     Mpo dapo minaa.

     The sea does not sleep;
     The sea shell does not sleep.

Singer: Ashiaklẹ wulọmọ.
Occasion: Recording songs, 1968.
Exegesis: It means that when the sea ebbs and when the sea rises, it drags the beach shells forward and backward. When the sea is angry, these cowries, which are on the edge of the sea, do not get any rest, but when the sea is calm, the shells lie quietly.

     Version 2
     Mpo mina;
     Ngshọ wọ;
     Mpo mida,
     Ngshọ nglẹ hu wọọ.
     Mpo mida,
     Mpo nglẹ mida.

     The sea sleeps;
     The sea sleeps;
     The sea does not sleep,
     The sea cowry also does not sleep.
     The sea does not sleep,
     The sea cowry also does not sleep.

Singer: Olila wongtsẹ.
Occasion: Checking *kpele* songs, 1968.
Exegesis: When the sea sleeps, then I will sleep; when the sea does not sleep, I will not sleep. When the sea does not sleep, the cowry which is on the beach also will not sleep. Unless the sea sleeps, the cowry will not sleep. *Mpo nglẹ—*that is money; so if you have money and you sit down to do something, then your money also will not sleep; when you sleep, your money also will sleep. And also if you have a master whom you serve; if he does not sleep, will you sleep? If your master does not sleep, you will not sleep either.
Commentary: The second and fourth lines in Version 2 are in Ga.

[234]   Minya loo,
        Misa ngtwi di atọ.
        Krọbọdono lẹ,
        Misa ngtwi di atọ.

        Whenever you see a fish,
        Water is there.
        When a blanquillo[1] is there,
        Water is there.

1. *Krọbọdono,* blanquillo (*Latilus semifasciatus*).

Singer: Olila wọngtsẹ.
Occasion: Recording songs, 1968.
Exegesis: Whenever you see a blanquillo, there is water which will quench your thirst.
Commentary: According to Irvine, the striped body markings of the blanquillo "account for its vernacular names, and refer to the whitish parallel stripes made on the body and arms with the scented gum [*krọbọ*]" (Irvine, *The Fishes and Fisheries*, p. 135). *Krọbọ* is used as a cosmetic by women in secular society and by mediums and women of the *agbaa* on ritual occasions.

An analogous association between an animal species and its habitat and the pragmatic implications of this association for human beings is expressed in song 217.

The words of the *kpele* text are non-Ga, with the exception of *loo* and *krobodono*.

[235] Ngsholoo, woloo, woloobii;
Tẹtẹ, mashi tẹ.

They are the sea fish, the sea fish, the children of
the sea fish;
Tẹtẹ, I strike the stone.

Singer: Ashiaklẹ wulọmọ.
Occasion: Recording songs, 1968.
Commentary: The words of the *kpele* text are Ga.

[236] Tsukwe loo ana brobro ona;
Tsukwe kẹẹ misa awale mli loo;
Ekẹẹ lẹ engọ.

The threadfin[1] fish is sweet to the mouth;
The threadfin sings I am a suitable fish to put
in a spoon;
He says as for him, he is sweet.

1. *Tsukwe*, threadfin (*Galeoides decadactylus*).

Singer: Kle agbaayoo.
Occasion: Recording songs, 1968.
Commentary: The words of the *kpele* text are Ga.

[237] Potsiri Kofi namọ ba,
Namọ ba;
Osẹrẹ Kofi namọ ba.

It is Friday-born eagle ray[1] who came,
Who came;
It is Friday-born guitar fish[2] who came.

1. *Potsiri*, eagle ray (*Myliobatis aquila*).
2. *Osęrę*, guitar fish (*Rhinobatua rasus*).

Singer: Kle agbaayoo.
Occasion: Recording songs, 1968.
Commentary: The words of the *kpele* text are Ga.

[238] Kangkamba,
      Miyę odehem;
      Ase bu.

      Sardine,[1]
      I am a noble child;
      The year has come.

1. *Kangkamba*, sardine (*Sardinella awuta*).

Singer: Kle agbaayoo.
Occasion: Recording songs, 1968.
Exegesis: An edible fish says that it is noble.
Commentary: Although "the year has come" (*afi eshę*) usually refers to the commencement of the annual set of agricultural rites (song 108), in this song the phrase refers to the
homǫwǫ rite. On the Tuesday preceding *Lante Dzan we homǫwǫ*, a rite is performed to open the bream fishing season
(song 239). After this rite is completed, seven boats representing the seven quarters of Accra set out to catch sardines
(*kangkamba*) which are used as bait for catching bream.

    The words of the *kpele* text are non-Ga, with the excep-
tion of *kangkamba*.

[239] Tsile ani pǫ.
      Etsi pǫ;
      Enya pǫ.

The sea bream[1] is sweet.
When it is roasted, it is sweet;
When it is boiled, it is sweet.

1. *Tsile*, sea bream (*Dentex macrophtalmus*).

Singer: Ashiaklẹ wulọmọ.
Occasion: Recording songs, 1968.
Exegesis: The sea bream is used for *họmọwọ* food.
Commentary: The sea bream which comes in August is used
in the *họmọwọ* stew which accompanies *kpekpei.* The season
for bream fishing is opened by the *ngshọ bulemọ* rite on Tues-
day preceding *Lante Dzan we họmọwọ* in Accra (song 238).
    With the exception of *tsile*, the words of the text are non-
Ga.

[240] Kokobli, madzira mpona,
        Miyẹ ohene nam.

        Pampano,[1] I stand on the sea shore,
        I am a chief's fish.

1. *Kokobli*, pampano (*Trachinotus goreensis*).

Singer: Ashiaklẹ wulọmọ.
Occasion: Recording songs, 1968.
Exegesis: The pampano says I am on the beach. I am the fish
for chiefs; they eat me.
Commentary: The words of the *kpele* text are non-Ga, with
the exception of *kokobli.*

[241] Kokobli,
        Ngkẹ gbaa dzẹ nyẹ;
        Ngkẹ lẹ dzẹẹ tsẹ.

        It is the pampano,

The horse mackerel[1] and I came from one mother;
He and I did not come from one father.

1. *Gbaa,* horse mackerel (*Caranx hippos*).

Singer: Ashiaklẹ wulọmọ.
Occasion: Recording songs, 1968.
Commentary: According to Linnaean taxonomy, these two
fish belong to the same family. They grow to the same size,
have the same silvery color, except that the horse mackerel
has a yellow caudal fin, and they have similar body shapes,
although the nose of the horse mackerel is blunter and the
dorsal fin of the pampano is longer. Since in Ga thought a
child may resemble either parent, the physiognomic similarities between pampano and horse mackerel probably underlie
this song.
The words of the *kpele* text are Ga.

[242] Manya lo;
Odoi manya lo;
Odoi Kọbla manya;
Odoi manya lo;
Odi nam pa.

I have got;
A barracuda[1] I have got;
Barracuda Kọbla I have got;
A barracuda I have got;
You eat a good fish.

1. *Odoi,* barracuda (*Sphyraena guachancho*).

Singer: Olila wọngtsẹ.
Occasion: Checking *kpele* songs, 1968.
Exegesis: When you eat a barracuda, you eat a good fish.
Commentary: A shorter version of the song was sung by *Ash-
iaklẹ wulọmọ* in 1968.

The words of the *kpele* text are non-Ga, with the exception of *odoi* and *kǫbla.*

[243] Ablekwi, lo, tsęmęi engmę saa;
Niimęi engmę saa;
Naamęi engmę saa.
Ngkę ablekwi lo ba wǫwǫnǫ.

Painted eel,[1] lo, the fathers have spread a mat;
The grandfathers have spread a mat;
'The grandmothers have spread a mat.
Painted eel come with me, let us sleep on it.

1. *Ablekwi* (lit., *ablekui,* grains of maize), painted eel (*Gymnothorax vicinus*).

Singer: Ashiaklę wulǫmǫ.
Occasion: Recording songs, 1968.
Exegesis: Grandfather painted eel said that it is dark; the grandfather has spread a mat, come let us lie down. When mediums are possessed, they will invoke the sea people; all of them will sing. They will make things so that they will work god-things. The mediums will call all *Nai's* family.
Commentary: This song exemplifies the utilization of anthropomorphic analogy to describe the behavior of animal species (see Chapter 4).
The words of the *kpele* text are Ga.

Bibliography

Index

Bibliography

Ackah, C. A. "The Historical Significance of Some Ghanaian Festivals." *Ghana Notes and Queries* 5:16-27 (1963).

Acquah, Ioné. *Accra Survey*. London: University of London Press, 1958.

Adjei, Ako. "Mortuary Usages of the Ga Peoples of the Gold Coast." *American Anthropologist* 45:84-98 (1943).

Akrofi, C. A., and G. L. Botchey. *English-Twi-Ga Dictionary*. Accra: Waterville Publishing House, 1965.

Allott, A. N. "A Note on the Ga Law of Succession." *Bulletin of the School of Oriental and African Studies* 15:164-169 (1953).

Amarteifio, G. W., D. A. P. Butcher, and David Whitman. *Tema Manhean: A Study of Resettlement*. Accra: Ghana Universities Press, 1966.

Amartey, A. A. *Adzenuloo!* Accra: Bureau of Ghana Languages, 1961.

Ammah, Charles. *The Ga Homowo*. Accra: Advance Publishing, 1968.

Ammah, E. A. "Field Notebooks, 1937." MS.

—— "Annual Festival of the Ga People." *The Ghanaian*, August 1961, pp. 9-11; September 1961, pp. 25-26.

—— "Festivals of Gas and Jews." *The Ghanaian*, October 1961, p. 20.

—— "Ghanaian Philosophy." *The Ghanaian*, October 1961-June 1962.

—— *Materialism in Ga Society*. Accra: Institute of African Studies, University of Ghana, 1965.

Beidelman, T. O. "Pig (*Guluwe*): An Essay on Ngulu Sexual Symbolism and Ceremony." *Southwestern Journal of Anthropology* 20:359-392 (1964).

—— "Swazi Royal Ritual." *Africa* 36:373-405 (1966).

—— "The Ox and Nuer Sacrifice: Some Freudian Hypotheses about Nuer Symbolism." *Man*, n.s. 1:453-467 (1966).

303

Berry, J. *Pronunciation of Ga.* Cambridge: Heffer, 1951.

—— "The Place-names of Ghana," Xerox, 1958.

Boateng, E. A. "The Growth and Functions of Accra." *Bulletin of the Ghana Geographical Association* 4:4-15 (1959).

Brown, A. Addo-Aryee. "Signs and Omens." *Gold Coast Review* 2:285-289 (1926).

Bruce-Myers, J. M. "The Connubial Institutions of the Gas." *Journal of the African Society* 30:399-409 (1931).

—— "The Origin of the Gas." *Journal of the African Society* 27:69-76, 167-173 (1927, 1928).

Cansdale, G. S. *Animals of West Africa.* London: Longmans, Green, 1960.

Cassirer, Ernst. *An Essay on Man: An Introduction to a Philosophy of Human Culture.* New Haven: Yale University Press, 1944.

Christensen, J. B. *Double Descent among the Fanti.* New Haven: Human Relations Area Files, 1954.

Cunnison, Ian. "History and Genealogies in a Conquest State." *American Anthropologist* 59:20-31 (1957).

Danniell, William F. "On the Ethnography of Akkrah and Adampe, Gold Coast." *Journal of the Ethnological Society of London* 4:1-32 (1856).

Douglas, Mary. *Purity and Danger: An Analysis of Concepts of Pollution and Taboo.* New York: Frederick A. Praeger, 1966.

Durkheim, Emile, and Marcel Mauss. *Primitive Classification.* Trans. Rodney Needham. London: Cohen and West, 1963.

Engmann, E. A. W. *Ganyobi.* Accra: Bureau of Ghana Languages, 1961.

Evans-Pritchard, E. E. *The Nuer.* Oxford: Clarendon Press, 1940.

Field, M. J. *Social Organisation of the Ga People.* London: Crown Agents, 1940.

—— *Religion and Medicine of the Ga People.* London: Oxford University Press, 1937. Rev. ed., 1961.

—— "The Investigation of the Ancient Settlements of the Accra Plain." *Ghana Notes and Queries* 4:4-5 (1962).

Fitzgerald, Dale K. "The Question of Duo-locality Among the Ga: A Preliminary Study." MS, 1968.

—— "Prophetic Speech in Ga Spirit Mediumship." MS, 1970.

Fleischer, Rev. C., and M. B. Wilkie. "Specimens of Folk-lore of the Ga-people on the Gold Coast." *Africa* 3:360-368 (1930).

Ghana (Gold Coast) Government. "Proceedings Government Enquiry into Ga Constitution, 1907." MS, Ghana National Archives.

—— *Special Report 'E': Tribes in Ghana, 1960 Population Census of Ghana.* Accra: Census Office, 1964.

Goody, Jack, and Esther Goody. "Cross-cousin Marriage in Northern Ghana." *Man*, n.s. 1:343-355 (1966).

Greenberg, Joseph H. *The Languages of Africa.* Bloomington: Indiana University Press, 1966.

Horton, Robin. "Ritual Man in Africa." *Africa* 34:85-104 (1964).

—— *Kalabari Sculpture.* Apapa: Department of Antiquities, Federal Republic of Nigeria, 1965.

—— "African Traditional Thought and Western Science." *Africa* 37: 50-71, 155-187 (1967).

—— "Neo-Tylorianism: Sound Sense or Sinister Prejudice?" *Man*, n.s. 3:625-634 (1968).

Irvine, F. R. *The Fishes and Fisheries of the Gold Coast.* London: Crown Agents, 1947.

—— *Woody Plants of Ghana.* London: Oxford University Press, 1961.

Kaye, Barrington. *Bringing Up Children in Ghana.* London: Allen and Unwin, 1962.

Kilson, Marion D. de B. "Ga and Non-Ga Populations of Central Accra." *Ghana Journal of Sociology* 2:18-25 (1966).

—— "Urban Tribesmen: Social Continuity and Change Among the Ga in Accra, Ghana." Ph.D. diss., Harvard University, 1967.

—— "Continuity and Change in the Ga Residential System." *Ghana Journal of Sociology* 3:81-97 (1967).

—— ed. *Excerpts from the Diary of Kwaku Niri.* Legon: Institute of African Studies, University of Ghana, 1967.

—— "Variations in Ga Culture in Central Accra." *Ghana Journal of Sociology* 3:33-54 (1967).

—— "Possession in Ga Ritual." *Transcultural Psychiatric Research* 5: 67-69 (1968).

—— "The Ga Naming Rite." *Anthropos* 63/64:904-920 (1968/69).

—— "Libation in Ga Ritual." *Journal of Religion in Africa* 2:161-178 (1969).

—— "Taxonomy and Form in Ga Ritual." *Journal of Religion in Africa* (in press).

—— "Twin Beliefs and Ceremony in Ga Culture." *Journal of Religion in Africa* (forthcoming).

Kropp, Mary Esther. "European Loan-Words in Accra Ga." MS, 1965.

—— *Ga, Adangme and Ewe (Lomé) with English Gloss: Comparative Wordlists no. 2.* Legon: Institute of African Studies, University of Ghana, 1966.

Leach, E. R. "Lévi-Strauss in the Garden of Eden." *Transactions of the New York Academy of Sciences* 23:386-396 (1961).

Lévi-Strauss, Claude. *The Savage Mind.* Chicago: University of Chicago Press, 1967.

Lévy-Bruhl, Lucien. *Primitive Mentality.* Trans. Lilian A. Clare. Boston: Beacon Press, 1966.

Lewis, I. M. "Spirit Possession and Deprivation Cults." *Man,* n.s. 1:307-329 (1966).

Manoukian, Madeline. *Akan and Ga-Adangme Peoples of the Gold Coast.* Ethnographic Survey of Western Africa no. 1. London: International African Institute, 1950.

Middleton, John. *Lugbara Religion.* London: Oxford University Press, 1960.

Munger, E. S. "Land Use in Accra." *Zaire* 8:911-919 (1954).

Needham, Rodney. "The Left Hand of the Mugwe." *Africa* 30:20-33 (1960).

—— "Right and Left in Nyoro Symbolic Classification." *Africa* 37:425-452 (1967).

—— "Percussion and Transition." *Man,* n.s. 2:606-614 (1967).

Nketia, J. H. K. "Traditional Music of the Ga People." *Universitas* 3:76-81 (1958).

—— *African Music in Ghana.* Accra: Longmans, Green, 1962.

—— "Prayers at Kple Worship." *The Ghana Bulletin of Theology* 2:19-29, 1-7 (1963).

—— "Historical Evidence in Ga Religious Music." In *The Historian in Tropical Africa,* ed. Jan Vansina, Raymond Mauny, and L. V. Thomas, pp. 265-283. London: Oxford University Press, 1964.

Nypan, Astrid. *Market Trade: A Sample Survey of Market Traders in Accra.* African Business Series no. 2. Accra: University College of Ghana, 1960.

Okunor, Vincent. *Tone in the Ga Verb.* Legon: Institute of African Studies, University of Ghana, 1967.

Ozanne, Paul. "Notes on the Early Historic Archaeology of Accra." *Transactions of the Historical Society of Ghana* 6:51-70 (1962).

—— "Notes on the Later Prehistory of Accra." *Journal of the Historical Society of Nigeria* 3:3-23 (1964).

Page, R. E. "The Osu and Kindred Peoples." *Gold Coast Review* 1:66-70 (1925).

Pogucki, R. J. H. *Land Tenure in Ga Customary Law.* Gold Coast Land Tenure, vol. 3. Accra: Government Printer, 1955.

Quarcoo, A. K. "The Lakpa-Principal Deity of Labadi." *Research Review* (Institute of African Studies, University of Ghana), 3:2-43 (1967).

Quartey-Papafio, A. B. "Law of Succession among the Akras or the Ga Tribes Proper of the Gold Coast." *Journal of the African Society* 10:64-72 (1910-1911).

—— "The Native Tribunals of the Akras of the Gold Coast." *Journal of the African Society* 10:320-330, 434-446; 11:75-94 (1911).

—— "The Use of Names among the Gas or Accra People of the Gold Coast." *Journal of the African Society* 13:167-182 (1913).

—— "Apprenticeship amongst the Gas." *Journal of the African Society* 13:415-422 (1914).

—— "The Ga Homowo Festival." *Journal of the African Society* 19:126-134, 227-232 (1920).

Redfield, Robert. *The Primitive World and Its Transformation*. Ithaca: Cornell University Press, 1953.

Rigby, Peter. "Dual Symbolic Classification among the Gogo of Central Tanzania." *Africa* 36:1-17 (1966).

—— "Some Gogo Rituals of 'Purification': An Essay on Social and Moral Categories." In *Dialectic in Practical Religion*, ed. E. R. Leach, pp. 153-178. Cambridge: Cambridge University Press, 1968.

Rosaldo, Renato I., Jr. "Metaphors of Hierarchy in a Mayan Ritual." *American Anthropologist* 70:524-536 (1968).

Turner, Victor W. *Chihamba, The White Spirit: A Ritual Drama of the Ndembu*. Manchester: Manchester University Press, 1962.

—— *The Forest of Symbols*. Ithaca: Cornell University Press, 1967.

—— *The Drums of Affliction: A Study of Religious Processes among the Ndembu of Zambia*. Oxford: Clarendon Press, 1968.

Welman, C. W. "James Fort, Accra, and the Oyeni Fetish." *Gold Coast Review* 3:73-88 (1927).

Wilks, Ivor. "The Rise of the Akwamu Empire, 1650-1710." *Transactions of the Historical Society of Ghana* 3:99-136 (1957).

—— "Akwamu and Otublohum: An Eighteenth Century Akan Marriage Arrangement." *Africa* 29:391-404 (1959).

—— "Some Glimpses into the Early History of Accra." MS.

Wilson, Peter J. "Status Ambiguity and Spirit Possession." *Man*, n.s. 2:366-378 (1967).

Wright, V. "Some Ga Customs." *Gold Coast Review* 3:224-228 (1927).

Index

309